Deep Learning with PyTorch Step-by-Step: A Beginner's Guide
Volume I—Fundamentals

Daniel Voigt Godoy

Version 1.1.1

Deep Learning with PyTorch Step-by-Step: A Beginner's Guide

Volume I—Fundamentals

by Daniel Voigt Godoy

Copyright © 2020-2022 by Daniel Voigt Godoy. All rights reserved.

May 2021: First Edition

Revision History for the First Edition:

- 2021-05-18: v1.0
- 2021-12-15: v1.1
- 2022-02-12: v1.1.1

For more information, please send an email to contact @ dvgodoy.com

Although the author has used his best efforts to ensure that the information and instructions contained in this book are accurate, under no circumstances shall the author be liable for any loss, damage, liability, or expense incurred or suffered as a consequence, directly or indirectly, of the use and/or application of any of the contents of this book. Any action you take upon the information in this book is strictly at your own risk. If any code samples or other technology this book contains or describes is subject to open source licenses or the intellectual property rights of others, it is your responsibility to ensure that your use thereof complies with such licenses and/or rights. The author does not have any control over and does not assume any responsibility for third-party websites or their content. All trademarks are the property of their respective owners. Screenshots are used for illustrative purposes only.

No part of this book may be reproduced or transmitted in any form or by any means (electronic, mechanical, photocopying, recording, or otherwise), or by any information storage and retrieval system without the prior written permission of the copyright owner, except where permitted by law. Please purchase only authorized electronic editions. Your support of the author's rights is appreciated.

"What I cannot create, I do not understand."

Richard P. Feynman

Table of Contents

Preface xi
Acknowledgements xiii
About the Author xiv
Frequently Asked Questions (FAQ) 1
    Why PyTorch? 1
    Why This Book? 2
    Who Should Read This Book? 3
    What Do I Need to Know? 3
    How to Read This Book 4
    What's Next? 6
Setup Guide 8
    Official Repository 8
    Environment 8
        Google Colab 8
        Binder 9
        Local Installation 10
            1. Anaconda 11
            2. Conda (Virtual) Environments 11
            3. PyTorch 13
            4. TensorBoard 15
            5. GraphViz and Torchviz (optional) 16
            6. Git 17
            7. Jupyter 19
    Moving On 19
Chapter 0: Visualizing Gradient Descent 21
    Spoilers 21
    Jupyter Notebook 21
        Imports 22
    Visualizing Gradient Descent 22
    Model 23
    Data Generation 24
        Synthetic Data Generation 24
        Train-Validation-Test Split 26

Step 0 - Random Initialization	27
Step 1 - Compute Model's Predictions	28
Step 2 - Compute the Loss	29
Loss Surface	31
Cross-Sections	35
Step 3 - Compute the Gradients	36
Visualizing Gradients	38
Backpropagation	39
Step 4 - Update the Parameters	40
Learning Rate	42
Low Learning Rate	43
High Learning Rate	45
Very High Learning Rate	46
"Bad" Feature	47
Scaling / Standardizing / Normalizing	50
Step 5 - Rinse and Repeat!	54
The Path of Gradient Descent	55
Recap	57
Chapter 1: A Simple Regression Problem	59
Spoilers	59
Jupyter Notebook	59
Imports	60
A Simple Regression Problem	60
Data Generation	61
Synthetic Data Generation	61
Gradient Descent	62
Step 0 - Random Initialization	63
Step 1 - Compute Model's Predictions	63
Step 2 - Compute the Loss	63
Step 3 - Compute the Gradients	64
Step 4 - Update the Parameters	65
Step 5 - Rinse and Repeat!	66
Linear Regression in Numpy	66
PyTorch	70
Tensor	70
Loading Data, Devices, and CUDA	75

- Creating Parameters 80
- Autograd 84
  - backward 84
  - grad 86
  - zero_ 87
  - Updating Parameters 88
  - no_grad 91
- Dynamic Computation Graph 91
- Optimizer 95
  - step / zero_grad 96
- Loss 98
- Model 102
  - Parameters 104
  - state_dict 105
  - Device 106
  - Forward Pass 106
  - train 108
  - Nested Models 108
  - Sequential Models 111
  - Layers 112
- Putting It All Together 114
  - Data Preparation 115
  - Model Configuration 116
  - Model Training 117
- Recap 120

Chapter 2: Rethinking the Training Loop 122
- Spoilers 122
- Jupyter Notebook 122
  - Imports 123
- Rethinking the Training Loop 123
  - Training Step 129
- Dataset 133
  - TensorDataset 135
- DataLoader 135
  - Mini-Batch Inner Loop 141
  - Random Split 144

- Evaluation 146
  - Plotting Losses 150
- TensorBoard 151
  - Running It Inside a Notebook 151
  - Running It Separately (Local Installation) 153
  - Running It Separately (Binder) 154
  - SummaryWriter 154
  - add_graph 156
  - add_scalars 157
- Saving and Loading Models 163
  - Model State 163
  - Saving 163
  - Resuming Training 164
  - Deploying / Making Predictions 167
  - Setting the Model's Mode 168
- Putting It All Together 169
- Recap 172
- Chapter 2.1: Going Classy 174
  - Spoilers 174
  - Jupyter Notebook 174
    - Imports 174
  - Going Classy 175
    - The Class 175
    - The Constructor 176
      - Arguments 176
      - Placeholders 177
      - Variables 179
      - Functions 179
    - Training Methods 186
    - Saving and Loading Models 190
    - Visualization Methods 191
    - The Full Code 192
  - Classy Pipeline 193
    - Model Training 196
    - Making Predictions 198
    - Checkpointing 198

- Resuming Training...199
- Pulling It All Together...201
- Recap...204
- Chapter 3: A Simple Classification Problem........................205
  - Spoilers..205
  - Jupyter Notebook..205
    - Imports...205
  - A Simple Classification Problem..................................206
  - Data Generation...207
  - Data Preparation..208
  - Model...209
    - Logits..210
    - Probabilities..211
    - Odds Ratio...211
    - Log Odds Ratio...213
    - From Logits to Probabilities....................................214
    - Sigmoid..216
    - Logistic Regression...217
  - Loss...220
    - BCELoss...222
    - BCEWithLogitsLoss..224
    - Imbalanced Dataset..227
  - Model Configuration...230
  - Model Training..231
  - Decision Boundary..235
  - Classification Threshold...240
    - Confusion Matrix..242
    - Metrics..244
      - True and False Positive Rates................................244
      - Precision and Recall...247
      - Accuracy..248
    - Trade-offs and Curves...249
      - Low Threshold..249
      - High Threshold..251
      - ROC and PR Curves...252
      - The Precision Quirk..254

    Best and Worst Curves 255
    Comparing Models 256
Putting It All Together 258
Recap 260
Thank You! 262
Index 263

Preface

If you're reading this, I probably don't need to tell you that deep learning is amazing and PyTorch is cool, right?

But I will tell you, briefly, how this series of books came to be. In 2016, I started teaching a class on machine learning with Apache Spark and, a couple of years later, another class on the fundamentals of machine learning.

At some point, I tried to find a blog post that would visually explain, in a clear and concise manner, the concepts behind binary cross-entropy so that I could show it to my students. Since I could not find any that fit my purpose, I decided to write one myself. Although I thought of it as a fairly basic topic, it turned out to be my most popular blog post[1]! My readers have welcomed the simple, straightforward, and conversational way I explained the topic.

Then, in 2019, I used the same approach for writing another blog post: "Understanding PyTorch with an example: a step-by-step tutorial."[2] Once again, I was amazed by the reaction from the readers!

It was their positive feedback that motivated me to write this series of books to help beginners start their journey into deep learning and PyTorch.

In this first volume, I cover the basics of gradient descent, the fundamentals of PyTorch, training linear and logistic regressions, evaluation metrics, and more. If you have absolutely no experience with PyTorch, this is your starting point.

The second volume is mostly focused on computer vision: deeper models and activation functions, convolutional neural networks, initialization schemes, schedulers, and transfer learning. If your goal is to learn about deep learning models for computer vision, and you're already comfortable training simple models in PyTorch, the second volume is the right one for you.

Then, the third volume focuses on all things sequence: recurrent neural networks and their variations, sequence-to-sequence models, attention, self-attention, and the Transformer architecture. The very last chapter of the third volume is a crash course on natural language processing: from the basics of word tokenization all the way up to fine-tuning large models (BERT and GPT-2) using the HuggingFace library. This volume is more demanding than the other two, and you're going to enjoy it more if you already have a solid understanding of deep learning models.

These books are meant to be read in order, and, although they *can* be read independently, I strongly recommend you read them as the one, long book I originally wrote :-)

I hope you enjoy reading this series as much as I enjoyed writing it.

[1] https://bit.ly/2UW5iTg
[2] https://bit.ly/2TpzwxR

Acknowledgements

First and foremost, I'd like to thank YOU, my reader, for making this book possible. If it weren't for the amazing feedback I got from the thousands of readers of my blog post about PyTorch, I would have never mustered the strength to start *and finish* such a major undertaking as writing a 1,000-page book series!

I'd like to thank my good friends Jesús Martínez-Blanco (who managed to read absolutely *everything* that I wrote), Jakub Cieslik, Hannah Berscheid, Mihail Vieru, Ramona Theresa Steck, Mehdi Belayet Lincon, and António Góis for helping me out and dedicating a good chunk of their time to reading, proofing, and suggesting improvements to my drafts. I'm forever grateful for your support! I'd also like to thank my friend José Luis Lopez Pino for the initial push I needed to actually *start* writing this book.

Many thanks to my friends José Quesada and David Anderson for taking me as a student at the Data Science Retreat in 2015 and, later on, for inviting me to be a teacher there. That was the starting point of my career both as a data scientist and as teacher.

I'd also like to thank the PyTorch developers for developing such an amazing framework, and the teams from Leanpub and Towards Data Science for making it incredibly easy for content creators like me to share their work with the community.

Finally, I'd like to thank my wife, Jerusa, for always being supportive throughout the entire writing of this series of books, and for taking the time to read *every* single page in it :-)

About the Author

Daniel is a data scientist, developer, writer, and teacher. He has been teaching machine learning and distributed computing technologies at Data Science Retreat, the longest-running Berlin-based bootcamp, since 2016, helping more than 150 students advance their careers.

Daniel is also the main contributor of two Python packages: HandySpark[3] and DeepReplay.[4]

His professional background includes 20 years of experience working for companies in several industries: banking, government, fintech, retail, and mobility.

[3] https://github.com/dvgodoy/handyspark
[4] https://github.com/dvgodoy/deepreplay

Frequently Asked Questions (FAQ)

Why PyTorch?

First, coding in PyTorch is **fun** :-) Really, there is something to it that makes it very enjoyable to write code in. Some say it is because it is very **pythonic**, or maybe there is something else, who knows? I hope that, by the end of this book, you feel like that too!

Second, maybe there are even some *unexpected benefits* to your health—check Andrej Karpathy's tweet[5] about it!

Jokes aside, PyTorch is the **fastest-growing**[6] framework for developing deep learning models and it has a **huge ecosystem**.[7] That is, there are many *tools* and *libraries* developed on top of PyTorch. It is the **preferred framework**[8] in academia already and is making its way in the industry.

Several companies are already powered by PyTorch;[9] to name a few:

- **Facebook**: The company is the original developer of PyTorch, released in October 2016.
- **Tesla**: Watch Andrej Karpathy (AI director at Tesla) speak about "*how Tesla is using PyTorch to develop full self-driving capabilities for its vehicles.*"[10]
- **OpenAI**: In January 2020, OpenAI decided to standardize its deep learning framework on PyTorch.[11]
- **fastai**: fastai is a library[12] built on top of PyTorch to simplify model training and is used in its "*Practical Deep Learning for Coders*"[13] course. The fastai library is deeply connected to PyTorch and "*you can't become really proficient at using fastai if you don't know PyTorch well, too.*"
- **Uber**: The company is a significant contributor to PyTorch's ecosystem, having developed libraries like Pyro[14] (probabilistic programming) and Horovod[15] (a distributed training framework).
- **Airbnb**: PyTorch sits at the core of the company's dialog assistant for customer service.[16]

This series of books **aims to get you started with PyTorch** while giving you a **solid understanding of how it works**.

Why This Book?

If you're looking for a book where you can learn about deep learning and PyTorch without having to spend hours deciphering cryptic text and code, and one that's easy and enjoyable to read, this is it :-)

First, this is **not** a typical book: most tutorials *start* with some nice and pretty *image classification problem* to illustrate how to use PyTorch. It may seem cool, but I believe it **distracts** you from the **main goal**: learning **how PyTorch works**. In this book, I present a **structured, incremental,** and **from-first-principles** approach to learn PyTorch.

Second, this is **not** a **formal book** in any way: I am writing this book **as if I were having a conversation with you**, the reader. I will ask you **questions** (and give you answers shortly afterward), and I will also make (silly) **jokes**.

My job here is to make you **understand** the topic, so I will **avoid fancy mathematical notation** as much as possible and **spell it out in plain English**.

In this first book of the *Deep Learning with PyTorch Step-by-Step* series, I will **guide** you through the **development** of many models in PyTorch, showing you why PyTorch makes it much **easier** and more **intuitive** to build models in Python: *autograd, dynamic computation graph, model classes*, and much, much more.

We will build, **step-by-step**, not only the models themselves but also your **understanding** as I show you both the **reasoning** behind the code and **how to avoid** some **common pitfalls** and **errors** along the way.

There is yet another advantage of **focusing on the basics**: this book is likely to have a **longer shelf life**. It is fairly common for technical books, especially those focusing on cutting-edge technology, to become outdated quickly. Hopefully, this is not going to be the case here, since the **underlying mechanics are not changing and neither are the concepts**. It is expected that some syntax changes over time, but I do not see backward compatibility-breaking changes coming anytime soon.

 One more thing: If you hadn't noticed already, I **really** like to make use of **visual cues**, that is, **bold** and *italic* highlights. I firmly believe this helps the reader to **grasp** the **key ideas** I am trying to convey in a sentence more easily. You can find more on that in the section "**How to Read This Book.**"

Who Should Read This Book?

I wrote this book for **beginners in general**—not only PyTorch beginners. Every now and then, I will spend some time explaining some **fundamental concepts** that I believe are **essential** to have a proper **understanding of what's going on in the code**.

The best example is **gradient descent**, which most people are familiar with at some level. Maybe you know its general idea, perhaps you've seen it in Andrew Ng's Machine Learning course, or maybe you've even **computed some partial derivatives yourself**!

In real life, the **mechanics** of gradient descent will be **handled automatically by PyTorch** (uh, spoiler alert!). But, I will walk you through it anyway (unless you choose to skip Chapter 0 altogether, of course), because lots of **elements in the code**, as well as **choices of hyper-parameters** (learning rate, mini-batch size, etc.), can be much more easily understood if you know **where they come from**.

Maybe you already know some of these concepts well: If this is the case, you can simply *skip* them, since I've made these explanations as *independent* as possible from the rest of the content.

But **I want to make sure everyone is on the same page**, so, if you have just heard about a given concept or if you are unsure if you have entirely understood it, these explanations are for you.

What Do I Need to Know?

This is a book for beginners, so I am assuming as **little prior knowledge** as possible; as mentioned in the previous section, I will take the time to explain fundamental concepts whenever needed.

That being said, this is what I expect from you, the reader:

- to be able to code in **Python** (if you are familiar with object-oriented programming [OOP], even better)
- to be able to work with PyData stack (**numpy**, **matplotlib**, and **pandas**) and **Jupyter notebooks**
- to be familiar with some basic concepts used in **machine learning**, like:

- supervised learning: regression and classification
- loss functions for regression and classification (mean squared error, cross-entropy, etc.)
- training-validation-test split
- underfitting and overfitting (bias-variance trade-off)

Even so, I am still briefly touching on **some** of these topics, but I need to draw a line somewhere; otherwise, this book would be gigantic!

How to Read This Book

Since this book is a **beginner's guide**, it is meant to be read **sequentially**, as ideas and concepts are progressively built. The same holds true for the **code** inside the book—you should be able to *reproduce* all outputs, provided you execute the chunks of code in the same order as they are introduced.

This book is **visually** different than other books: As I've mentioned already in the "**Why This Book?**" section, I **really** like to make use of **visual cues**. Although this is not, *strictly speaking*, a **convention**, this is how you can interpret those cues:

- I use **bold** to highlight what I believe to be the **most relevant words** in a sentence or paragraph, while *italicized* words are considered *important* too (not important enough to be bold, though)
- *Variables*, *coefficients*, and *parameters* in general, are *italicized*
- `Classes` and `methods` are written in a `monospaced` font
- Every **code cell** is followed by *another* cell showing the corresponding **outputs** (if any)
- **All code** presented in the book is available at its **official repository** on GitHub:

    https://github.com/dvgodoy/PyTorchStepByStep

Code cells with **titles** are an important piece of the workflow:

Title Goes Here

```
1 # Whatever is being done here is going to impact OTHER code
2 # cells. Besides, most cells have COMMENTS explaining what
3 # is happening
4 x = [1., 2., 3.]
5 print(x)
```

If there is any output to the code cell, titled or not, there *will* be another code cell depicting the corresponding **output** so you can *check* if you successfully reproduced it or not.

Output

```
[1.0, 2.0, 3.0]
```

Some code cells **do not** have titles—running them does not affect the workflow:

```
# Those cells illustrate HOW TO CODE something, but they are
# NOT part of the main workflow
dummy = ['a', 'b', 'c']
print(dummy[::-1])
```

But even these cells have their outputs shown!

Output

```
['c', 'b', 'a']
```

I use asides to communicate a variety of things, according to the corresponding icon:

WARNING

Potential **problems** or things to **look out** for.

How to Read This Book | 5

TIP

Key aspects I really want you to **remember**.

INFORMATION

Important information to **pay attention** to.

IMPORTANT

Really important information to **pay attention** to.

TECHNICAL

Technical aspects of **parameterization** or **inner workings of algorithms**.

QUESTION AND ANSWER

Asking myself **questions** (pretending to be you, the reader) and answering them, either in the same block or shortly after.

DISCUSSION

Really brief discussion on a concept or topic.

LATER

Important topics that will be covered in more detail later.

SILLY

Jokes, puns, memes, quotes from movies.

What's Next?

It's time to **set up** an environment for your learning journey using the **Setup Guide**.

[5] https://bit.ly/2MQoYRo
[6] https://bit.ly/37uZgLB
[7] https://pytorch.org/ecosystem/
[8] https://bit.ly/2MTN0Lh
[9] https://bit.ly/2UFHFve
[10] https://bit.ly/2XXJkyo
[11] https://openai.com/blog/openai-pytorch/

[12] https://docs.fast.ai/
[13] https://course.fast.ai/
[14] http://pyro.ai/
[15] https://github.com/horovod/horovod
[16] https://bit.ly/30CPhm5

Setup Guide

Official Repository

This book's official repository is available on GitHub:

https://github.com/dvgodoy/PyTorchStepByStep

It contains **one Jupyter notebook** for every **chapter** in this book. Each notebook contains **all the code shown** in its corresponding chapter, and you should be able to **run its cells in sequence** to get the **same outputs**, as shown in the book. I strongly believe that being able to **reproduce the results** brings **confidence** to the reader.

 Even though I did my best to ensure the **reproducibility** of the results, you may **still** find some minor differences in your outputs (especially during model training). Unfortunately, completely reproducible results are not guaranteed across PyTorch releases, and results may not be reproducible between CPU and GPU executions, even when using identical seeds.[17]

Environment

There are **three options** for you to run the Jupyter notebooks:

- Google Colab (*https://colab.research.google.com*)
- Binder (*https://mybinder.org*)
- Local Installation

Let's briefly explore the **pros** and **cons** of each of these options.

Google Colab

Google Colab "*allows you to write and execute Python in your browser, with zero configuration required, free access to GPUs and easy sharing.*"[18].

You can easily **load notebooks directly from GitHub** using Colab's special URL (*https://colab.research.google.com/github/*). Just type in the GitHub's user or organization (like mine, **dvgodoy**), and it will show you a list of all its public repositories (like this book's, PyTorchStepByStep).

After choosing a repository, it will list the available notebooks and corresponding links to open them in a new browser tab.

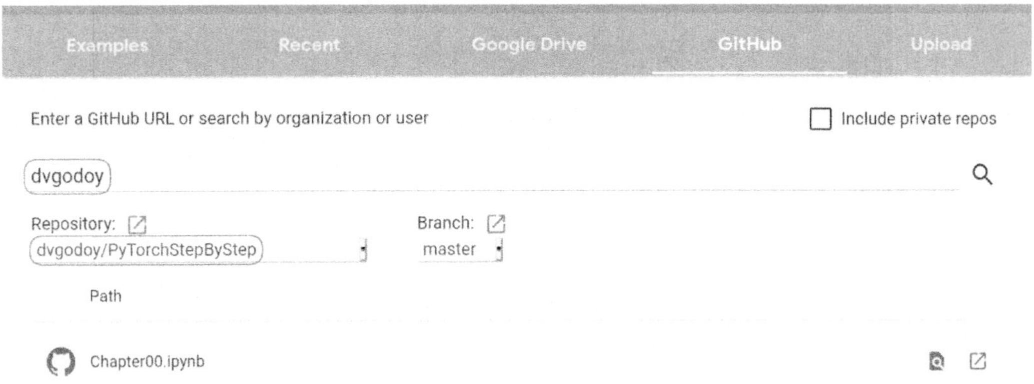

Figure S.1 - Google Colab's special URL

You also get access to a **GPU**, which is very useful to train deep learning models **faster**. More important, if you **make changes** to the notebook, Google Colab will **keep them**. The whole setup is very convenient; the only **cons** I can think of are:

- You need to be **logged in** to a Google account.
- You need to (re)install Python packages that are not part of Google Colab's default configuration.

Binder

Binder "*allows you to create custom computing environments that can be shared and used by many remote users.*"[19]

You can also **load notebooks directly from GitHub**, but the process is slightly different. Binder will create something like a *virtual machine* (technically, it is a container, but let's leave it at that), clone the repository, and start Jupyter. This allows you to have access to **Jupyter's home page** in your browser, just like you would if you were running it locally, but everything is running in a JupyterHub server on their end.

Just go to Binder's site (*https://mybinder.org/*) and type in the URL to the GitHub repository you want to explore (for instance, `https://github.com/dvgodoy/PyTorchStepByStep`) and click on **Launch**. It will take a couple of minutes to build the image and open Jupyter's home page.

You can also **launch Binder** for this book's repository directly using the following link: *https://mybinder.org/v2/gh/dvgodoy/PyTorchStepByStep/master*.

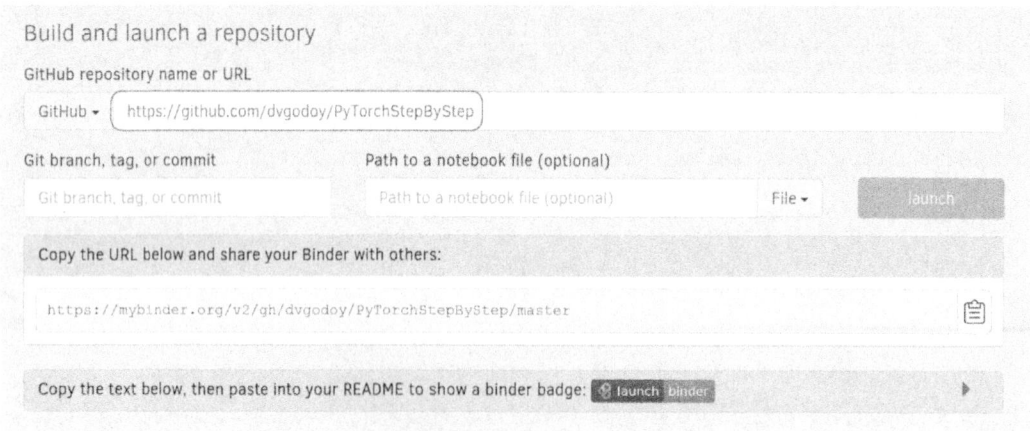

Figure S.2 - Binder's page

Binder is very convenient since it **does not require a prior setup** of any kind. Any Python packages needed to successfully run the environment are likely installed during launch (if provided by the author of the repository).

On the other hand, it may **take time** to start, and it **does not keep your changes** after your session expires (so, make sure you **download** any notebooks you modify).

Local Installation

This option will give you more **flexibility**, but it will require **more effort to set up**. I encourage you to try setting up your own environment. It may seem daunting at first, but you can surely accomplish it by following **seven easy steps**:

Checklist

- ☐ 1. Install **Anaconda**.
- ☐ 2. Create and activate a **virtual environment**.
- ☐ 3. Install **PyTorch** package.
- ☐ 4. Install **TensorBoard** package.
- ☐ 5. Install **GraphViz** software and **TorchViz** package (**optional**).
- ☐ 6. Install **git** and **clone** the repository.
- ☐ 7. Start **Jupyter** notebook.

1. Anaconda

If you don't have **Anaconda's Individual Edition**[20] installed yet, this would be a good time to do it. It is a convenient way to start since it contains most of the Python libraries a data scientist will ever need to develop and train models.

Please follow the **installation instructions** for your OS:

- Windows (*https://docs.anaconda.com/anaconda/install/windows/*)
- macOS (*https://docs.anaconda.com/anaconda/install/mac-os/*)
- Linux (*https://docs.anaconda.com/anaconda/install/linux/*)

 Make sure you choose **Python 3.X** version since Python 2 was discontinued in January 2020.

After installing Anaconda, it is time to create an **environment**.

2. Conda (Virtual) Environments

Virtual environments are a convenient way to isolate Python installations associated with different projects.

 "What is an environment?"

It is pretty much a **replication of Python itself and some (or all) of its libraries**, so, effectively, you'll end up with multiple Python installations on your computer.

 "Why can't I just use one single Python installation for everything?"

With so many independently developed Python **libraries**, each having many different **versions** and each version having various **dependencies** (on other libraries), **things can get out of hand** real quick.

It is beyond the scope of this guide to debate these issues, but take my word for it (or Google it!)—you'll benefit a great deal if you pick up the habit of **creating a different environment for every project you start working on**.

 "How do I create an environment?"

First, you need to choose a **name** for your environment :-) Let's call ours pytorchbook (or anything else you find easy to remember). Then, you need to open a **terminal** (in Ubuntu) or **Anaconda Prompt** (in Windows or macOS) and type the following command:

```
$ conda create -n pytorchbook anaconda
```

The command above creates a Conda environment named pytorchbook and includes **all Anaconda packages** in it (time to get a coffee, it will take a while...). If you want to learn more about creating and using Conda environments, please check Anaconda's "Managing Environments"[21] user guide.

Did it finish creating the environment? Good! It is time to **activate it**, meaning, making **that Python installation** the one to be used now. In the same terminal (or Anaconda prompt), just type:

```
$ conda activate pytorchbook
```

Your prompt should look like this (if you're using Linux):

```
(pytorchbook)$
```

or like this (if you're using Windows):

```
(pytorchbook)C:\>
```

Done! You are using a **brand new Conda environment** now. You'll need to **activate it** every time you open a new terminal, or, if you're a Windows or macOS user, you can open the corresponding Anaconda prompt (it will show up as **Anaconda Prompt (pytorchbook)**, in our case), which will have it activated from the start.

 IMPORTANT: From now on, I am assuming you'll activate the pytorchbook environment every time you open a terminal or Anaconda prompt. Further installation steps **must** be executed inside the environment.

3. PyTorch

PyTorch is the coolest **deep learning framework**, just in case you skipped the introduction.

It is "*an open source machine learning framework that accelerates the path from research prototyping to production deployment.*"[22] Sounds good, right? Well, I probably don't have to convince you at this point :-)

It is time to install the star of the show :-) We can go straight to the **Start Locally** (*https://pytorch.org/get-started/locally/*) section of PyTorch's website, and it will automatically select the options that best suit your local environment, and it will show you the **command to run**.

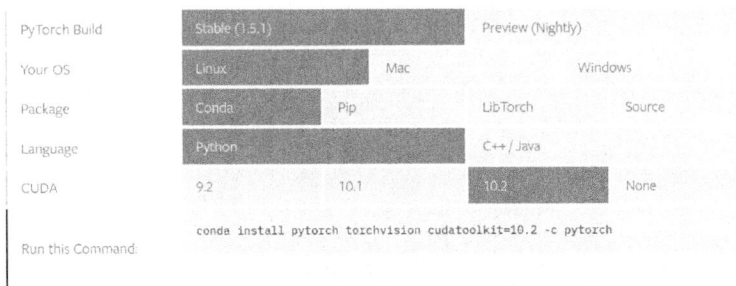

Figure S.3 - PyTorch's Start Locally page

Some of these options are given:

- PyTorch Build: Always select a **Stable** version.
- Package: I am assuming you're using **Conda**.
- Language: Obviously, **Python**.

So, two options remain: **Your OS** and **CUDA**.

 "*What is CUDA?*" you ask.

Environment | 13

Using GPU / CUDA

CUDA "*is a parallel computing platform and programming model developed by NVIDIA for general computing on graphical processing units (GPUs).*"[23]

If you have a **GPU** in your computer (likely a *GeForce* graphics card), you can leverage its power to train deep learning models **much faster** than using a CPU. In this case, you should choose a PyTorch installation that includes CUDA support.

This is not enough, though: If you haven't done so yet, you need to install up-to-date drivers, the CUDA Toolkit, and the CUDA Deep Neural Network library (cuDNN). Unfortunately, more detailed installation instructions for CUDA are outside the scope of this book.

The **advantage** of using a GPU is that it allows you to **iterate faster** and **experiment with more-complex models and a more extensive range of hyper-parameters**.

In my case, I use **Linux**, and I have a **GPU** with CUDA version 10.2 installed. So I would run the following command in the **terminal** (after activating the environment):

```
(pytorchbook)$ conda install pytorch torchvision\
cudatoolkit=10.2 -c pytorch
```

Using CPU

If you **do not** have a **GPU**, you should choose **None** for CUDA.

 "Would I be able to run the code without a GPU?" you ask.

Sure! The code and the examples in this book were designed to allow **all readers** to follow them promptly. Some examples may demand a bit more computing power, but we are talking about a **couple of minutes** in a CPU, not hours. If you do not have a GPU, **don't worry**! Besides, you can always use Google Colab if you need to use a GPU for a while!

If I had a **Windows** computer, and **no GPU**, I would have to run the following command in the **Anaconda prompt (pytorchbook)**:

```
(pytorchbook) C:\> conda install pytorch torchvision cpuonly\
-c pytorch
```

Installing CUDA

CUDA: Installing drivers for a GeForce graphics card, NVIDIA's cuDNN, and CUDA Toolkit can be challenging and is highly dependent on which model you own and which OS you use.

For installing GeForce's drivers, go to GeForce's website (*https://www.geforce.com/drivers*), select your OS and the model of your graphics card, and follow the installation instructions.

For installing NVIDIA's CUDA Deep Neural Network library (cuDNN), you need to register at *https://developer.nvidia.com/cudnn*.

For installing CUDA Toolkit (*https://developer.nvidia.com/cuda-toolkit*), please follow instructions for your OS and choose a local installer or executable file.

macOS: If you're a macOS user, please beware that PyTorch's binaries **DO NOT** support **CUDA**, meaning you'll need to install PyTorch **from source** if you want to use your GPU. This is a somewhat **complicated** process (as described in *https://github.com/pytorch/pytorch#from-source*), so, if you don't feel like doing it, you can choose to proceed **without CUDA**, and you'll still be able to execute the code in this book promptly.

4. TensorBoard

TensorBoard is TensorFlow's **visualization toolkit**, and "*provides the visualization and tooling needed for machine learning experimentation.*"[24]

TensorBoard is a powerful tool, and we can use it even if we are developing models in PyTorch. Luckily, you don't need to install the whole TensorFlow to get it; you can easily **install TensorBoard alone** using **Conda**. You just need to run this command in your **terminal** or **Anaconda prompt** (again, after activating the environment):

```
(pytorchbook)$ conda install -c conda-forge tensorboard
```

5. GraphViz and Torchviz (optional)

 This step is optional, mostly because the installation of GraphViz can sometimes be *challenging* (especially on Windows). If for any reason you do not succeed in installing it correctly, or if you decide to skip this installation step, you will still be **able to execute the code in this book** (except for a couple of cells that generate images of a model's structure in the "Dynamic Computation Graph" section of Chapter 1).

GraphViz is an open source graph visualization software. It is "*a way of representing structural information as diagrams of abstract graphs and networks.*"[25]

We need to install GraphViz to use **TorchViz**, a neat package that allows us to visualize a model's structure. Please check the **installation instructions** for your OS at *https://www.graphviz.org/download/*.

 If you are using Windows, please use the **GraphViz's Windows Package** installer at *https://graphviz.gitlab.io/_pages/Download/windows/graphviz-2.38.msi*.

 You also need to add GraphViz to the PATH (environment variable) in Windows. Most likely, you can find the GraphViz executable file at `C:\ProgramFiles(x86)\Graphviz2.38\bin`. Once you find it, you need to set or change the PATH accordingly, adding GraphViz's location to it.

For more details on how to do that, please refer to "How to Add to Windows PATH Environment Variable."[26]

For additional information, you can also check the "How to Install Graphviz Software"[27] guide.

After installing GraphViz, you can install the **torchviz**[28] package. This package is **not** part of Anaconda Distribution Repository[29] and is only available at **PyPI**[30], the Python Package Index, so we need to `pip install` it.

Once again, open a **terminal** or **Anaconda prompt** and run this command (just once more: after activating the environment):

```
(pytorchbook)$ pip install torchviz
```

To check your GraphViz / TorchViz installation, you can try the Python code below:

```
(pytorchbook)$ python

Python 3.7.5 (default, Oct 25 2019, 15:51:11)
[GCC 7.3.0] :: Anaconda, Inc. on linux
Type "help", "copyright", "credits" or "license" for more
information.
>>> import torch
>>> from torchviz import make_dot
>>> v = torch.tensor(1.0, requires_grad=True)
>>> make_dot(v)
```

If everything is **working correctly**, you should see something like this:

Output

```
<graphviz.dot.Digraph object at 0x7ff540c56f50>
```

If you get an **error** of any kind (the one below is pretty common), it means there is still some kind of **installation issue** with GraphViz.

Output

```
ExecutableNotFound: failed to execute ['dot', '-Tsvg'], make
sure the Graphviz executables are on your systems' PATH
```

6. Git

It is *way* beyond this guide's scope to introduce you to version control and its most popular tool: `git`. If you are familiar with it already, great, you can skip this section altogether!

Otherwise, I'd recommend you to learn more about it; it will **definitely** be useful for you later down the line. In the meantime, I will show you the bare minimum so you can use `git` to **clone the repository** containing all code used in this book and get your **own**, **local copy** of it to modify and experiment with as you please. First, you need to install it. So, head to its downloads page (*https://git-scm.com/downloads*) and follow instructions for your OS. Once the installation is complete, please open a **new terminal** or **Anaconda prompt** (it's OK to close the previous one). In the new terminal or Anaconda prompt, you should be able to **run `git` commands**.

To clone this book's repository, you only need to run:

```
(pytorchbook)$ git clone https://github.com/dvgodoy/\
PyTorchStepByStep.git
```

The command above will create a `PyTorchStepByStep` folder that contains a local copy of everything available on GitHub's repository.

> ### conda install vs pip install
>
> Although they may seem equivalent at first sight, you should **prefer `conda install`** over `pip install` when working with Anaconda and its virtual environments.
>
> This is because `conda install` is sensitive to the active virtual environment: The package will be installed only for that environment. If you use `pip install`, and `pip` itself is not installed in the active environment, it will fall back to the **global `pip`**, and you definitely **do not** want that.
>
> Why not? Remember the problem with **dependencies** I mentioned in the virtual environment section? That's why! The `conda` installer assumes it handles all packages that are part of its repository and keeps track of the complicated network of dependencies among them (to learn more about this, check the "Install with Conda"[31] article).
>
> To learn more about the differences between `conda` and `pip`, read "Understanding Conda and Pip."[32]
>
> As a rule, first try to `conda install` a given package and, only if it does not exist there, fall back to `pip install`, as we did with `torchviz`.

7. Jupyter

After cloning the repository, navigate to the `PyTorchStepByStep` folder and, **once inside it**, **start Jupyter** on your terminal or Anaconda prompt:

```
(pytorchbook)$ jupyter notebook
```

This will open your browser, and you will see **Jupyter's home page** containing the repository's notebooks and code.

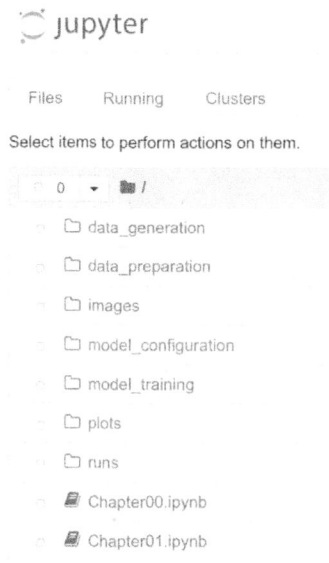

Figure S.4 - Running Jupyter

Moving On

Regardless of which of the three environments you chose, now you are ready to move on and tackle the development of your first PyTorch model, **step-by-step**!

[17] https://pytorch.org/docs/stable/notes/randomness.html
[18] https://colab.research.google.com/notebooks/intro.ipynb
[19] https://mybinder.readthedocs.io/en/latest/
[20] https://www.anaconda.com/products/individual
[21] https://bit.ly/2MVk0CM
[22] https://pytorch.org/
[23] https://developer.nvidia.com/cuda-zone
[24] https://www.tensorflow.org/tensorboard
[25] https://www.graphviz.org/
[26] https://bit.ly/3fIwYA5

[27] https://bit.ly/3OAyct3
[28] https://github.com/szagoruyko/pytorchviz
[29] https://docs.anaconda.com/anaconda/packages/pkg-docs/
[30] https://pypi.org/
[31] https://bit.ly/37onBTt
[32] https://bit.ly/2AAh8J5

Chapter 0
Visualizing Gradient Descent

Spoilers

In this chapter, we will:

- define a **simple linear regression model**
- walk through **every step of gradient descent**: initializing parameters, performing a forward pass, computing errors and loss, computing gradients, and updating parameters
- understand **gradients** using **equations**, **code**, and **geometry**
- understand the difference between **batch**, **mini-batch**, and **stochastic** gradient descent
- visualize the **effects on the loss** of using different **learning rates**
- understand the importance of **standardizing / scaling features**
- and much, much more!

There is **no** actual PyTorch code in this chapter… it is *Numpy* all along because our focus here is to understand, inside and out, how gradient descent works. PyTorch will be introduced in the next chapter.

Jupyter Notebook

The Jupyter notebook corresponding to Chapter 0[33] is part of the official ***Deep Learning with PyTorch Step-by-Step*** repository on GitHub. You can also run it directly in **Google Colab**[34].

If you're using a *local installation*, open your terminal or Anaconda prompt and navigate to the `PyTorchStepByStep` folder you cloned from GitHub. Then, *activate* the `pytorchbook` environment and run `jupyter notebook`:

```
$ conda activate pytorchbook

(pytorchbook)$ jupyter notebook
```

If you're using Jupyter's default settings,

`http://localhost:8888/notebooks/Chapter00.ipynb` should open Chapter 0's notebook. If not, just click on `Chapter00.ipynb` on your Jupyter's home page.

Imports

For the sake of organization, all libraries needed throughout the code used in any given chapter are imported at its very beginning. For this chapter, we'll need the following imports:

```
import numpy as np
from sklearn.linear_model import LinearRegression
from sklearn.preprocessing import StandardScaler
```

Visualizing Gradient Descent

According to Wikipedia: "*Gradient descent* is a first-order iterative optimization algorithm for finding a local minimum of a differentiable function."[35]

But I would go with: "**Gradient descent** is an iterative technique commonly used in machine learning and deep learning to find the best possible set of parameters / coefficients for a given model, data points, and loss function, starting from an initial, and usually random, guess."

"*Why visualizing gradient descent?*"

I believe *the way gradient descent is usually explained lacks intuition*. Students and beginners are left with a *bunch of equations* and *rules of thumb*—**this is not the way one should learn such a fundamental topic.**

If you **really understand** how gradient descent works, you will also understand how the **characteristics of your data** and your **choice of hyper-parameters** (mini-batch size and learning rate, for instance) have an **impact** on how **well** and how **fast** the model training is going to be.

By *really understanding*, I do not mean working through the equations manually: this does not develop intuition either. I mean **visualizing** the effects of different settings; I mean **telling a story** to illustrate the concept. That's how you **develop** intuition.

That being said, I'll cover the **five basic steps** you'd need to go through to use gradient descent. I'll show you the corresponding *Numpy* code while explaining lots of **fundamental concepts** along the way.

But first, we need some **data** to work with. Instead of using some *external dataset*, let's

- define which **model** we want to train to better understand gradient descent; and
- generate **synthetic data** for that model.

Model

The model must be **simple** and **familiar**, so you can focus on the **inner workings** of gradient descent.

So, I will stick with a model as simple as it can be: a **linear regression with a single feature, x**!

$$y = b + wx + \epsilon$$

Equation 0.1 - Simple linear regression model

In this model, we use a **feature (x)** to try to predict the value of a **label (y)**. There are three elements in our model:

- **parameter b**, the *bias* (or *intercept*), which tells us the expected average value of y when x is zero
- **parameter w**, the *weight* (or *slope*), which tells us how much y increases, on average, if we increase x by one unit
- and that **last term** (why does it *always* have to be a Greek letter?), *epsilon*, which is there to account for the inherent **noise**; that is, the **error** we cannot get rid of

We can also conceive the very same model structure in a less abstract way:

salary = minimum wage + increase per year * years of experience + noise

And to make it even more concrete, let's say that the **minimum wage** is **$1,000** (whatever the currency or time frame, this is not important). So, if you have **no** experience, your salary is going to be the **minimum wage** (parameter **b**).

Also, let's say that, **on average**, you get a **$2,000 increase** (parameter **w**) for every year of experience you have. So, if you have **two years of experience**, you are expected to earn a salary of **$5,000**. But your actual salary is **$5,600** (lucky you!). Since the model cannot account for those **extra $600**, your extra money is, technically speaking, **noise**.

Data Generation

We know our model already. In order to generate **synthetic data** for it, we need to pick values for its **parameters**. I chose **b = 1** and **w = 2** (as in thousands of dollars) from the example above.

First, let's generate our **feature (x)**: We use *Numpy*'s rand() method to randomly generate 100 (**N**) points between 0 and 1.

Then, we plug our **feature (x)** and our **parameters b and w** into our **equation** to compute our **labels (y)**. But we need to add some **Gaussian noise**[36] (**epsilon**) as well; otherwise, our synthetic dataset would be a perfectly straight line. We can generate noise using *Numpy*'s randn() method, which draws samples from a normal distribution (of mean 0 and variance 1), and then multiply it by a **factor** to adjust for the **level of noise**. Since I don't want to add too much noise, I picked 0.1 as my factor.

Synthetic Data Generation

Data Generation

```
1  true_b = 1
2  true_w = 2
3  N = 100
4
5  # Data Generation
6  np.random.seed(42)
7  x = np.random.rand(N, 1)
8  epsilon = (.1 * np.random.randn(N, 1))
9  y = true_b + true_w * x + epsilon
```

Did you notice the np.random.seed(42) at line 6? This line of code is actually more important than it looks. It guarantees that, every time we run this code, the **same** random numbers will be generated.

> *"Wait; what?! Aren't the numbers supposed to be **random**? How could they possibly be the **same** numbers?"* you ask, perhaps even a bit annoyed by this.

> ### (Not So) Random Numbers
>
> Well, you know, random numbers are not **quite** random... They are really **pseudo-random**, which means *Numpy*'s number generator spits out a **sequence of numbers** that **looks like it's random**. But it is not, really.
>
> The **good** thing about this behavior is that we can tell the generator to **start a particular sequence of pseudo-random numbers**. To some extent, it works as if we tell the generator: *"please generate sequence #42,"* and it will spill out a sequence of numbers. That number, 42, which works like the *index* of the sequence, is called a **seed**. Every time we give it the **same seed**, it generates the **same numbers**.
>
> This means we have the **best of both worlds**: On the one hand, we do **generate** a sequence of numbers that, for all intents and purposes, is **considered to be random**; on the other hand, we have the **power to reproduce any given sequence**. I cannot stress enough how convenient that is for **debugging** purposes!
>
> Moreover, you can guarantee that **other people will be able to reproduce your results**. Imagine how annoying it would be to run the code in this book and get different outputs every time, having to wonder if there is anything wrong with it. But since I've set a seed, you and I can achieve the very same outputs, even if it involved generating random data!

Next, let's **split** our synthetic data into **train** and **validation** sets, shuffling the array of indices and using the first 80 shuffled points for training.

> *"Why do you need to **shuffle** randomly generated data points? Aren't they random enough?"*

Yes, they **are** random enough, and shuffling them is indeed redundant in this example. But it is best practice to **always shuffle** your data points before training a model to improve the performance of gradient descent.

> There is one **exception** to the "always shuffle" rule, though: **time series** problems, where shuffling can lead to data leakage.

Train-Validation-Test Split

It is beyond the scope of this book to explain the reasoning behind the **train-validation-test split**, but there are two points I'd like to make:

1. The split should **always** be the **first thing** you do—no preprocessing, no transformations; **nothing happens before the split**. That's why we do this **immediately after the synthetic data generation**.

2. In this chapter we will use **only the training set**, so I did not bother to create a **test set**, but I performed a split nonetheless to **highlight point #1** :-)

Train-Validation Split

```
1  # Shuffles the indices
2  idx = np.arange(N)
3  np.random.shuffle(idx)
4
5  # Uses first 80 random indices for train
6  train_idx = idx[:int(N*.8)]
7  # Uses the remaining indices for validation
8  val_idx = idx[int(N*.8):]
9
10 # Generates train and validation sets
11 x_train, y_train = x[train_idx], y[train_idx]
12 x_val, y_val = x[val_idx], y[val_idx]
```

> *"Why didn't you use* `train_test_split()` *from Scikit-Learn?"* you may be asking.

That's a fair point. Later on, we will refer to the **indices of the data points** belonging to either train or validation sets, instead of the points themselves. So, I thought of using them from the very start.

26 | Chapter 0: Visualizing Gradient Descent

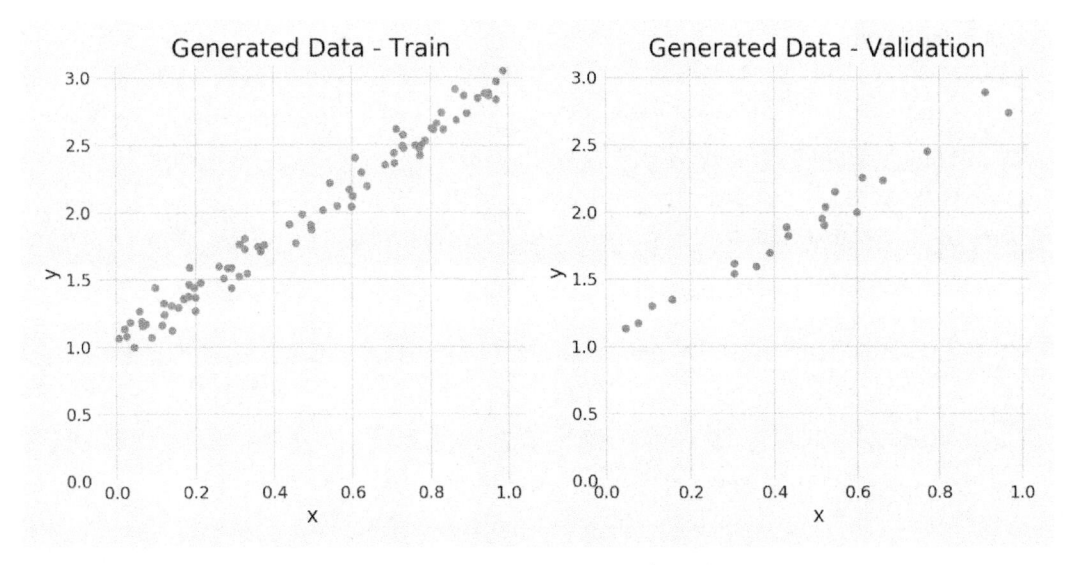

Figure 0.1 - Synthetic data: train and validation sets

We **know** that *b* = 1, *w* = 2, but now let's see **how close** we can get to the true values by using **gradient descent** and the 80 points in the **training set** (for training, *N* = 80).

Step 0 - Random Initialization

In our example, we already **know** the **true values** of the **parameters**, but this will obviously never happen in real life: If we *knew* the true values, why even bother to train a model to find them?!

OK, given that **we'll never know** the **true values** of the parameters, we need to set **initial values** for them. How do we choose them? It turns out a **random guess** is as good as any other.

> Even though the initialization is **random**, there are some clever **initialization schemes** that should be used when training more-complex models. We'll get back to them (much) later, in the second volume of the series.

For training a model, you need to **randomly initialize the parameters / weights** (we have only two, *b* and *w*).

Step 0 - Random Initialization | 27

Random Initialization

```
1 # Step 0 - Initializes parameters "b" and "w" randomly
2 np.random.seed(42)
3 b = np.random.randn(1)
4 w = np.random.randn(1)
5
6 print(b, w)
```

Output

```
[0.49671415] [-0.1382643]
```

Step 1 - Compute Model's Predictions

This is the **forward pass**; it simply *computes the model's predictions using the current values of the parameters / weights*. At the very beginning, we will be producing **really bad predictions**, as we started with **random values in Step 0**.

Step 1

```
1 # Step 1 - Computes our model's predicted output - forward pass
2 yhat = b + w * x_train
```

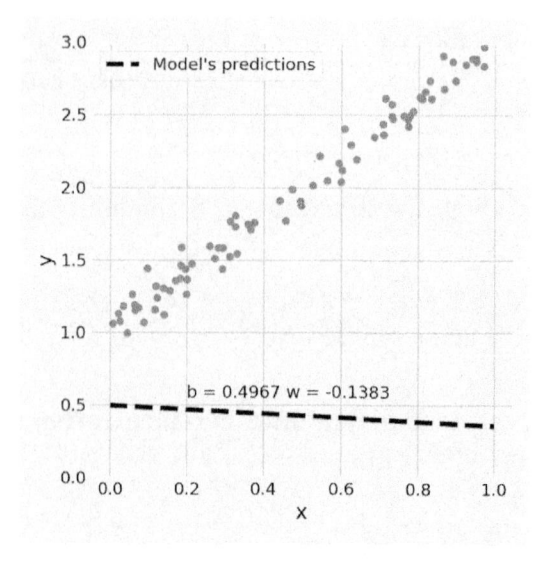

Figure 0.2 - Model's predictions (with random parameters)

28 | Chapter 0: Visualizing Gradient Descent

Step 2 - Compute the Loss

There is a subtle but fundamental difference between **error** and **loss**.

The **error** is the difference between the **actual value (label)** and the **predicted value** computed for a single data point. So, for a given *i*-th point (from our dataset of N points), its error is:

$$\text{error}_i = \hat{y}_i - y_i$$

Equation 0.2 - Error

The error of the **first point** in our dataset (*i* = 0) can be represented like this:

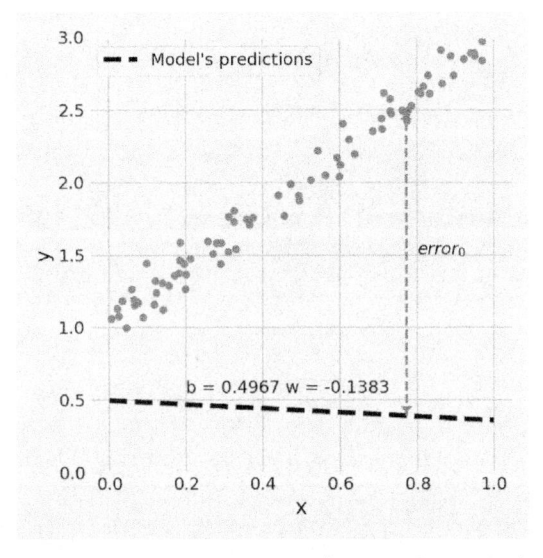

Figure 0.3 - Prediction error (for one data point)

The **loss**, on the other hand, is some sort of **aggregation of errors for a set of data points**.

It seems rather obvious to compute the loss for **all** (*N*) data points, right? Well, yes and no. Although it will surely yield a **more stable path** from the initial **random parameters** to the parameters that **minimize the loss**, it will also surely be **slow**.

This means one *needs to sacrifice (a bit of) stability for the sake of speed*. This is easily accomplished by randomly choosing (*without replacement*) a subset of *n* out of *N* data points each time we compute the loss.

Batch, Mini-batch, *and* Stochastic Gradient Descent

- If we use **all points** in the training set (n = N) to compute the loss, we are performing a **batch** gradient descent;
- If we were to use a **single point** (n = 1) each time, it would be a **stochastic** gradient descent;
- Anything else (n) **in between 1 and N** characterizes a **mini-batch** gradient descent;

For a regression problem, the **loss** is given by the **mean squared error (MSE)**; that is, the average of all squared errors; that is, the average of all squared differences between **labels** (y) and **predictions** (b + wx).

$$\text{MSE} = \frac{1}{n} \sum_{i=1}^{n} \text{error}_i^2$$

$$= \frac{1}{n} \sum_{i=1}^{n} (\hat{y}_i - y_i)^2$$

$$= \frac{1}{n} \sum_{i=1}^{n} (b + wx_i - y_i)^2$$

Equation 0.3 - Loss: mean squared error (MSE)

In the code below, we are using **all data points** of the training set to compute the **loss**, so n = N = 80, meaning we are indeed performing **batch gradient descent**.

Step 2

```
1  # Step 2 - Computing the loss
2  # We are using ALL data points, so this is BATCH gradient
3  # descent. How wrong is our model? That's the error!
4  error = (yhat - y_train)
5
6  # It is a regression, so it computes mean squared error (MSE)
7  loss = (error ** 2).mean()
8
9  print(loss)
```

Output

```
2.7421577700550976
```

Loss Surface

We have just computed the **loss** (2.74) corresponding to our **randomly initialized parameters** (*b* = 0.49 and *w* = -0.13). What if we did the same for **ALL** possible values of *b* and *w*? Well, not *all* possible values, but *all combinations of evenly spaced values in a given range*, like:

```
# Reminder:
# true_b = 1
# true_w = 2

# we have to split the ranges in 100 evenly spaced intervals each
b_range = np.linspace(true_b - 3, true_b + 3, 101)
w_range = np.linspace(true_w - 3, true_w + 3, 101)
# meshgrid is a handy function that generates a grid of b and w
# values for all combinations
bs, ws = np.meshgrid(b_range, w_range)
bs.shape, ws.shape
```

Output

```
((101, 101), (101, 101))
```

The result of the `meshgrid()` operation was two (101, 101) matrices representing the values of each parameter inside a grid. What does one of these matrices look like?

```
bs
```

Output

```
array([[-2.  , -1.94, -1.88, ...,  3.88,  3.94,  4.  ],
       [-2.  , -1.94, -1.88, ...,  3.88,  3.94,  4.  ],
       [-2.  , -1.94, -1.88, ...,  3.88,  3.94,  4.  ],
       ...,
       [-2.  , -1.94, -1.88, ...,  3.88,  3.94,  4.  ],
       [-2.  , -1.94, -1.88, ...,  3.88,  3.94,  4.  ],
       [-2.  , -1.94, -1.88, ...,  3.88,  3.94,  4.  ]])
```

Sure, we're somewhat *cheating* here, since we *know* the **true** values of b and w, so we can choose the **perfect ranges** for the parameters. But it is for educational purposes only :-)

Next, we could use those values to compute the corresponding **predictions**, **errors**, and **losses**. Let's start by taking a **single data point** from the training set and computing the predictions for every combination in our grid:

```
dummy_x = x_train[0]
dummy_yhat = bs + ws * dummy_x
dummy_yhat.shape
```

Output

```
(101, 101)
```

Thanks to its broadcasting capabilities, *Numpy* is able to understand we want to multiply the **same x value** by **every entry** in the **ws** matrix. This operation resulted in a **grid of predictions** for that **single data point**. Now we need to do this for **every one of our 80 data points** in the training set.

We can use *Numpy*'s `apply_along_axis()` to accomplish this:

> Look ma, no loops!

```
all_predictions = np.apply_along_axis(
    func1d=lambda x: bs + ws * x,
    axis=1,
    arr=x_train,
)
all_predictions.shape
```

Output

```
(80, 101, 101)
```

Cool! We got **80 matrices** of shape (101, 101), **one matrix for each data point**, each matrix containing a **grid of predictions**.

The **errors** are the difference between the predictions and the labels, but we cannot perform this operation right away—we need to work a bit on our **labels (y)**, so they have the proper **shape** for it (broadcasting is good, but not *that* good):

```
all_labels = y_train.reshape(-1, 1, 1)
all_labels.shape
```

Output

```
(80, 1, 1)
```

Our **labels** turned out to be **80 matrices of shape (1, 1)**—the most boring kind of matrix—but that is enough for broadcasting to work its magic. We can compute the **errors** now:

```
all_errors = (all_predictions - all_labels)
all_errors.shape
```

Output

```
(80, 101, 101)
```

Each prediction has its own error, so we get **80 matrices** of shape (101, 101), again, one matrix for each data point, each matrix containing a **grid of errors**.

The only step missing is to compute the **mean squared error**. First, we take the square of all errors. Then, we **average the squares over all data points**. Since our data points are in the **first dimension**, we use axis=0 to compute this average:

```
all_losses = (all_errors ** 2).mean(axis=0)
all_losses.shape
```

Output

```
(101, 101)
```

The result is a **grid of losses**, a matrix of shape (101, 101), **each loss** corresponding to a **different combination of the parameters b and w**.

These losses are our **loss surface**, which can be visualized in a 3D plot, where the vertical axis (z) represents the loss values. If we **connect** the combinations of b and w that yield the **same loss value**, we'll get an **ellipse**. Then, we can draw this ellipse in the original b x w plane (in blue, for a loss value of 3). This is, in a nutshell, what a **contour plot** does. From now on, we'll always use the contour plot, instead of the corresponding 3D version.

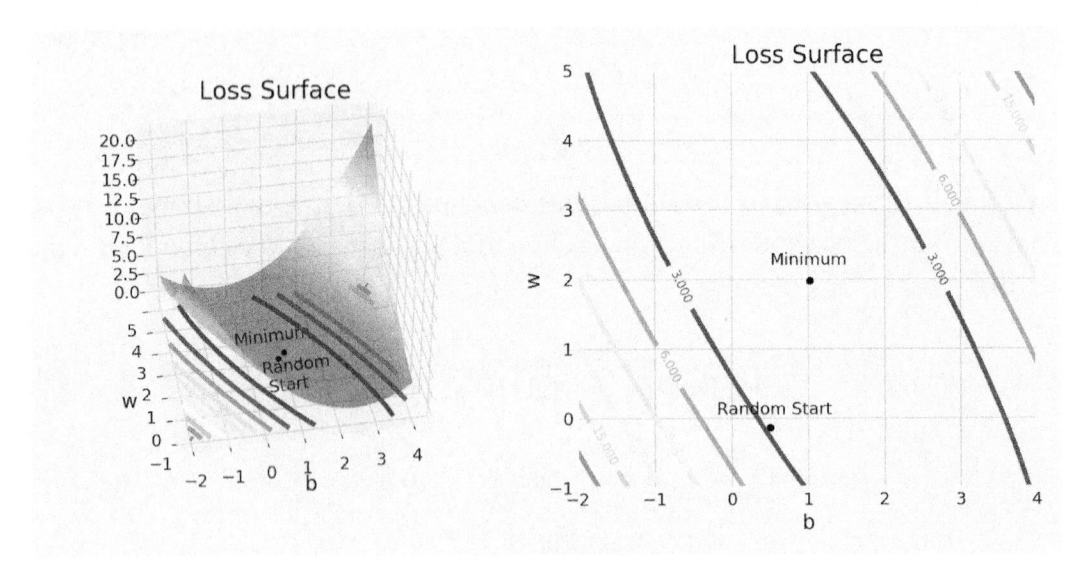

Figure 0.4 - Loss surface

In the center of the plot, where parameters (b, w) have values close to (1, 2), the loss is at its **minimum** value. This is the point we're trying to reach using gradient descent.

In the bottom, slightly to the left, there is the **random start** point, corresponding to our randomly initialized parameters.

This is one of the nice things about tackling a simple problem like a linear regression with a single feature: We have only **two parameters**, and thus **we can compute and visualize the loss surface**.

> Unfortunately, for the absolute majority of problems, **computing the loss surface is not going to be feasible**: we have to rely on gradient descent's ability to reach a point of minimum, even if it starts at some random point.

Cross-Sections

Another nice thing is that we can cut a **cross-section** in the loss surface to check what the **loss** would look like if **the other parameter were held constant**.

Let's start by making **b = 0.52** (the value from b_range that is closest to our initial random value for b, 0.4967). We cut a cross-section *vertically* (the red dashed line) on our loss surface (left plot), and we get the resulting plot on the right:

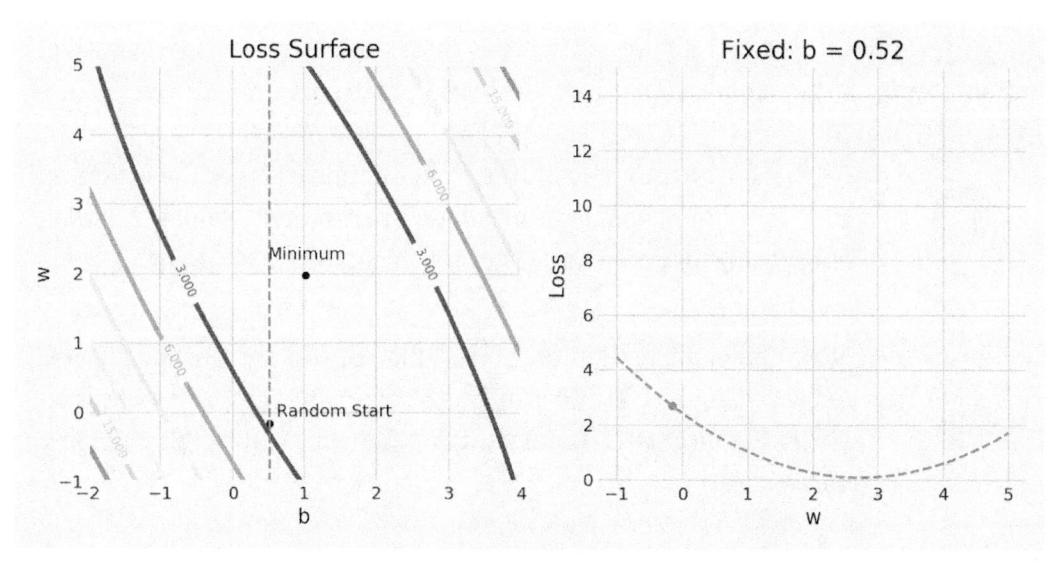

Figure 0.5 - Vertical cross-section; parameter b is fixed

What does this cross-section tell us? It tells us that, **if we keep b constant** (at 0.52), the **loss**, seen from the **perspective of parameter w**, can be minimized if **w gets increased** (up to some value between 2 and 3).

Sure, **different values of b** produce **different cross-section loss curves for w**. And those curves will depend on the **shape of the loss surface** (more on that later, in the "**Learning Rate**" section).

OK, so far, so good... What about the *other* cross-section? Let's cut it *horizontally* now, making **w = -0.16** (the value from w_range that is closest to our initial random value for *b*, -0.1382). The resulting plot is on the right:

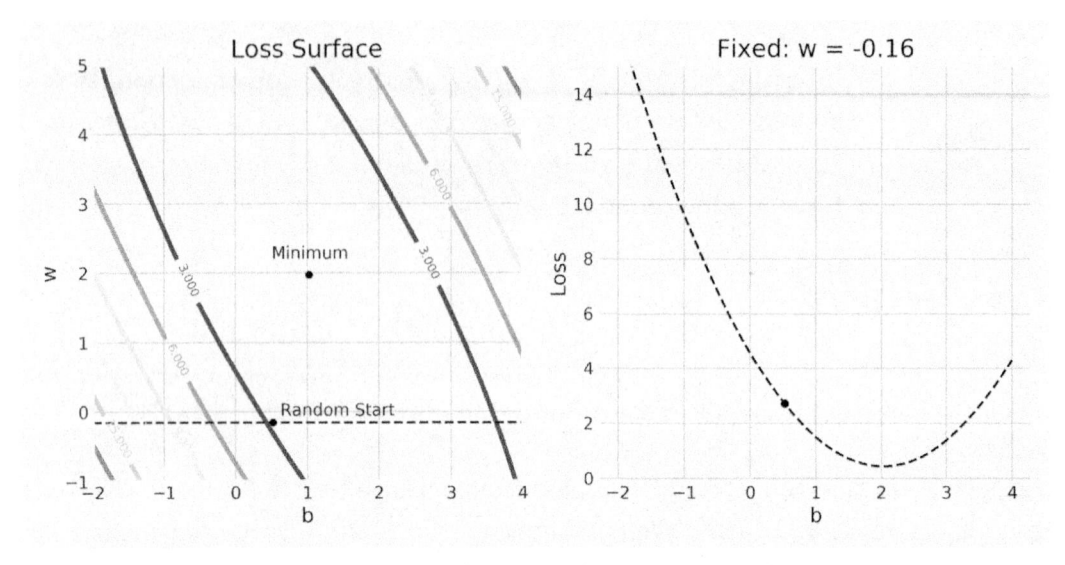

Figure 0.6 - Horizontal cross-section; parameter w is fixed

Now, **if we keep w constant** (at -0.16), the **loss**, seen from the **perspective of parameter b**, can be minimized if **b gets increased** (up to some value close to 2).

> In general, the purpose of this cross-section is to get the **effect on the loss** of **changing a single parameter**, while keeping everything else constant. This is, in a nutshell, a **gradient** :-)

> Now I have a question for you: **Which** of the two dashed curves, red (*w* changes, *b* is constant) or black (*b* changes, *w* is constant) yields the **largest changes in loss** when we modify the changing parameter?

The answer is coming right up in the next section!

Step 3 - Compute the Gradients

A **gradient** is a **partial derivative**—*why* **partial**? Because one computes it *with* respect to (w.r.t.) a **single parameter**. We have two parameters, **b** and **w**, so we must compute two partial derivatives.

A **derivative** tells you *how much* a given quantity changes when you *slightly* **vary** some **other quantity**. In our case, how much does our **MSE loss** change when we vary **each of our two parameters separately**?

> 💡 Gradient = **how much** the **loss** changes if **ONE** parameter changes **a little bit!**

The *right-most* part of the equations below is what you usually see in implementations of gradient descent for simple linear regression. In the **intermediate step**, I show you **all elements** that pop up from the application of the chain rule,[37] so you know how the final expression came to be.

$$\frac{\partial MSE}{\partial b} = \frac{\partial MSE}{\partial \hat{y}_i}\frac{\partial \hat{y}_i}{\partial b} = \frac{1}{n}\sum_{i=1}^{n} 2(b + wx_i - y_i)$$

$$= 2\frac{1}{n}\sum_{i=1}^{n}(\hat{y}_i - y_i)$$

$$\frac{\partial MSE}{\partial w} = \frac{\partial MSE}{\partial \hat{y}_i}\frac{\partial \hat{y}_i}{\partial w} = \frac{1}{n}\sum_{i=1}^{n} 2(b + wx_i - y_i)x_i$$

$$= 2\frac{1}{n}\sum_{i=1}^{n} x_i(\hat{y}_i - y_i)$$

Equation 0.4 - Computing gradients w.r.t coefficients b and w using n points

Just to be clear: We will always **use our "*regular*" error computed at the beginning of Step 2**. The loss surface is surely eye candy, but, as I mentioned before, it is only feasible to use it for educational purposes.

Step 3

```
1 # Step 3 - Computes gradients for both "b" and "w" parameters
2 b_grad = 2 * error.mean()
3 w_grad = 2 * (x_train * error).mean()
4 print(b_grad, w_grad)
```

Output

```
-3.044811379650508 -1.8337537171510832
```

Visualizing Gradients

Since the **gradient for b** is **larger** (in absolute value, 3.04) than the gradient for *w* (in absolute value, 1.83), the answer for the question I posed you in the "**Cross-Sections**" section is: The **black** curve (*b* changes, *w* is constant) yields the largest changes in loss.

> *"Why is that?"*

To answer that, let's first put both cross-section plots side-by-side, so we can more easily compare them. What is the **main difference** between them?

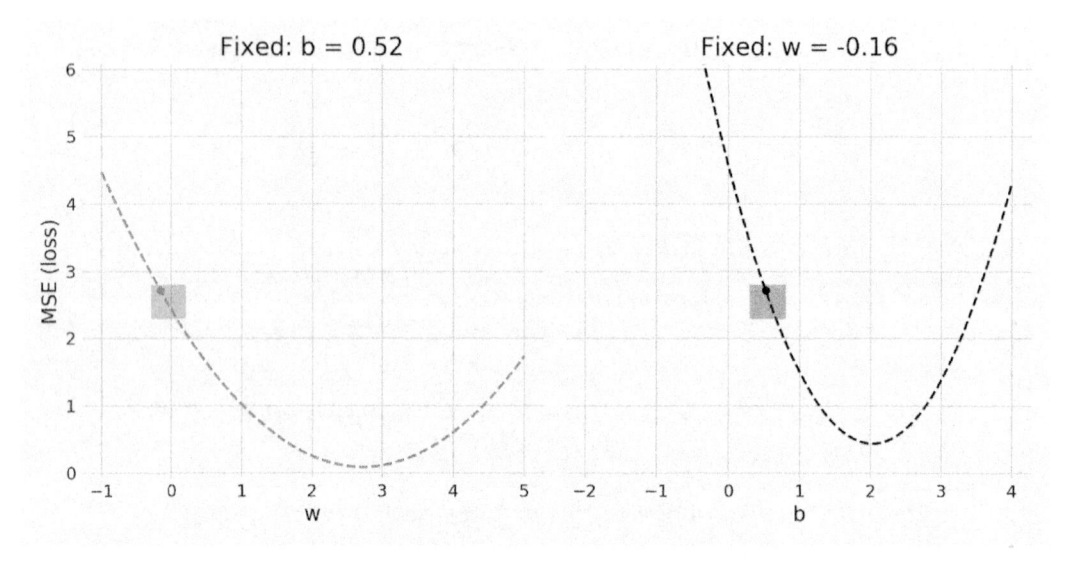

Figure 0.7 - Cross-sections of the loss surface

The curve on the right is **steeper**. That's your answer! **Steeper curves** have **larger gradients**.

Cool! That's the intuition... Now, let's get a bit more *geometrical*. So, I am **zooming in** on the regions given by the *red* and *black* squares of Figure 0.7.

From the "**Cross-Sections**" section, we already know that to *minimize the loss*, both *b* and *w* needed to be **increased**. So, keeping in the spirit of using gradients, let's **increase each parameter a *little bit*** (always keeping the other one fixed!). By the way, in this example, *a little bit* equals 0.12 (for convenience's sake, so it results in a nicer plot).

What effect do these increases have on the loss? Let's check it out:

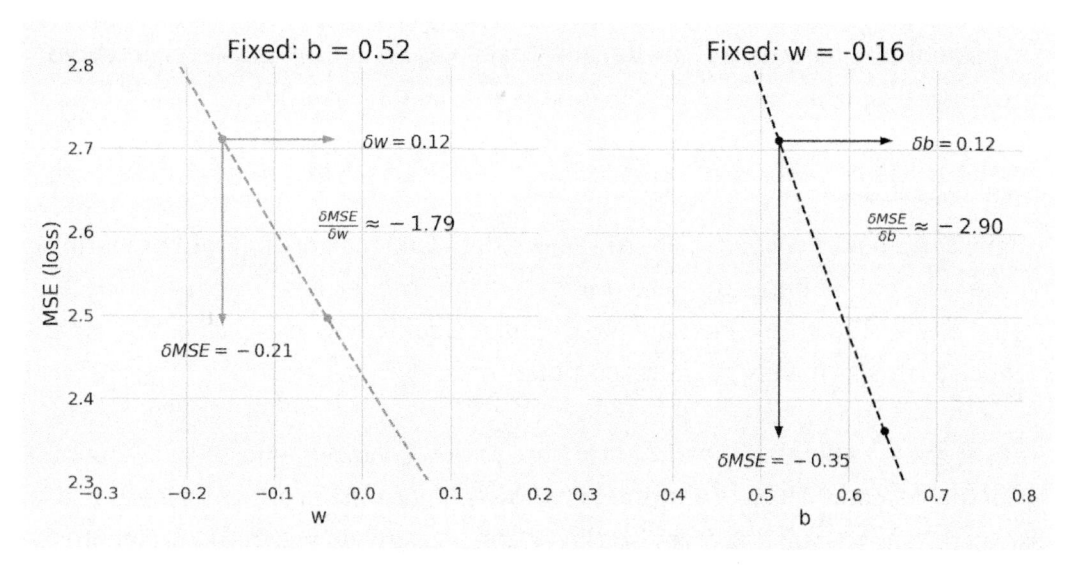

Figure 0.8 - Computing (approximate) gradients, geometrically

On the left plot, **increasing w by 0.12** yields a **loss reduction of 0.21**. The geometrically computed and roughly approximate gradient is given by the ratio between the two values: **-1.79**. How does this result compare to the actual value of the gradient (-1.83)? It is actually not bad for a crude approximation. Could it be better? Sure, if we make the **increase in w smaller and smaller** (like 0.01, instead of 0.12), we'll get **better and better** approximations. In the limit, as the **increase approaches zero**, we'll arrive at the **precise value of the gradient**. Well, that's the definition of a derivative!

The same reasoning goes for the plot on the right: **increasing b by the same 0.12** yields a **larger loss reduction of 0.35**. Larger loss reduction, larger ratio, larger gradient—and larger error, too, since the geometric approximation (-2.90) is farther away from the actual value (-3.04).

Time for another question: **Which curve**, red or black, do you like **best** to **reduce the loss**? It should be the **black one**, right? Well, yes, but it is not as straightforward as we'd like it to be. We'll dig deeper into this in the "**Learning Rate**" section.

Backpropagation

Now that you've learned about *computing the gradient of the loss function w.r.t. to each parameter using the chain rule*, let me show you how *Wikipedia* describes **backpropagation** (highlights are mine):

> The backpropagation algorithm works by **computing the gradient of the loss function with respect to each weight by the chain rule**, computing the gradient one layer at a time, iterating backward from the last layer to avoid redundant calculations of intermediate terms in the chain rule;
>
> ...
>
> The term *backpropagation* strictly refers only to the algorithm for computing the gradient, not how the gradient is used; but the term is often used loosely to refer to the entire learning algorithm, including how the gradient is used, such as by stochastic gradient descent.

Does it seem familiar? That's it; **backpropagation** is nothing more than **"chained" gradient descent**. That's, in a nutshell, how a neural network is trained: It uses backpropagation, starting at its **last layer** and working its way back, to update the weights through all the layers.

In our example, we have a **single layer**, even a **single neuron**, so there is no need to backpropagate anything (more on that in the next chapter).

Step 4 - Update the Parameters

In the final step, we **use the gradients to update** the parameters. Since we are trying to **minimize** our **losses**, we **reverse the sign** of the gradient for the update.

There is still another (hyper-)parameter to consider: the **learning rate**, denoted by the *Greek letter eta* (that looks like the letter *n*), which is the **multiplicative factor** that we need to apply to the gradient for the parameter update.

$$b = b - \eta \frac{\partial \text{MSE}}{\partial b}$$
$$w = w - \eta \frac{\partial \text{MSE}}{\partial w}$$

*Equation 0.5 - Updating coefficients **b** and **w** using computed gradients and a learning rate*

We can also interpret this a bit differently: **Each parameter** is going to have its value **updated by a constant value** *eta* (the learning rate), but this constant is going to be **weighted by how much that parameter contributes to minimizing the loss** (its gradient).

Honestly, I believe this way of thinking about the parameter update makes more sense. First, you decide on a *learning rate* that specifies your **step size**, while the *gradients* tell you the **relative impact** (on the loss) of taking a step for each parameter. Then, you take a given **number of steps** that's **proportional** to that **relative impact**: **more impact, more steps**.

"*How do you **choose** a learning rate?*"

That is a topic on its own and beyond the scope of this section as well. We'll get back to it later on, in the second volume of the series.

In our example, let's start with a value of **0.1** for the learning rate (which is a relatively *high value*, as far as learning rates are concerned).

Step 4

```
1  # Sets learning rate - this is "eta" ~ the "n"-like Greek letter
2  lr = 0.1
3  print(b, w)
4
5  # Step 4 - Updates parameters using gradients and the
6  # learning rate
7  b = b - lr * b_grad
8  w = w - lr * w_grad
9
10 print(b, w)
```

Output

```
[0.49671415] [-0.1382643]
[0.80119529] [0.04511107]
```

What's the **impact of one update** on our model? Let's visually check its predictions.

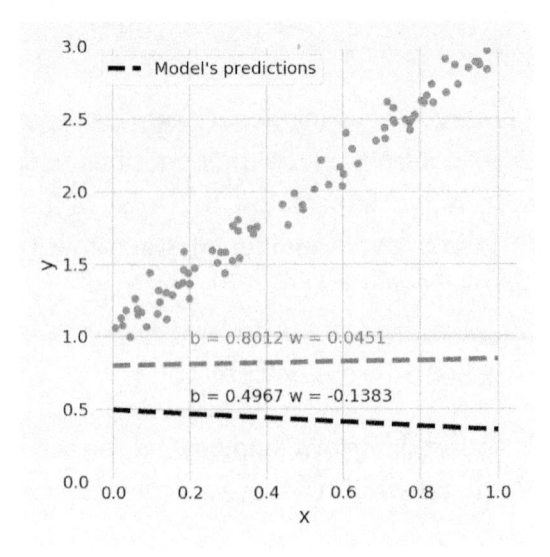

Figure 0.9 - Updated model's predictions

It looks better ... at least it started pointing in the right direction!

Learning Rate

The **learning rate** is the most important hyper-parameter. There is a gigantic amount of material on how to *choose* a learning rate, how to *modify* the learning rate during the training, and how the *wrong* learning rate can completely ruin the model training.

Maybe you've seen this famous graph[38] (from Stanford's CS231n class) that shows how a learning rate that is **too high** or **too low** affects the **loss** during training. Most people will see it (or have seen it) at some point in time. This is pretty much general knowledge, but I think it needs to be **thoroughly explained and visually demonstrated** to be *truly* understood. So, let's start!

I will tell you a little story (trying to build an analogy here, please bear with me!): Imagine you are coming back from hiking in the mountains and you want to get back home as quickly as possible. At some point in your path, you can either choose to *go ahead* or to *make a right turn*.

The path *ahead* is almost *flat*, while the path to your *right* is kinda *steep*. The **steepness** is the **gradient**. If you take a single step one way or the other, it will lead to different outcomes (you'll descend more if you take one step to the right instead of going ahead).

But, here is the thing: You know that the path to your *right* is getting you home **faster**, so you don't take just one step, but **multiple steps** in that direction. **The steeper the path, the more steps you take**! Remember, "*more impact, more steps*!" You just cannot resist the urge to take that many steps; your behavior seems to be completely determined by the landscape (This analogy is getting weird, I know...)

But, you still have **one choice**: You **can adjust the size of your step**. You can choose to take steps of any size, from *tiny steps* to *long strides*. That's your **learning rate**.

OK, let's see where this little story brought us so far. That's how you'll move, in a nutshell:

updated location = previous location + step size * number of steps

Now, compare it to what we did with the parameters:

updated value = previous value - learning rate * gradient

You get the point, right? I hope so, because the analogy completely falls apart now. At this point, after moving in one direction (say, the *right turn* we talked about), you'd have to stop and move in the *other* direction (for just a fraction of a step, because the path was almost *flat*, remember?). And so on and so forth. Well, I don't think anyone has ever returned from hiking in such an orthogonal zig-zag path!

Anyway, let's explore further the **only choice** you have: the size of your *step*—I mean, the **learning rate**.

> "*Choose your learning rate wisely.*"
>
> Grail Knight

Low Learning Rate

It makes sense to start with *baby steps*, right? This means using a **low learning rate**. Low learning rates are **safe(r)**, as expected. If you were to take *tiny steps* while returning home from your hiking, you'd be more likely to arrive there safe and sound—but it would take a **lot of time**. The same holds true for training models: Low learning rates will likely get you to (some) minimum point, **eventually**. Unfortunately, time is money, especially when you're paying for GPU time in the cloud, so, there is an *incentive* to try **higher learning rates**.

How does this reasoning apply to our model? From computing our (geometric) gradients, we know we need to take a given **number of steps**: **1.79** (parameter w) and **2.90** (parameter b), respectively. Let's set our **step size to 0.2** (low-ish). It means we **move 0.36 for w** and **0.58 for b**.

> **IMPORTANT**: In real life, a learning rate of 0.2 is usually considered *HIGH*—but in our very simple linear regression example, it still qualifies as low-ish.

Where does this movement lead us? As you can see in the plots below (as shown by the **new dots** to the right of the original ones), in both cases, the movement took us closer to the minimum; more so on the right because the curve is **steeper**.

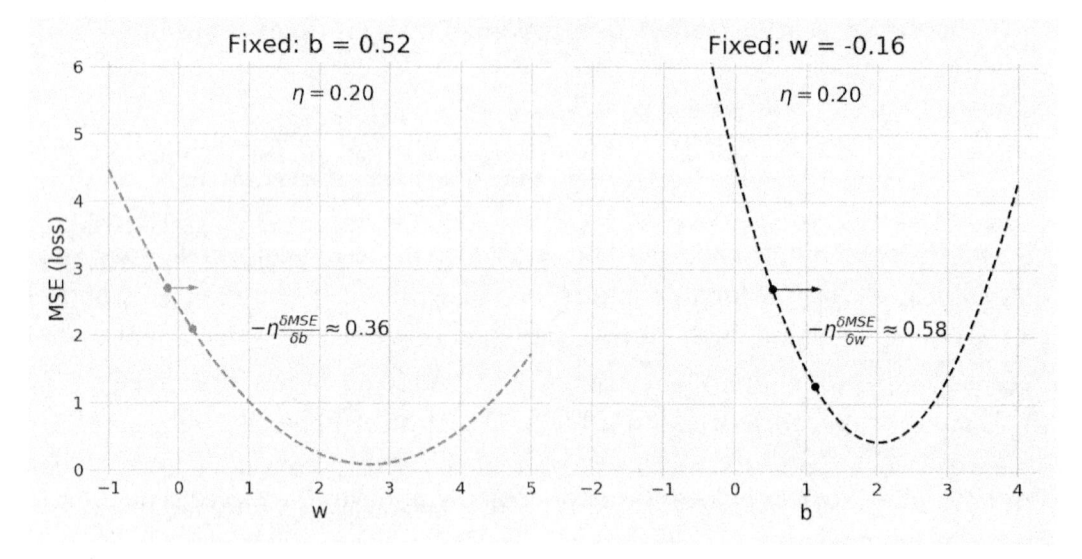

Figure 0.10 - Using a low-ish learning rate

44 | Chapter 0: Visualizing Gradient Descent

High Learning Rate

What would have happened if we had used a **high** learning rate instead, say, a **step size of 0.8**? As we can see in the plots below, we start to, literally, **run into trouble**.

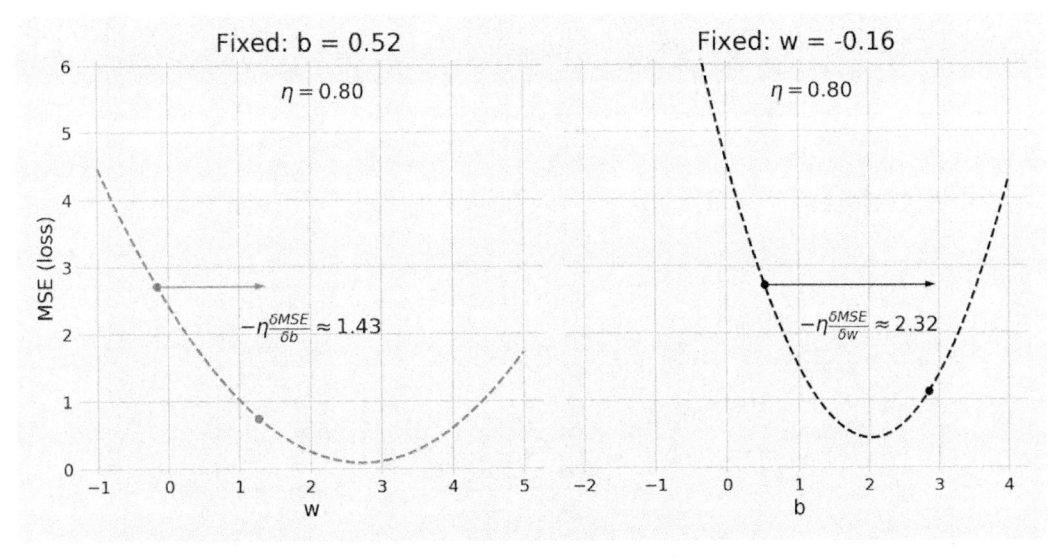

Figure 0.11 - Using a high learning rate

Even though everything is still OK on the left plot, the right plot shows us a completely different picture: **We ended up on the other side of the curve**. That is *not* good... You'd be going **back and forth**, alternately hitting both sides of the curve.

> "Well, even so, I **still** may reach the minimum; why is it so bad?"

In our simple example, yes, you'd eventually reach the minimum because the **curve is nice and round**.

But, in real problems, the "curve" has a really **weird shape** that allows for **bizarre outcomes**, such as going back and forth **without ever approaching the minimum**.

In our analogy, you **moved so fast** that you **fell down** and hit the **other side of the valley**, then kept going down like a *ping-pong*. Hard to believe, I know, but you definitely don't want that!

Very High Learning Rate

Wait, it may get **worse** than that! Let's use a **really high learning rate**, say, a **step size of 1.1!**

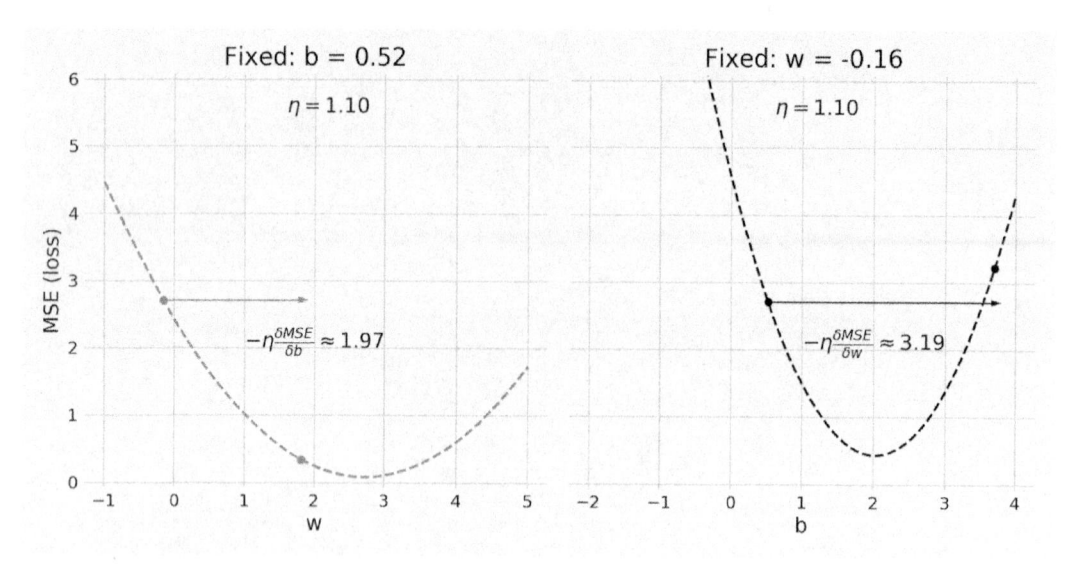

Figure 0.12 - Using a really high learning rate

"He chose ... poorly."

Grail Knight

Ok, that *is* bad. On the right plot, not only did we end up on the *other side of the curve* again, but we actually **climbed up**. This means **our loss increased**, instead of decreased! How is that even possible? *You're moving so fast downhill that you end up climbing it back up?!* Unfortunately, the analogy cannot help us anymore. We need to think about this particular case in a different way.

First, notice that everything is *fine* on the left plot. The *enormous learning rate* **did not cause any issues**, because the left curve is **less steep** than the one on the right. In other words, the curve on the left **can take higher learning rates** than the curve on the right.

What can we learn from it?

Too high, for a **learning rate**, is a relative concept: It depends on **how steep** the curve is, or, in other words, it depends on **how large the gradient is**.

We do have *many curves*, **many gradients**: one for each parameter. But we only have **one single learning rate** to choose (sorry, that's the way it is!).

It means that the **size of the learning rate is limited by the steepest curve**. All other curves must follow suit, meaning they'd be using a *suboptimal* learning rate, given their shapes.

The reasonable conclusion is: It is **best** if all the **curves are equally steep**, so the **learning rate** is closer to optimal for all of them!

"Bad" Feature

How do we achieve *equally steep curves*? I'm on it! First, let's take a look at a *slightly modified* example, which I am calling the "bad" dataset:

- I **multiplied our feature (x) by 10**, so it is in the range [0, 10] now, and renamed it bad_x.

- But since I **do not want the labels (y) to change**, I **divided the original true_w parameter by 10** and renamed it bad_w—this way, both bad_w * bad_x and w * x yield the same results.

```
true_b = 1
true_w = 2
N = 100

# Data Generation
np.random.seed(42)

# We divide w by 10
bad_w = true_w / 10
# And multiply x by 10
bad_x = np.random.rand(N, 1) * 10

# So, the net effect on y is zero - it is still
# the same as before
y = true_b + bad_w * bad_x + (.1 * np.random.randn(N, 1))
```

Then, I performed the same split as before for both *original* and *bad* datasets and plotted the training sets side-by-side, as you can see below:

```
# Generates train and validation sets
# It uses the same train_idx and val_idx as before,
# but it applies to bad_x
bad_x_train, y_train = bad_x[train_idx], y[train_idx]
bad_x_val, y_val = bad_x[val_idx], y[val_idx]
```

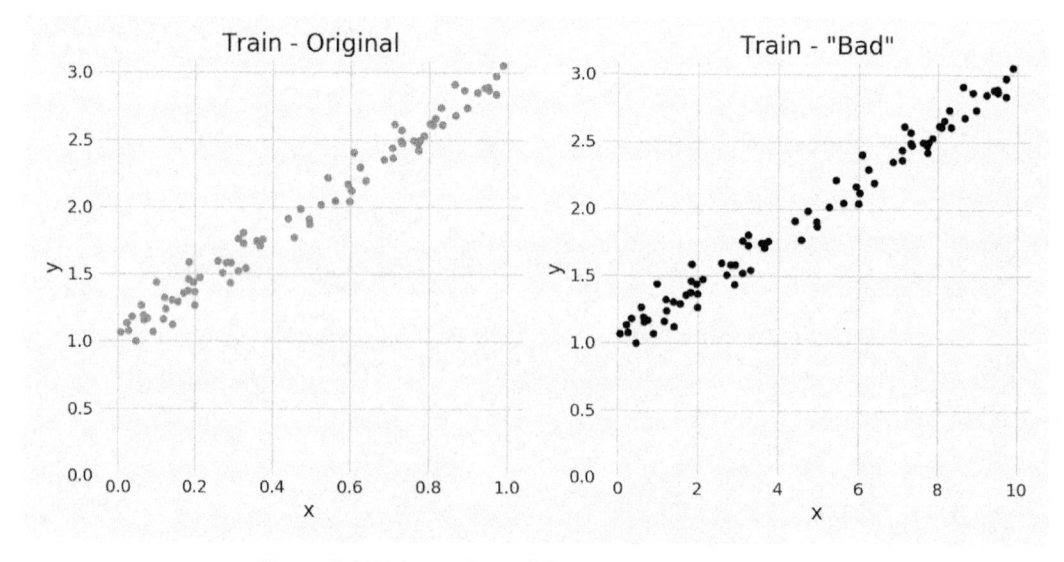

Figure 0.13 - Same data, different scales for feature x

The **only** difference between the two plots is the **scale of feature x**. Its range was [0, 1], now it is [0, 10]. The label y hasn't changed, and I did not touch `true_b`.

Does this simple **scaling** have any meaningful impact on our gradient descent? Well, if it hadn't, I wouldn't be asking it, right? Let's compute a new **loss surface** and compare to the one we had before.

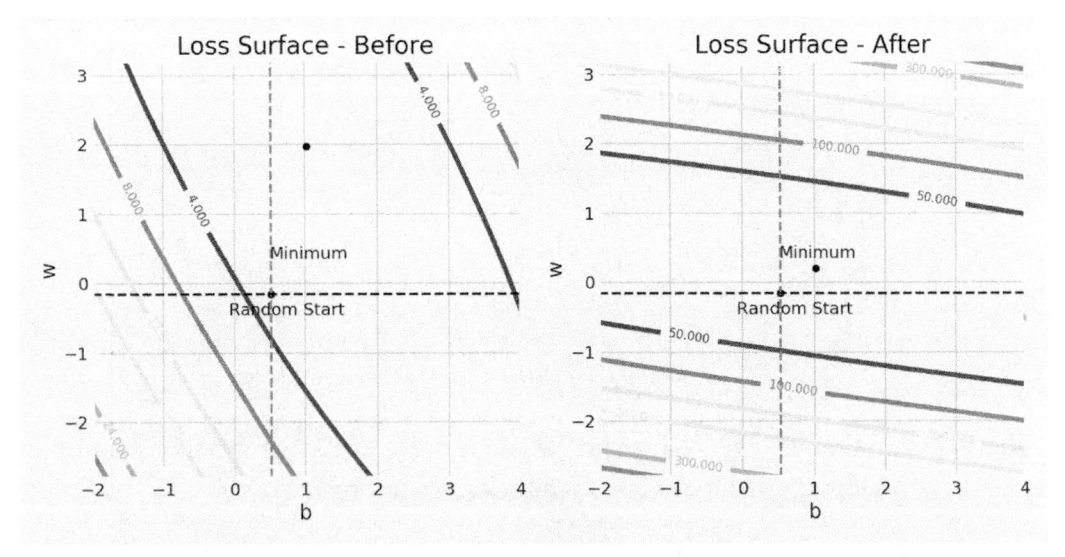

Figure 0.14 - Loss surface—before and after scaling feature x (Obs.: left plot looks a bit different than Figure 0.6 because it is centered at the "after" minimum)

Look at the **contour values** of Figure 0.14: The *dark blue* line was 3.0, and now it is 50.0! For the same range of parameter values, **loss values are much higher**.

Step 4 - Update the Parameters | 49

Let's look at the *cross-sections* before and after we multiplied feature *x* by 10.

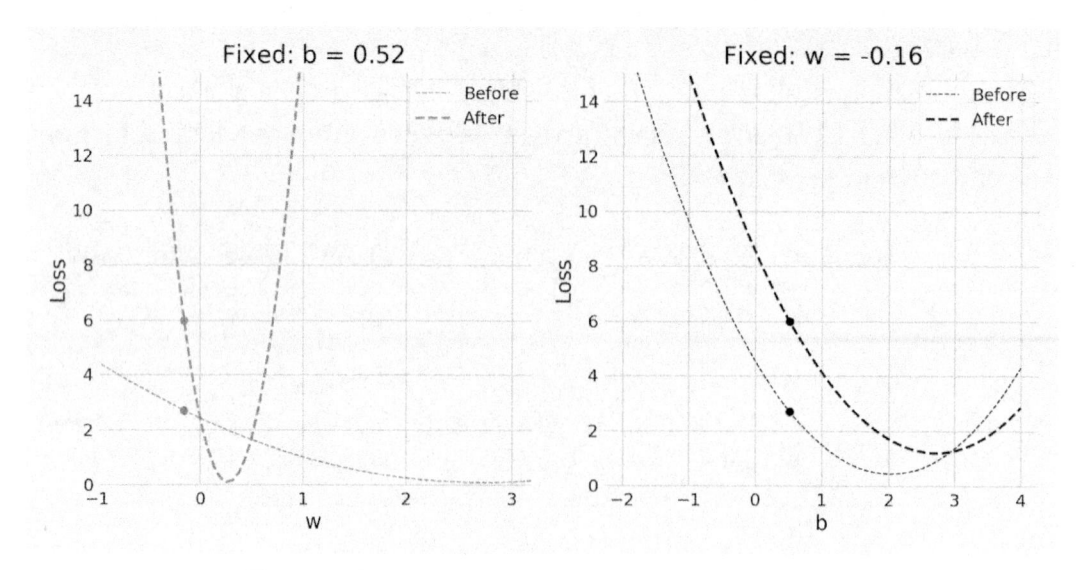

Figure 0.15 - Comparing cross-sections: before and after

What happened here? The **red curve** got much **steeper** (larger gradient), and thus we must use a **lower learning rate** to safely descend along it.

> More important, the **difference** in **steepness** between the red and the black curves **increased**.
>
> This is exactly what **WE NEED TO AVOID!**
>
> Do you remember why?
>
> Because the **size of the learning rate is limited by the steepest curve!**

How can we fix it? Well, we *ruined* it by **scaling it 10x larger**. Perhaps we can make it better if we **scale it in a different way**.

Scaling / Standardizing / Normalizing

Different how? There is this *beautiful* thing called the `StandardScaler`, which transforms a **feature** in such a way that it ends up with **zero mean** and **unit standard deviation**.

How does it achieve that? First, it computes the *mean* and the *standard deviation* of a given **feature (x)** using the training set (**N** points):

$$\overline{X} = \frac{1}{N} \sum_{i=1}^{N} x_i$$

$$\sigma(X) = \sqrt{\frac{1}{N} \sum_{i=1}^{N} (x_i - \overline{X})^2}$$

Equation 0.6 - Computing mean and standard deviation

Then, it uses both values to **scale** the feature:

$$\text{scaled } x_i = \frac{x_i - \overline{X}}{\sigma(X)}$$

Equation 0.7 - Standardizing

If we were to recompute the mean and the standard deviation of the scaled feature, we would get 0 and 1, respectively. This pre-processing step is commonly referred to as *normalization*, although, technically, it should always be referred to as *standardization*.

> **IMPORTANT**: Pre-processing steps like the StandardScaler **MUST** be performed **AFTER** the train-validation-test split; otherwise, you'll be **leaking** information from the validation and / or test sets to your model!
>
> After using the **training set only** to fit the StandardScaler, you should use its transform() method to apply the pre-processing step to **all datasets**: training, validation, and test.

Zero Mean and Unit Standard Deviation

Let's start with the **unit standard deviation**; that is, scaling the feature values such that its **standard deviation** equals **one**. This is one of the **most important pre-processing steps**, not only for the sake of improving the performance of **gradient descent**, but for other techniques such as **principal component analysis (PCA)** as well. The **goal** is to have **all numerical features** in a **similar scale**, so the results are not affected by the original **range** of each feature.

Think of two common features in a model: *age* and *salary*. While *age* usually varies between 0 and 110, salaries can go from the low hundreds (say, 500) to several thousand (say, 9,000). If we compute the corresponding standard deviations, we may get values like 25 and 2,000, respectively. Thus, we need to **standardize** both features to have them on **equal footing**.

And then there is the **zero mean**; that is, **centering** the feature at **zero**. **Deeper neural networks** may suffer from a very serious condition called **vanishing gradients**. Since the gradients are used to update the parameters, smaller and smaller (that is, vanishing) gradients mean smaller and smaller updates, up to the point of a standstill: The network simply stops learning. One way to help the network to fight this condition is to **center its inputs**, the features, at **zero**. We'll get back to this later on, in the second volume of the series, while discussing *activation functions*.

The code below will illustrate this well.

```
scaler = StandardScaler(with_mean=True, with_std=True)
# We use the TRAIN set ONLY to fit the scaler
scaler.fit(x_train)

# Now we can use the already fit scaler to TRANSFORM
# both TRAIN and VALIDATION sets
scaled_x_train = scaler.transform(x_train)
scaled_x_val = scaler.transform(x_val)
```

Notice that we are **not** regenerating the data—we are using the **original feature *x*** as input for the `StandardScaler` and transforming it into a **scaled *x***. The labels (*y*) are left untouched.

Let's plot the three of them—*original*, *"bad"*, and *scaled*—side-by-side to illustrate the differences.

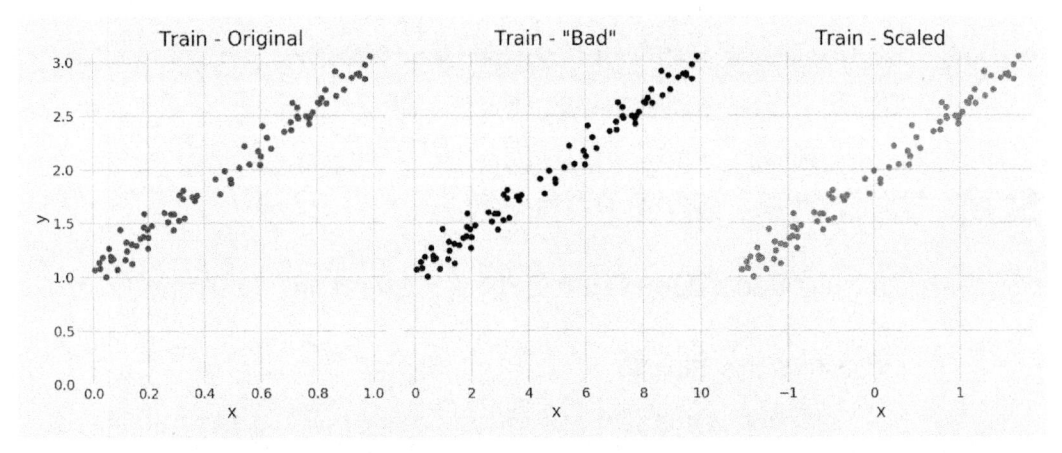

Figure 0.16 - Same data, three different scales for feature x

Once again, the **only** difference between the plots is the **scale of feature** x. Its range was originally [0, 1], then we made it [0, 10], and now the `StandardScaler` made it [-1.5, 1.5].

OK, time to check the **loss surface**: To illustrate the differences, I am plotting the three of them side-by-side: *original*, *"bad"*, and *scaled*. It looks like Figure 0.17.

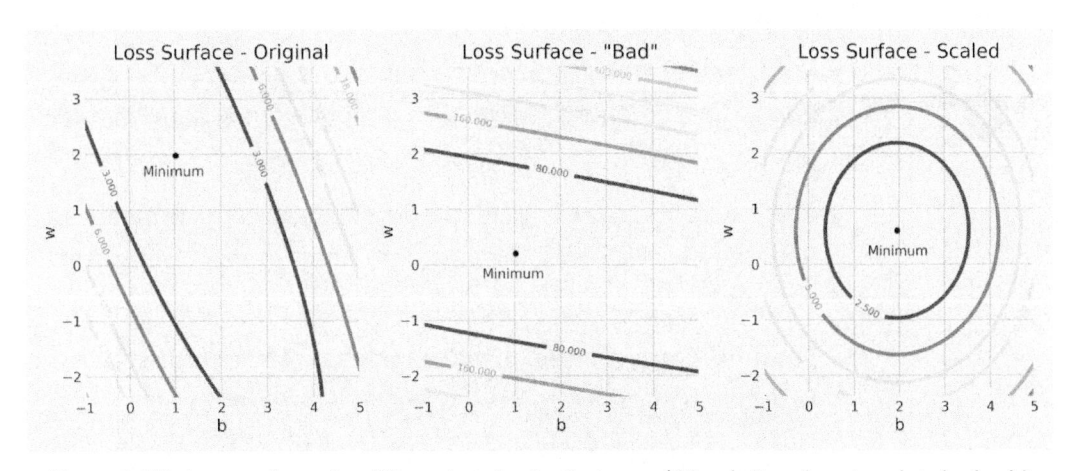

Figure 0.17 - Loss surfaces for different scales for feature x (Obs.: left and center plots look a bit different than Figure 0.14 because they are centered at the "scaled" minimum)

BEAUTIFUL, isn't it? The textbook definition of a **bowl** :-)

In practice, this is the **best surface** one could hope for: The **cross-sections** are going to be **similarly steep**, and a **good learning rate** for one of them is also good for the other.

Sure, in the real world, you'll never get a *pretty bowl* like that. But our conclusion still holds:

1. **Always standardize (scale) your features.**
2. **DO NOT EVER FORGET #1!**

Step 5 - Rinse and Repeat!

Now we use the **updated parameters** to go back to **Step 1** and restart the process.

Definition of Epoch

An **epoch** is complete whenever every point in the training set (*N*) has already been used in all steps: forward pass, computing loss, computing gradients, and updating parameters.

During **one epoch**, we perform at least **one update**, but no more than *N* **updates**.

The number of **updates** (*N/n*) will depend on the type of gradient descent being used:

- For **batch** (*n = N*) gradient descent, this is trivial, as it uses all points for computing the loss—**one epoch** is the same as **one update**.
- For **stochastic** (*n = 1*) gradient descent, **one epoch** means *N* updates, since every individual data point is used to perform an update.
- For **mini-batch** (of size *n*), **one epoch** has *N/n* **updates**, since a mini-batch of *n* data points is used to perform an update.

Repeating this process over and over for **many epochs** is, in a nutshell, **training** a model.

What happens if we run it over **1,000 epochs**?

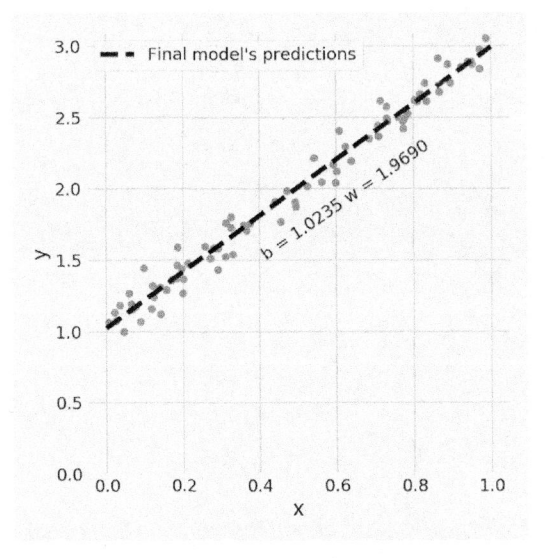

Figure 0.18 - Final model's predictions

In the next chapter, we'll put all these steps together and run it for 1,000 epochs, so we'll get to the parameters depicted in the figure above, b = 1.0235 and w = 1.9690.

"Why 1,000 epochs?"

No particular reason, but this is a fairly simple model, and we can afford to run it over a large number of epochs. In more-complex models, though, a couple of dozen epochs may be enough. We'll discuss this a bit more in Chapter 1.

The Path of Gradient Descent

In Step 3, we have seen the **loss surface** and both random start and minimum points.

Which **path** is gradient descent going to take to go from **random start** to a **minimum**? **How long** will it take? Will it actually **reach the minimum**?

The answers to all these questions depend on many things, like the *learning rate*, the *shape of the loss surface*, and the **number of points** we use to compute the loss.

Depending on whether we use **batch**, **mini-batch**, or **stochastic** gradient descent, the path is going to be more or less **smooth**, and it is likely to reach the minimum in more or less **time**.

To illustrate the differences, I've generated paths over 100 **epochs** using either 80 data points (*batch*), 16 data points (*mini-batch*), or a single data point (*stochastic*) for computing the loss, as shown in the figure below.

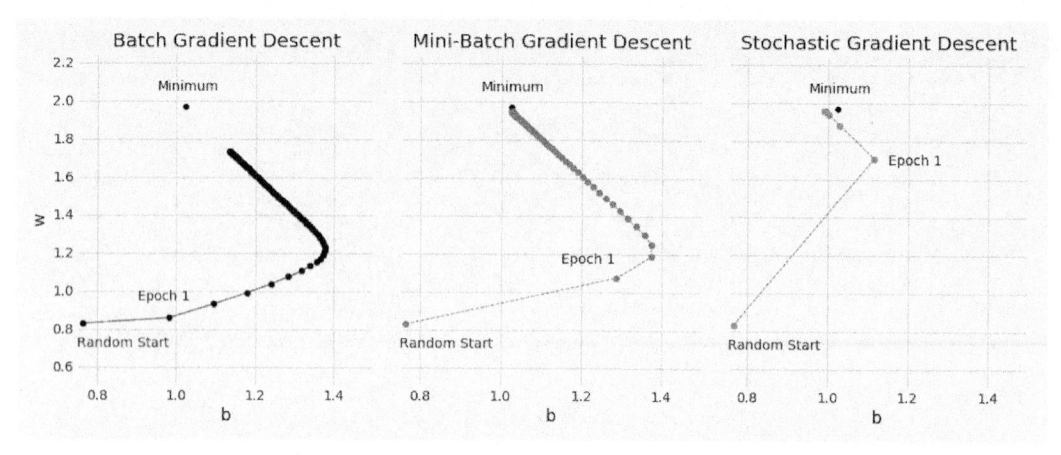

Figure 0.19 - The paths of gradient descent (Obs.: random start is different from Figure 0.4)

You can see that the resulting parameters at the end of **Epoch 1** differ greatly from one another. This is a direct consequence of the **number of updates** happening during **one epoch**, according to the batch size. In our example, for 100 epochs:

- 80 data points (*batch*): 1 update / epoch, totaling **100 updates**
- 16 data points (*mini-batch*): 5 updates / epoch, totaling **500 updates**
- 1 data point (*stochastic*): 80 updates / epoch, totaling **8,000 updates**

So, for both *center* and *right* plots, the **path between random start and Epoch 1** contains **multiple updates**, which are not depicted in the plot (otherwise it would be *very* cluttered)—that's why the line connecting two epochs is **dashed**, instead of solid. In reality, there would be **zig-zagging lines** connecting every two epochs.

There are two things to notice:

- It should be no surprise that **mini-batch** gradient descent is able to get **closer to the minimum point** (using the same number of epochs) since it benefits from a *larger number of updates* than batch gradient descent.

- The **stochastic** gradient descent path is somewhat weird: It gets quite close to the **minimum point** at the end of Epoch 1 already, but then it seems to **fail to actually reach it**. But this is *expected* since it uses a *single data point for each update*; it will never stabilize, forever **hovering** in the neighborhood of the **minimum point**.

Clearly, there is a **trade-off** here: Either we have a **stable and smooth** trajectory, or we **move faster toward the minimum**.

Recap

This finishes our journey through the inner workings of **gradient descent**. By now, I hope you have developed better **intuition** about the many different aspects involved in the process.

In time, with practice, you'll observe the behaviors described here in your own models. Make sure to try plenty of different combinations: mini-batch sizes, learning rates, etc. This way, not only will your models learn, but so will you :-)

This is a (not so) short recap of everything we covered in this chapter:

- defining a **simple linear regression model**
- generating **synthetic data** for it
- performing a **train-validation split** on our dataset
- **randomly initializing the parameters** of our model
- performing a **forward pass**; that is, *making predictions* using our model
- computing the **errors** associated with our **predictions**
- *aggregating* the errors into a **loss** (mean squared error)
- learning that the **number of points** used to compute the **loss** defines the kind of gradient descent we're using: **batch** (all), **mini-batch**, or **stochastic** (one)
- visualizing an example of a **loss surface** and using its **cross-sections** to get the **loss curves** for individual parameters
- learning that a **gradient is a partial derivative** and it represents **how much the loss changes if one parameter changes a little bit**
- computing the **gradients** for our model's parameters using **equations**, **code**, and **geometry**
- learning that **larger gradients** correspond to **steeper loss curves**
- learning that **backpropagation** is nothing more than "**chained**" gradient descent
- using the **gradients** and a **learning rate** to **update the parameters**
- comparing the **effects on the loss** of using **low**, **high**, and **very high learning rates**
- learning that **loss curves** for all parameters should be, ideally, **similarly steep**

- visualizing the effects of using a **feature with a larger range**, making the loss curve for the corresponding parameter **much steeper**

- using Scikit-Learn's `StandardScaler` to bring a feature to a reasonable range and thus making the **loss surface more bowl-shaped** and its cross-sections **similarly steep**

- learning that **preprocessing steps** like scaling should be applied **after the train-validation split** to prevent **leakage**

- figuring out that performing **all steps** (forward pass, loss, gradients, and parameter update) makes **one epoch**

- visualizing the **path of gradient descent** over many epochs and realizing it is heavily **dependent on the kind of gradient descent** used: batch, mini-batch, or stochastic

- learning that there is a **trade-off** between the *stable and smooth path* of batch gradient descent and the *fast and somewhat chaotic path* of stochastic gradient descent, making the use of **mini-batch gradient descent a good compromise** between the other two

You are now **ready** to put it all together and actually **train a model using PyTorch**!

[33] https://github.com/dvgodoy/PyTorchStepByStep/blob/master/Chapter00.ipynb

[34] https://colab.research.google.com/github/dvgodoy/PyTorchStepByStep/blob/master/Chapter00.ipynb

[35] https://en.wikipedia.org/wiki/Gradient_descent

[36] https://en.wikipedia.org/wiki/Gaussian_noise

[37] https://en.wikipedia.org/wiki/Chain_rule

[38] https://bit.ly/2BxCxTO

Chapter 1
A Simple Regression Problem

Spoilers

In this chapter, we will:

- briefly **review** the steps of gradient descent (*optional*)
- use gradient descent to implement a **linear regression** in *Numpy*
- create **tensors in PyTorch** (finally!)
- understand the difference between **CPU** and **GPU tensors**
- understand PyTorch's main feature, **autograd**, used to perform automatic differentiation
- visualize the **dynamic computation graph**
- create a **loss function**
- define an **optimizer**
- implement our **own model class**
- implement **nested** and **sequential** models, using PyTorch's layers
- organize our code into three parts: **data preparation**, **model configuration**, and **model training**

Jupyter Notebook

The Jupyter notebook corresponding to Chapter 1[39] is part of the official *Deep Learning with PyTorch Step-by-Step* repository on GitHub. You can also run it directly in **Google Colab**[40].

If you're using a *local installation*, open your terminal or Anaconda prompt and navigate to the `PyTorchStepByStep` folder you cloned from GitHub. Then, *activate* the `pytorchbook` environment and run `jupyter notebook`:

```
$ conda activate pytorchbook
(pytorchbook)$ jupyter notebook
```

If you're using Jupyter's default settings, `http://localhost:8888/notebooks/Chapter01.ipynb` should open Chapter 1's notebook. If not, just click on `Chapter01.ipynb` on your Jupyter's home page.

Imports

For the sake of organization, all libraries needed throughout the code used in any given chapter are imported at its very beginning. For this chapter, we'll need the following imports:

```
import numpy as np
from sklearn.linear_model import LinearRegression

import torch
import torch.optim as optim
import torch.nn as nn
from torchviz import make_dot
```

A Simple Regression Problem

Most tutorials start with some nice and *pretty image classification problem* to illustrate how to use PyTorch. It may seem cool, but I believe it **distracts** you from the **main goal**: learning **how PyTorch works**.

For this reason, in this first example, I will stick with a **simple** and **familiar** problem: a **linear regression with a single feature *x*!** It doesn't get much simpler than that!

$$y = b + wx + \epsilon$$

Equation 1.1 - Simple linear regression model

It is also possible to think of it as the **simplest neural network** possible: **one** input, **one** output, and **no** activation function (that is, **linear**).

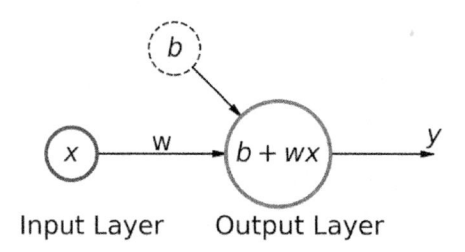

Figure 1.1 - The simplest of all neural networks

> If you have read **Chapter 0**, you can either choose to skip to the "**Linear Regression in Numpy**" section or to use the **next two sections as a review**.

Data Generation

Let's start **generating** some synthetic data. We start with a vector of 100 (*N*) points for our **feature (x)** and create our **labels (y)** using *b* = 1, *w* = 2, and some **Gaussian noise**[41] (*epsilon*).

Synthetic Data Generation

Data Generation

```
1  true_b = 1
2  true_w = 2
3  N = 100
4
5  # Data Generation
6  np.random.seed(42)
7  x = np.random.rand(N, 1)
8  epsilon = (.1 * np.random.randn(N, 1))
9  y = true_b + true_w * x + epsilon
```

Next, let's **split** our synthetic data into **train** and **validation** sets, shuffling the array of indices and using the first 80 shuffled points for training.

Notebook Cell 1.1 - *Splitting synthetic dataset into train and validation sets for linear regression*

```
1  # Shuffles the indices
2  idx = np.arange(N)
3  np.random.shuffle(idx)
4
5  # Uses first 80 random indices for train
6  train_idx = idx[:int(N*.8)]
7  # Uses the remaining indices for validation
8  val_idx = idx[int(N*.8):]
9
10 # Generates train and validation sets
11 x_train, y_train = x[train_idx], y[train_idx]
12 x_val, y_val = x[val_idx], y[val_idx]
```

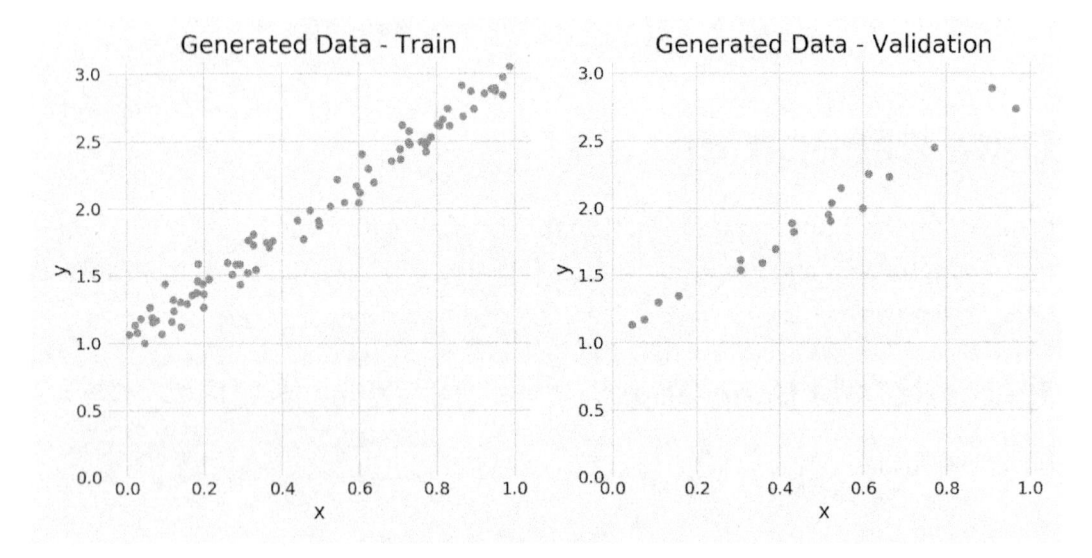

Figure 1.2 - Synthetic data: train and validation sets

We **know** that b = 1, w = 2, but now let's see **how close** we can get to the true values by using **gradient descent** and the 80 points in the **training set** (for training, N = 80).

Gradient Descent

I'll cover the **five basic steps** you'll need to go through to use gradient descent and the corresponding *Numpy* code.

Step 0 - Random Initialization

For training a model, you need to **randomly initialize the parameters / weights** (we have only two, **b** and **w**).

Step 0

```
# Step 0 - Initializes parameters "b" and "w" randomly
np.random.seed(42)
b = np.random.randn(1)
w = np.random.randn(1)

print(b, w)
```

Output

```
[0.49671415] [-0.1382643]
```

Step 1 - Compute Model's Predictions

This is the **forward pass**; it simply *computes the model's predictions using the current values of the parameters / weights*. At the very beginning, we will be producing **really bad predictions**, as we started with **random values from Step 0**.

Step 1

```
# Step 1 - Computes our model's predicted output - forward pass
yhat = b + w * x_train
```

Step 2 - Compute the Loss

For a regression problem, the **loss** is given by the **mean squared error (MSE)**; that is, the average of all squared errors; that is, the average of all squared differences between **labels** (y) and **predictions** (b + wx).

In the code below, we are using **all data points** of the training set to compute the **loss**, so $n = N = 80$, meaning we are performing **batch gradient descent**.

Step 2

```
# Step 2 - Computing the loss
# We are using ALL data points, so this is BATCH gradient
# descent. How wrong is our model? That's the error!
error = (yhat - y_train)

# It is a regression, so it computes mean squared error (MSE)
loss = (error ** 2).mean()

print(loss)
```

Output

```
2.7421577700550976
```

Batch, Mini-batch, *and* **Stochastic Gradient Descent**

- If we use **all points** in the training set ($n = N$) to compute the loss, we are performing a **batch** gradient descent.
- If we were to use a **single point** ($n = 1$) each time, it would be a **stochastic** gradient descent.
- Anything else (n) **in between 1 and N** characterizes a **mini-batch** gradient descent.

Step 3 - Compute the Gradients

A **gradient** is a **partial derivative**. *Why* **partial**? Because one computes it *with respect to* (w.r.t.) a **single parameter**. We have two parameters, *b* and *w*, so we must compute two partial derivatives.

A **derivative** tells you *how much* **a given quantity changes** when you *slightly vary* some **other quantity**. In our case, how much does our *MSE* **loss** change when we vary **each of our two parameters separately**?

Gradient = **how much** the **loss** changes if **ONE parameter** changes **a little bit**!

Step 3

```
# Step 3 - Computes gradients for both "b" and "w" parameters
b_grad = 2 * error.mean()
w_grad = 2 * (x_train * error).mean()
print(b_grad, w_grad)
```

Output

```
-3.044811379650508 -1.8337537171510832
```

Step 4 - Update the Parameters

In the final step, we **use the gradients to update** the parameters. Since we are trying to **minimize** our **losses**, we **reverse the sign** of the gradient for the update.

There is still another (hyper-)parameter to consider: the **learning rate**, denoted by the *Greek letter eta* (that looks like the letter *n*), which is the **multiplicative factor** that we need to apply to the gradient for the parameter update.

> *"How do you **choose** a learning rate?"*
>
> That is a topic on its own and beyond the scope of this section as well. We'll get back to it in the second volume of the series.

In our example, let's start with a value of **0.1** for the learning rate (which is a relatively *high value*, as far as learning rates are concerned!).

Step 4

```
# Sets learning rate - this is "eta" ~ the "n"-like Greek letter
lr = 0.1
print(b, w)

# Step 4 - Updates parameters using gradients and
# the learning rate
b = b - lr * b_grad
w = w - lr * w_grad

print(b, w)
```

Output

```
[0.49671415] [-0.1382643]
[0.80119529] [0.04511107]
```

Step 5 - Rinse and Repeat!

Now we use the **updated parameters** to go back to **Step 1** and restart the process.

> **Definition of Epoch**
>
> An **epoch is complete** whenever every point in the training set (*N*) has already been used in all steps: forward pass, computing loss, computing gradients, and updating parameters.
>
> During **one epoch**, we perform at least **one update**, but no more than *N* **updates**.
>
> The number of **updates** (*N/n*) will depend on the type of gradient descent being used:
>
> - For **batch** (*n* = *N*) gradient descent, this is trivial, as it uses all points for computing the loss—**one epoch** is the same as **one update**.
> - For **stochastic** (*n* = 1) gradient descent, **one epoch** means *N* updates, since every individual data point is used to perform an update.
> - For **mini-batch** (of size *n*), **one epoch** has *N/n* **updates**, since a mini-batch of *n* data points is used to perform an update.

Repeating this process over and over for **many epochs** is, in a nutshell, **training** a model.

Linear Regression in Numpy

It's time to implement our linear regression model using gradient descent and *Numpy* only.

"Wait a minute ... I thought this book was about PyTorch!" Yes, it is, but this serves **two purposes**: *first*, to introduce the **structure** of our task, which will remain largely the same and, *second*, to show you the main **pain points** so you can fully appreciate how much PyTorch makes your life easier :-)

For training a model, there is a first **initialization step** (line numbers refer to **Notebook Cell 1.2** code below):

- Random initialization of parameters / weights (we have only two, *b* and *w*)—lines 3 and 4
- Initialization of hyper-parameters (in our case, only *learning rate* and *number of epochs*)—lines 9 and 11

Make sure to *always initialize your random seed* to ensure the **reproducibility** of your results. As usual, the random seed is 42[42], the **(second) least random**[43] of all random seeds one could possibly choose.

For each epoch, there are **four training steps** (line numbers refer to **Notebook Cell 1.2** code below):

- Compute model's predictions—this is the **forward pass**—line 15
- Compute the loss, using *predictions* and *labels* and the appropriate **loss function** for the task at hand—lines 20 and 22
- Compute the **gradients** for every parameter—lines 25 and 26
- **Update** the parameters—lines 30 and 31

For now, we will be using **batch** gradient descent only, meaning, we'll use **all data points** for each one of the four steps above. It also means that going **once** through all of the steps is already **one epoch**. Then, if we want to train our model over 1,000 epochs, we just need to add a **single loop**.

In Chapter 2, we'll introduce **mini-batch** gradient descent, and then we'll have to include a second *inner loop*.

Notebook Cell 1.2 - Implementing gradient descent for linear regression using Numpy

```
1  # Step 0 - Initializes parameters "b" and "w" randomly
2  np.random.seed(42)
3  b = np.random.randn(1)                                      ①
4  w = np.random.randn(1)                                      ①
5
6  print(b, w)
7
8  # Sets learning rate - this is "eta" ~ the "n"-like Greek letter
9  lr = 0.1                                                    ②
10 # Defines number of epochs
11 n_epochs = 1000                                             ②
12
13 for epoch in range(n_epochs):
14     # Step 1 - Computes model's predicted output - forward pass
15     yhat = b + w * x_train                                  ③
16
17     # Step 2 - Computes the loss
18     # We are using ALL data points, so this is BATCH gradient
19     # descent. How wrong is our model? That's the error!
20     error = (yhat - y_train)                                ④
21     # It is a regression, so it computes mean squared error (MSE)
22     loss = (error ** 2).mean()                              ④
23
24     # Step 3 - Computes gradients for both "b" and "w" parameters
25     b_grad = 2 * error.mean()                               ⑤
26     w_grad = 2 * (x_train * error).mean()                   ⑤
27
28     # Step 4 - Updates parameters using gradients and
29     # the learning rate
30     b = b - lr * b_grad                                     ⑥
31     w = w - lr * w_grad                                     ⑥
32
33 print(b, w)
```

① Step 0: Random initialization of parameters / weights

② Initialization of hyper-parameters

③ Step 1: Forward pass

④ Step 2: Computing loss

⑤ Step 3: Computing gradients

⑥ Step 4: Updating parameters

Output

```
# b and w after initialization
[0.49671415] [-0.1382643]
# b and w after our gradient descent
[1.02354094] [1.96896411]
```

> *"Do we need to run it for 1,000 epochs? Shouldn't it **stop** automatically after getting close enough to the minimum loss?"*

Good question: We **don't** need to run it for 1,000 epochs. There are ways of **stopping** it earlier, once the progress is considered negligible (for instance, if the loss was barely reduced). These are called, most appropriately, **early stopping** methods. For now, since our model is a very simple one, we can afford to train it for 1,000 epochs.

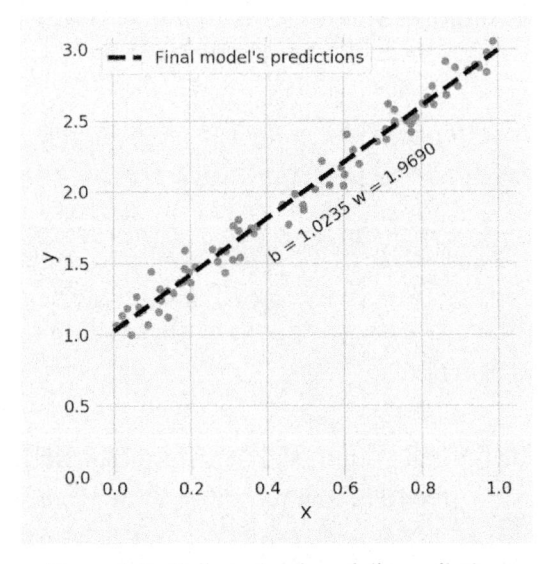

Figure 1.3 - Fully trained model's predictions

Just to make sure we haven't made any mistakes in our code, we can use Scikit-Learn's linear regression to fit the model and compare the coefficients.

```
# Sanity Check: do we get the same results as our
# gradient descent?
linr = LinearRegression()
linr.fit(x_train, y_train)
print(linr.intercept_, linr.coef_[0])
```

Output

```
# intercept and coef from Scikit-Learn
[1.02354075] [1.96896447]
```

They **match** up to six decimal places—we have a *fully working implementation of linear regression* using Numpy.

Time to **TORCH** it!

PyTorch

First, we need to cover a **few basic concepts** that may throw you off-balance if you don't grasp them well enough before going full-force on modeling.

In deep learning, we see **tensors** everywhere. Well, Google's framework is called *TensorFlow* for a reason! *What is a tensor, anyway?*

Tensor

In *Numpy*, you may have an **array** that has **three dimensions**, right? That is, technically speaking, a **tensor**.

> A **scalar** (a single number) **has zero** dimensions, a **vector has one** dimension, a **matrix has two** dimensions, and a **tensor has three or more** dimensions. That's it!

But, to keep things simple, it is commonplace to call vectors and matrices tensors as well—so, from now on, **everything is either a scalar or a tensor.**

Scalar   Vector   Matrix   Tensor

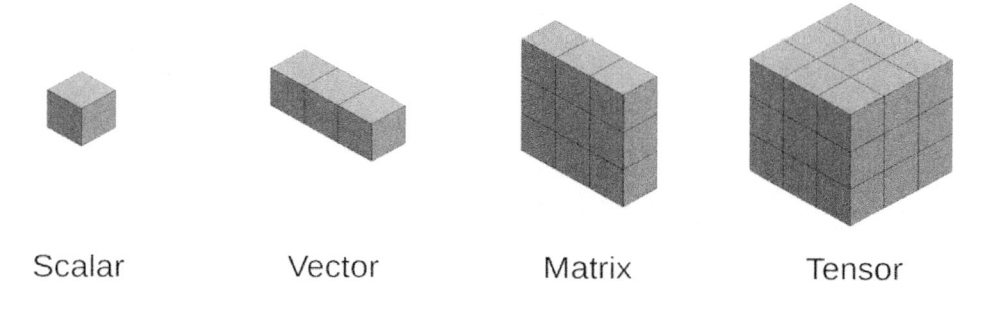

Figure 1.4 - Tensors are just higher-dimensional matrices

You can create **tensors** in PyTorch pretty much the same way you create **arrays** in *Numpy*. Using tensor() you can create either a scalar or a tensor.

PyTorch's tensors have equivalent functions to its *Numpy* counterparts, like ones(), zeros(), rand(), randn(), and many more. In the example below, we create one of each: scalar, vector, matrix, and tensor—or, saying it differently, one scalar and three tensors.

```
scalar = torch.tensor(3.14159)
vector = torch.tensor([1, 2, 3])
matrix = torch.ones((2, 3), dtype=torch.float)
tensor = torch.randn((2, 3, 4), dtype=torch.float)

print(scalar)
print(vector)
print(matrix)
print(tensor)
```

Output

```
tensor(3.1416)
tensor([1, 2, 3])
tensor([[1., 1., 1.],
        [1., 1., 1.]])
tensor([[[-1.0658, -0.5675, -1.2903, -0.1136],
         [ 1.0344,  2.1910,  0.7926, -0.7065],
         [ 0.4552, -0.6728,  1.8786, -0.3248]],

        [[-0.7738,  1.3831,  1.4861, -0.7254],
         [ 0.1989, -1.0139,  1.5881, -1.2295],
         [-0.5338, -0.5548,  1.5385, -1.2971]]])
```

You can get the shape of a tensor using its size() method or its shape attribute.

```
print(tensor.size(), tensor.shape)
```

Output

```
torch.Size([2, 3, 4]) torch.Size([2, 3, 4])
```

All tensors have shapes, but scalars have "empty" shapes, since they are **dimensionless** (or zero dimensions, if you prefer):

```
print(scalar.size(), scalar.shape)
```

Output

```
torch.Size([]) torch.Size([])
```

You can also reshape a tensor using its view() (*preferred*) or reshape() methods.

Beware: The `view()` method only returns a **tensor** with the desired shape that **shares the underlying data** with the original tensor—it **DOES NOT create a new, independent, tensor**!

The `reshape()` method **may** or **may not** create a copy! The reasons behind this apparently weird behavior are beyond the scope of this section, but this behavior is the reason why `view()` **is preferred**.

```
# We get a tensor with a different shape but it still is
# the SAME tensor
same_matrix = matrix.view(1, 6)
# If we change one of its elements...
same_matrix[0, 1] = 2.
# It changes both variables: matrix and same_matrix
print(matrix)
print(same_matrix)
```

Output

```
tensor([[1., 2., 1.],
        [1., 1., 1.]])
tensor([[1., 2., 1., 1., 1., 1.]])
```

If you want to copy all data, that is, **duplicate the data** in memory, you may use either its `new_tensor()` or `clone()` methods.

```
# We can use "new_tensor" method to REALLY copy it into a new one
different_matrix = matrix.new_tensor(matrix.view(1, 6))
# Now, if we change one of its elements...
different_matrix[0, 1] = 3.
# The original tensor (matrix) is left untouched!
# But we get a "warning" from PyTorch telling us
# to use "clone()" instead!
print(matrix)
print(different_matrix)
```

Output

```
tensor([[1., 2., 1.],
        [1., 1., 1.]])
tensor([[1., 3., 1., 1., 1., 1.]])
```

Output

```
UserWarning: To copy construct from a tensor, it is
recommended to use sourceTensor.clone().detach() or
sourceTensor.clone().detach().requires_grad_(True),
rather than tensor.new_tensor(sourceTensor).
  """Entry point for launching an IPython kernel.
```

It seems that PyTorch prefers that we use `clone()`—together with `detach()`—instead of `new_tensor()`. Both ways accomplish **exactly the same result**, but the code below is deemed cleaner and more readable.

```
# Let's follow PyTorch's suggestion and use "clone" method
another_matrix = matrix.view(1, 6).clone().detach()
# Again, if we change one of its elements...
another_matrix[0, 1] = 4.
# The original tensor (matrix) is left untouched!
print(matrix)
print(another_matrix)
```

Output

```
tensor([[1., 2., 1.],
        [1., 1., 1.]])
tensor([[1., 4., 1., 1., 1., 1.]])
```

> You're probably asking yourself: "*But, what about the* `detach()` *method—what does it do?*"

It *removes the tensor from the computation graph*, which probably raises more questions than it answers, right? Don't worry, we'll get back to it later in this chapter.

Loading Data, Devices, and CUDA

It is time to start converting our *Numpy* code to PyTorch: We'll start with the **training data**; that is, our x_train and y_train arrays.

"How do we go from Numpy's arrays to PyTorch's tensors?"

That's what as_tensor() is good for (which works like from_numpy()).

This operation **preserves the type** of the array:

```
x_train_tensor = torch.as_tensor(x_train)
x_train.dtype, x_train_tensor.dtype
```

Output

```
(dtype('float64'), torch.float64)
```

You can also easily **cast** it to a different type, like a *lower-precision* (32-bit) float, which will occupy *less space in memory*, using float():

```
float_tensor = x_train_tensor.float()
float_tensor.dtype
```

Output

```
torch.float32
```

IMPORTANT: Both as_tensor() and from_numpy() return a tensor that **shares the underlying data** with the original *Numpy* array. Similar to what happened when we used view() in the last section, if you **modify the original *Numpy* array**, you're modifying the corresponding **PyTorch tensor too**, and vice-versa.

PyTorch | 75

```
dummy_array = np.array([1, 2, 3])
dummy_tensor = torch.as_tensor(dummy_array)
# Modifies the numpy array
dummy_array[1] = 0
# Tensor gets modified too...
dummy_tensor
```

Output

```
tensor([1, 0, 3])
```

> *"What do I need* `as_tensor()` *for? Why can't I just use* `torch.tensor()`*?"*

Well, you could ... just keep in mind that `torch.tensor()` always **makes a copy of the data**, instead of sharing the underlying data with the *Numpy* array.

You can also perform the **opposite** operation, namely, transforming a PyTorch tensor back to a *Numpy* array. That's what `numpy()` is good for:

```
dummy_tensor.numpy()
```

Output

```
array([1, 0, 3])
```

So far, we have only created **CPU tensors**. What does it mean? It means the **data** in the tensor is **stored** in the computer's **main memory** and any operations performed on it are going to be **handled by its CPU** (the central processing **unit**; for instance, an Intel® Core™ i7 Processor). So, although the data is, technically speaking, in the memory, we're still calling this kind of tensor a **CPU tensor**.

> *"Is there any other kind of tensor?"*

Yes, there is also a **GPU tensor**. A **GPU** (which stands for graphics processing unit) is the **processor** of a **graphics card**. These tensors **store their data** in the **graphics card's memory**, and operations on top of them are performed by the **GPU**. For more information on the differences between CPUs and GPUs, please refer to the article "What's the Difference Between a CPU and a GPU?"[44]

If you have a graphics card from NVIDIA, you can use the **power of its GPU** to **speed up model training**. PyTorch supports the use of these GPUs for model training using **CUDA** (**C**ompute **U**nified **D**evice **A**rchitecture), which needs to be previously installed and configured (please refer to the **"Setup Guide"** for more information on this).

If you **do** have a **GPU** (and you managed to install CUDA), we're getting to the part where you get to use it with PyTorch. But, even if you **do not** have a **GPU**, you should stick around in this section anyway. Why? First, you can use a **free GPU from Google Colab**, and, second, you should always make your code *GPU-ready*; that is, it should **automatically run in a GPU, if one is available**.

"*How do I know if a GPU is available?*"

PyTorch has your back once more—you can use `cuda.is_available()` to find out if you have a GPU at your disposal and set your device accordingly. So, it is good practice to figure this out at the top of your code:

Defining Your Device

```
device = 'cuda' if torch.cuda.is_available() else 'cpu'
```

So, if you don't have a GPU, your `device` is called `cpu`. If you do have a GPU, your device is called `cuda` or `cuda:0`. Why isn't it called `gpu`, then? Don't ask me... The important thing is, your code will be able to always use the appropriate device.

"*Why* `cuda:0`? *Are there others, like* `cuda:1`, `cuda:2` *and so on?*"

There may be if you are lucky enough to have *multiple GPUs* in your computer. Since this is usually *not* the case, I am assuming you have either **one GPU** or **none**. So, when we tell PyTorch to send a tensor to `cuda` without any numbering, it will send it to the current CUDA device, which is device #0 by default.

If you are using someone else's computer and you don't know how many GPUs it has, or which model they are, you can figure it out using `cuda.device_count()` and `cuda.get_device_name()`:

```
n_cudas = torch.cuda.device_count()
for i in range(n_cudas):
    print(torch.cuda.get_device_name(i))
```

Output

```
GeForce GTX 1060 6GB
```

In my case, I have only *one GPU*, and it is a *GeForce GTX 1060* model with 6 GB RAM.

There is only one thing left to do: turn our tensor into a **GPU tensor**. That's what to() is good for. It sends a tensor to the specified **device**.

```
gpu_tensor = torch.as_tensor(x_train).to(device)
gpu_tensor[0]
```

Output - GPU

```
tensor([0.7713], device='cuda:0', dtype=torch.float64)
```

Output - CPU

```
tensor([0.7713], dtype=torch.float64)
```

In this case, there is no device information in the printed output because PyTorch simply assumes the default (cpu).

> ❓ *"Should I use* to(device), *even if I am using CPU only?"*

Yes, you should, because there is **no cost** in doing so. If you have only a CPU, your tensor is already a CPU tensor, so nothing will happen. But if you share your code with others on GitHub, whoever has a GPU will benefit from it.

Let's put it all together now and make our **training data ready for PyTorch**.

Notebook Cell 1.3 - Loading data: turning Numpy arrays into PyTorch tensors

```
1  device = 'cuda' if torch.cuda.is_available() else 'cpu'
2
3  # Our data was in Numpy arrays, but we need to transform them
4  # into PyTorch tensors and then send them to the
5  # chosen device
6  x_train_tensor = torch.as_tensor(x_train).float().to(device)
7  y_train_tensor = torch.as_tensor(y_train).float().to(device)
```

So, we defined a device, converted both *Numpy* arrays into PyTorch tensors, cast them to floats, and sent them to the device. Let's take a look at the types:

```
# Here we can see the difference - notice that .type() is more
# useful since it also tells us WHERE the tensor is (device)
print(type(x_train), type(x_train_tensor), x_train_tensor.type())
```

Output - GPU

```
<class 'numpy.ndarray'> <class 'torch.Tensor'>
torch.cuda.FloatTensor
```

Output - CPU

```
<class 'numpy.ndarray'> <class 'torch.Tensor'>
torch.FloatTensor
```

If you compare the **types** of both variables, you'll get what you'd expect: numpy.ndarray for the first one and torch.Tensor for the second one.

But where does the x_train_tensor "live"? Is it a CPU or a GPU tensor? You can't say, but if you use PyTorch's type(), it will reveal its **location** —torch.cuda.FloatTensor—a GPU tensor in this case (assuming the output using a GPU, of course).

There is one more thing to be aware of when using GPU tensors. Remember numpy()? What if we want to turn a GPU tensor back into a *Numpy* array? We'll get an **error**:

```
back_to_numpy = x_train_tensor.numpy()
```

Output

```
TypeError: can't convert CUDA tensor to numpy. Use
Tensor.cpu() to copy the tensor to host memory first.
```

Unfortunately, *Numpy* **cannot** handle GPU tensors! You need to make them CPU tensors first using `cpu()`:

```
back_to_numpy = x_train_tensor.cpu().numpy()
```

So, to avoid this error, use *first* `cpu()` and *then* `numpy()`, even if you are using a CPU. It follows the same principle of `to(device)`: You can share your code with others who may be using a GPU.

Creating Parameters

What distinguishes a *tensor* used for *training data (or validation, or test)*—like the ones we've just created—from a **tensor** used as a (*trainable*) **parameter / weight**?

The latter requires the **computation of its gradients**, so we can **update** their values (the parameters' values, that is). That's what the `requires_grad=True` argument is good for. It tells PyTorch to compute gradients for us.

> A tensor for a **learnable parameter** requires a **gradient**!

You may be tempted to create a simple tensor for a parameter and, later on, send it to your chosen device, as we did with our data, right? *Not so fast…*

In the next few pages, I will present **four** chunks of code showing different attempts at creating parameters.

> ⚠️ The first three attempts are shown to *build up* to a solution. The first one only works well if you never use a GPU. The second one doesn't work at all. The third one works, but it is too verbose.

The **recommended** way of creating parameters is the **last**: **Notebook Cell 1.4**.

The first chunk of code below creates two tensors for our parameters, including gradients and all. But they are **CPU** tensors, by default.

```
# FIRST
# Initializes parameters "b" and "w" randomly, ALMOST as we
# did in Numpy, since we want to apply gradient descent on
# these parameters we need to set REQUIRES_GRAD = TRUE
torch.manual_seed(42)
b = torch.randn(1, requires_grad=True, dtype=torch.float)
w = torch.randn(1, requires_grad=True, dtype=torch.float)
print(b, w)
```

Output

```
tensor([0.3367], requires_grad=True)
tensor([0.1288], requires_grad=True)
```

> 💡 Never forget to set the **seed** to ensure reproducibility,[45] just like we did before while using *Numpy*. PyTorch's equivalent is `torch.manual_seed()`.

> ❓ *"If I use the same seed in PyTorch as I used in Numpy (or, to put it differently, if I use 42 everywhere), will I get the same numbers?"*

Unfortunately, **NO**.

You'll get the **same numbers** for the **same seed** in the **same package**. PyTorch generates a number sequence that is different from the one generated by *Numpy*, even if you use the same seed in both.

PyTorch | 81

I am assuming you'd like to use your **GPU** (or the one from Google Colab), right? So we need to **send those tensors to the device**. We can try the **naive** approach, the one that worked well for sending the training data to the device. That's our second (and failed) attempt:

```
# SECOND
# But what if we want to run it on a GPU? We could just
# send them to device, right?
torch.manual_seed(42)
b = torch.randn(1, requires_grad=True, dtype=torch.float).to(device)
w = torch.randn(1, requires_grad=True, dtype=torch.float).to(device)
print(b, w)
# Sorry, but NO! The to(device) "shadows" the gradient...
```

Output

```
tensor([0.3367], device='cuda:0', grad_fn=<CopyBackwards>)
tensor([0.1288], device='cuda:0', grad_fn=<CopyBackwards>)
```

We succeeded in sending them to another device, but we **"lost"** the **gradients** somehow, since there is no more `requires_grad=True`, (don't bother with the weird `grad_fn`). Clearly, we need to do better...

In the third chunk, we **first** send our tensors to the **device** and **then** use the `requires_grad_()` method to set its `requires_grad` attribute to True in place.

> In PyTorch, every method that **ends** with an **underscore** (_), like the `requires_grad_()` method above, makes changes **in-place**, meaning, they will **modify** the underlying variable.

```
# THIRD
# We can create regular tensors and send them to
# the device (as we did with our data)
torch.manual_seed(42)
b = torch.randn(1, dtype=torch.float).to(device)
w = torch.randn(1, dtype=torch.float).to(device)
# and THEN set them as requiring gradients...
b.requires_grad_()
w.requires_grad_()
print(b, w)
```

Output

```
tensor([0.3367], device='cuda:0', requires_grad=True)
 tensor([0.1288], device='cuda:0', requires_grad=True)
```

This approach worked fine; we managed to end up with gradient-requiring **GPU tensors** for our parameters *b* and *w*. It seems a lot of work, though... Can we do better still?

Yes, we **can** do better: We can **assign** tensors to a **device** at the moment of their **creation**.

Notebook Cell 1.4 - Actually creating variables for the coefficients

```
# FINAL
# We can specify the device at the moment of creation
# RECOMMENDED!

# Step 0 - Initializes parameters "b" and "w" randomly
torch.manual_seed(42)
b = torch.randn(1, requires_grad=True, \
                dtype=torch.float, device=device)
w = torch.randn(1, requires_grad=True, \
                dtype=torch.float, device=device)
print(b, w)
```

Output

```
tensor([0.1940], device='cuda:0', requires_grad=True)
tensor([0.1391], device='cuda:0', requires_grad=True)
```

Much easier, right?

> 💡 Always **assign** tensors to a **device** at the moment of their **creation** to avoid unexpected behaviors!

If you **do not** have a **GPU**, your outputs are going to be slightly different:

Output - CPU

```
tensor([0.3367], requires_grad=True)
tensor([0.1288], requires_grad=True)
```

> ❓ *"Why are they different, even if I am using the **same seed**?"*

Similar to what happens when using the same seed in **different packages** (*Numpy* and *PyTorch*), we also get **different sequences of random numbers** if PyTorch generates them in **different devices** (CPU and GPU).

Now that we know how to create tensors that require gradients, let's see how PyTorch handles them. That's the role of the...

Autograd

Autograd is PyTorch's *automatic differentiation package*. Thanks to it, we **don't need to worry** about *partial derivatives*, *chain rule*, or anything like it.

backward

So, how do we tell PyTorch to do its thing and **compute all gradients**? That's the role of the `backward()` method. It will compute gradients for *all (gradient-requiring) tensors* involved in the computation of a given variable.

Do you remember the **starting point** for **computing the gradients**? It was the **loss**, as we computed its partial derivatives w.r.t. our parameters. Hence, we need to invoke the `backward()` method from the corresponding Python variable:

loss.backward().

Notebook Cell 1.5 - Autograd in action!

```
# Step 1 - Computes our model's predicted output - forward pass
yhat = b + w * x_train_tensor

# Step 2 - Computes the loss
# We are using ALL data points, so this is BATCH gradient
# descent. How wrong is our model? That's the error!
error = (yhat - y_train_tensor)
# It is a regression, so it computes mean squared error (MSE)
loss = (error ** 2).mean()

# Step 3 - Computes gradients for both "b" and "w" parameters
# No more manual computation of gradients!
# b_grad = 2 * error.mean()
# w_grad = 2 * (x_tensor * error).mean()
loss.backward() ①
```

① New "Step 3 - Computing Gradients" using backward()

Which tensors are going to be handled by the backward() method applied to the loss?

- b
- w
- yhat
- error

We have set requires_grad=True to both b and w, so they are obviously included in the list. We use them both to compute yhat, so it will also make it to the list. Then we use yhat to compute the error, which is also added to the list.

Do you see the pattern here? If a tensor in the list is used to compute another tensor, the latter will also be included in the list. Tracking these dependencies is exactly what the **dynamic computation graph** is doing, as we'll see shortly.

What about x_train_tensor and y_train_tensor? They are involved in the computation too, but we created them as **non**-gradient-requiring tensors, so backward() does not care about them.

```
print(error.requires_grad, yhat.requires_grad, \
      b.requires_grad, w.requires_grad)
print(y_train_tensor.requires_grad, x_train_tensor.requires_grad)
```

Output

```
True True True True
False False
```

grad

What about the **actual values** of the **gradients**? We can inspect them by looking at the grad **attribute** of a tensor.

```
print(b.grad, w.grad)
```

Output

```
tensor([-3.3881], device='cuda:0')
tensor([-1.9439], device='cuda:0')
```

If you check the method's documentation, it clearly states that **gradients are accumulated**. What does that mean? It means that, if we run **Notebook Cell 1.5**'s code (Steps 1 to 3) twice and check the grad attribute afterward, we will end up with:

Output

```
tensor([-6.7762], device='cuda:0')
tensor([-3.8878], device='cuda:0')
```

If you **do not** have a **GPU**, your outputs are going to be slightly different:

Output

```
tensor([-3.1125]) tensor([-1.8156])
```

86 | Chapter 1: A Simple Regression Problem

Output

```
tensor([-6.2250]) tensor([-3.6313])
```

These gradients' values are exactly **twice** as much as they were before, as expected!

OK, but that is actually a **problem**: We need to use the gradients corresponding to the **current** loss to perform the parameter update. We should **NOT** use **accumulated gradients**.

> "If **accumulating gradients** is a **problem**, why does PyTorch do it by default?"

It turns out this behavior can be useful to circumvent hardware limitations.

During the training of large models, the necessary number of data points in a mini-batch may be **too large to fit in memory** (of the graphics card). How can one solve this, other than buying more-expensive hardware?

One can **split a mini-batch** into "*sub-mini-batches*" (horrible name, I know, don't quote me on this!), compute the gradients for those "subs" and **accumulate** them to achieve the same result as computing the gradients on the **full** mini-batch.

Sounds confusing? No worries, this is fairly advanced already and somewhat outside of the scope of this book, but I thought this particular behavior of PyTorch needed to be explained.

Luckily, this is easy to solve!

zero_

Every time we use the **gradients** to **update** the parameters, we need to **zero the gradients afterward**. And that's what zero_() is good for.

```
# This code will be placed _after_ Step 4
# (updating the parameters)
b.grad.zero_(), w.grad.zero_()
```

Output

```
(tensor([0.], device='cuda:0'),
 tensor([0.], device='cuda:0'))
```

> What does the **underscore** (_) at the **end of the method's name** mean? Do you remember? If not, go back to the previous section and find out.

So, let's **ditch** the **manual computation of gradients** and use both the `backward()` and `zero_()` methods instead.

That's it? Well, pretty much ... but there is always a **catch**, and this time it has to do with the **update** of the **parameters**.

Updating Parameters

> *"One does not simply update parameters..."*
>
> Boromir

Unfortunately, our *Numpy*'s code for updating parameters is not enough. Why not?! Let's try it out, simply copying and pasting it (this is the *first attempt*), changing it slightly (*second attempt*), and then asking PyTorch to **back off** (yes, it is PyTorch's fault!).

Notebook Cell 1.6 - Updating parameters

```
1  # Sets learning rate - this is "eta" ~ the "n"-like Greek letter
2  lr = 0.1
3
4  # Step 0 - Initializes parameters "b" and "w" randomly
5  torch.manual_seed(42)
6  b = torch.randn(1, requires_grad=True, \
7                  dtype=torch.float, device=device)
8  w = torch.randn(1, requires_grad=True, \
9                  dtype=torch.float, device=device)
10
11 # Defines number of epochs
12 n_epochs = 1000
13
```

```
14  for epoch in range(n_epochs):
15      # Step 1 - Computes model's predicted output - forward pass
16      yhat = b + w * x_train_tensor
17
18      # Step 2 - Computes the loss
19      # We are using ALL data points, so this is BATCH gradient
20      # descent. How wrong is our model? That's the error!
21      error = (yhat - y_train_tensor)
22      # It is a regression, so it computes mean squared error (MSE)
23      loss = (error ** 2).mean()
24
25      # Step 3 - Computes gradients for both "b" and "w"
26      # parameters. No more manual computation of gradients!
27      # b_grad = 2 * error.mean()
28      # w_grad = 2 * (x_tensor * error).mean()
29      # We just tell PyTorch to work its way BACKWARDS
30      # from the specified loss!
31      loss.backward()
32
33      # Step 4 - Updates parameters using gradients and
34      # the learning rate. But not so fast...
35      # FIRST ATTEMPT - just using the same code as before
36      # AttributeError: 'NoneType' object has no attribute 'zero_'
37      # b = b - lr * b.grad                                    ①
38      # w = w - lr * w.grad                                    ①
39      # print(b)                                               ①
40
41      # SECOND ATTEMPT - using in-place Python assignment
42      # RuntimeError: a leaf Variable that requires grad
43      # has been used in an in-place operation.
44      # b -= lr * b.grad                                       ②
45      # w -= lr * w.grad                                       ②
46
47      # THIRD ATTEMPT - NO_GRAD for the win!
48      # We need to use NO_GRAD to keep the update out of
49      # the gradient computation. Why is that? It boils
50      # down to the DYNAMIC GRAPH that PyTorch uses...
51      with torch.no_grad():                                    ③
52          b -= lr * b.grad                                     ③
53          w -= lr * w.grad                                     ③
54
55      # PyTorch is "clingy" to its computed gradients; we
```

```
56      # need to tell it to let it go...
57      b.grad.zero_()                                    ④
58      w.grad.zero_()                                    ④
59
60 print(b, w)
```

① First Attempt: leads to an `AttributeError`

② Second Attempt: leads to a `RuntimeError`

③ Third Attempt: `no_grad()` solves the problem!

④ `zero_()` prevents gradient accumulation

In the **first attempt**, if we use the same update structure as in our *Numpy* code, we'll get the weird **error** below, but we can get a *hint* of what's going on by looking at the tensor itself. Once again, we **"lost"** the **gradient** while reassigning the update results to our parameters. Thus, the `grad` attribute turns out to be `None`, and it raises the error.

Output - First Attempt - Keeping the same code

```
tensor([0.7518], device='cuda:0', grad_fn=<SubBackward0>)
AttributeError: 'NoneType' object has no attribute 'zero_'
```

We then change it slightly, using a familiar **in-place Python assignment** in our **second attempt**. And, once again, PyTorch complains about it and raises an **error**.

Output - Second Attempt - In-place assignment

```
RuntimeError: a leaf Variable that requires grad has been used in an in-place operation.
```

Why?! It turns out to be a case of **"too much of a good thing."** The culprit is PyTorch's ability to build a **dynamic computation graph** from every **Python operation** that involves any **gradient-computing tensor** or **its dependencies**.

We'll go deeper into the inner workings of the dynamic computation graph in the next section.

Time for our **third attempt**...

no_grad

So, how do we tell PyTorch to **"back off"** and let us **update our parameters** without messing up its *fancy dynamic computation graph*? That's what `torch.no_grad()` is good for. It allows us to **perform regular Python operations on tensors without affecting PyTorch's computation graph**.

Finally, we managed to successfully run our model and get the **resulting parameters**. Surely enough, they **match** the ones we got in our *Numpy*-only implementation.

Output - Third Attempt - NO_GRAD for the win!

```
# THIRD ATTEMPT - NO_GRAD for the win!
tensor([1.0235], device='cuda:0', requires_grad=True)
tensor([1.9690], device='cuda:0', requires_grad=True)
```

Remember:

> *"One does not simply update parameters ... **without** no_grad"*
>
> Boromir

It was true for going into *Mordor*, and it is also true for updating parameters.

It turns out, `no_grad()` has another use case other than allowing us to update parameters; we'll get back to it in Chapter 2 when dealing with a model's evaluation.

Dynamic Computation Graph

> *"Unfortunately, no one can be told what the dynamic computation graph is. You have to see it for yourself."*
>
> Morpheus

How great was *The Matrix*? Right? Right? But, jokes aside, I want **you** to **see the graph for yourself** too!

The PyTorchViz package and its `make_dot(variable)` method allow us to easily visualize a graph associated with a given Python variable involved in the gradient computation.

> ℹ️ If you chose "Local Installation" in the "Setup Guide" and skipped or had issues with Step 5 ("Install GraphViz software and TorchViz package"), you will get an **error** when trying to visualize the graphs using `make_dot`.

So, let's stick with the **bare minimum**: two (*gradient-computing*) **tensors** for our parameters, predictions, errors, and loss—these are Steps 0, 1, and 2.

```
# Step 0 - Initializes parameters "b" and "w" randomly
torch.manual_seed(42)
b = torch.randn(1, requires_grad=True, \
                dtype=torch.float, device=device)
w = torch.randn(1, requires_grad=True, \
                dtype=torch.float, device=device)
# Step 1 - Computes our model's predicted output - forward pass
yhat = b + w * x_train_tensor
# Step 2 - Computes the loss
error = (yhat - y_train_tensor)
loss = (error ** 2).mean()
# We can try plotting the graph for any variable: yhat, error, loss
make_dot(yhat)
```

Running the code above will produce the **graph** below:

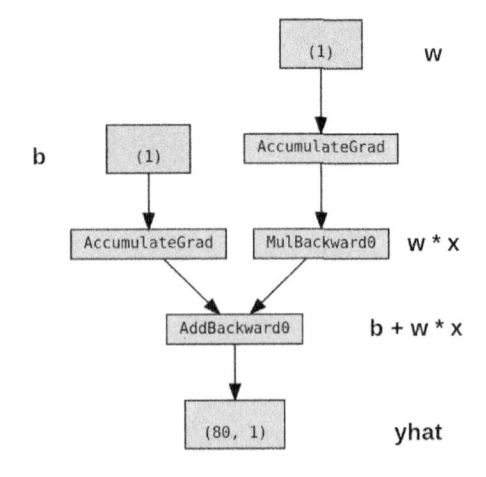

Figure 1.5 - Computation graph generated for yhat; Obs.: the corresponding variable names were inserted manually

Let's take a closer look at its components:

- **blue boxes** ((1)s): these boxes correspond to the **tensors** we use as **parameters**, the ones we're asking PyTorch to **compute gradients** for
- **gray boxes** (MulBackward0 and AddBackward0): **Python operations** that involve **gradient-computing tensors** or **its dependencies**
- **green box** ((80, 1)): the tensor used as the **starting point for the computation** of gradients (assuming the backward() method is called from the **variable used** to **visualize** the graph)—they are computed from the **bottom-up** in a graph

Now, take a closer look at the **gray box** at the bottom of the graph: **Two arrows** are pointing to it since it is **adding** up **two variables**, b and w*x. Seems obvious, right?

Then, look at the other **gray box** (MulBackward0) of the same graph: It is performing a **multiplication operation**, namely, w*x. But there is only one arrow pointing to it! The arrow comes from the **blue box** that corresponds to our **parameter w**.

> "**Why** don't we have a box for our **data** (x)?"

The answer is: We **do not compute gradients** for it!

So, even though there are *more* tensors involved in the operations performed by the computation graph, it **only** shows **gradient-computing tensors** and **their dependencies**.

What would happen to the computation graph if we set requires_grad to False for our **parameter b**?

```
b_nograd = torch.randn(1, requires_grad=False, \
                       dtype=torch.float, device=device)
w = torch.randn(1, requires_grad=True, \
                dtype=torch.float, device=device)

yhat = b_nograd + w * x_train_tensor

make_dot(yhat)
```

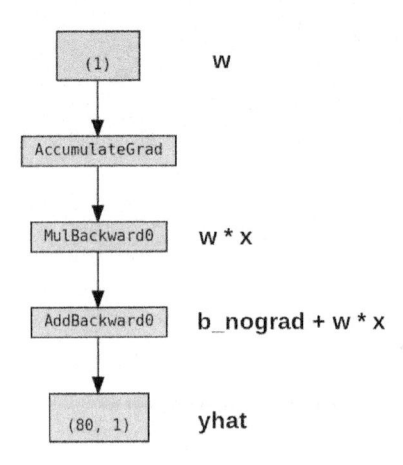

```
        (1)         w
         │
         ▼
   ┌──────────────┐
   │AccumulateGrad│
   └──────────────┘
         │
         ▼
   ┌──────────────┐
   │ MulBackward0 │    w * x
   └──────────────┘
         │
         ▼
   ┌──────────────┐
   │ AddBackward0 │    b_nograd + w * x
   └──────────────┘
         │
         ▼
      (80, 1)        yhat
```

Figure 1.6 - Now parameter "b" does NOT have its gradient computed, but it is STILL used in computation

Unsurprisingly, the **blue box** corresponding to **parameter b** is no more!

💡 Simple enough: **No gradients, no graph!**

The **best** thing about the *dynamic computation graph* is that you can make it **as complex as you want** it. You can even use *control flow statements* (e.g., if statements) to **control the flow of the gradients**.

Figure 1.7 shows an example of this. And yes, I do know that the computation itself is *complete* **nonsense**!

```
b = torch.randn(1, requires_grad=True, \
                dtype=torch.float, device=device)
w = torch.randn(1, requires_grad=True, \
                dtype=torch.float, device=device)
yhat = b + w * x_train_tensor
error = yhat - y_train_tensor
loss = (error ** 2).mean()
# this makes no sense!!
if loss > 0:
    yhat2 = w * x_train_tensor
    error2 = yhat2 - y_train_tensor
# neither does this!!
loss += error2.mean()
make_dot(loss)
```

94 | Chapter 1: A Simple Regression Problem

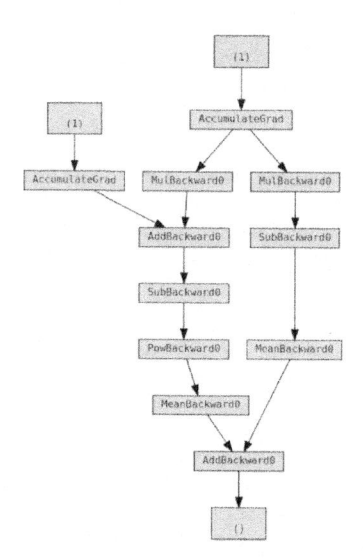

Figure 1.7 - Complex (and nonsensical!) computation graph just to make a point

Even though the computation is nonsensical, you can clearly see the **effect** of adding a **control flow statement** like `if loss > 0`: It **branches** the computation graph into two parts. The **right branch** performs the computation **inside the if statement**, which gets added to the result of the left branch in the end. Cool, right?

Even though we are not building more-complex models like that in this book, this small example illustrates very well PyTorch's capabilities and how easily they can be implemented in code.

Optimizer

So far, we've been **manually** updating the parameters using the computed gradients. That's probably fine for **two parameters**, but what if we had a **whole lot of them**? We need to use one of PyTorch's optimizers, like SGD, RMSprop, or Adam.

There are **many** optimizers: **SGD** is the most basic of them, and **Adam** is one of the most popular.

Different optimizers use different mechanics for **updating the parameters**, but they all achieve the same goal through, literally, **different paths**.

To see what I mean by this, check out this animated GIF (*https://bit.ly/2UDXDWM*) developed by Alec Radford[46], available at Stanford's "CS231n: Convolutional Neural Networks for Visual Recognition"[47] course. The animation shows a **loss surface**, just like the ones we computed in Chapter 0, and the **paths** traversed by some optimizers to achieve the **minimum** (represented by a star).

Remember, the **choice of mini-batch size** influences the **path of gradient descent**, and so does the **choice of an optimizer**.

step / zero_grad

An optimizer takes the **parameters** we want to update, the **learning rate** we want to use (and possibly many other hyper-parameters as well!), and **performs the updates** through its `step()` method.

```
# Defines an SGD optimizer to update the parameters
optimizer = optim.SGD([b, w], lr=lr)
```

Besides, we also don't need to *zero the gradients* one by one anymore. We just invoke the optimizer's `zero_grad()` method, and that's it!

In the code below, we create a *stochastic gradient descent* (SGD) optimizer to update our parameters **b** and **w**.

Don't be fooled by the **optimizer**'s name: If we use **all training data** at once for the update—as we are actually doing in the code—the optimizer is performing a **batch** gradient descent, despite its name.

96 | Chapter 1: A Simple Regression Problem

Notebook Cell 1.7 - PyTorch's optimizer in action—no more manual update of parameters!

```
 1  # Sets learning rate - this is "eta" ~ the "n"-like Greek letter
 2  lr = 0.1
 3
 4  # Step 0 - Initializes parameters "b" and "w" randomly
 5  torch.manual_seed(42)
 6  b = torch.randn(1, requires_grad=True, \
 7                  dtype=torch.float, device=device)
 8  w = torch.randn(1, requires_grad=True, \
 9                  dtype=torch.float, device=device)
10
11  # Defines a SGD optimizer to update the parameters
12  optimizer = optim.SGD([b, w], lr=lr)                       ①
13
14  # Defines number of epochs
15  n_epochs = 1000
16
17  for epoch in range(n_epochs):
18      # Step 1 - Computes model's predicted output - forward pass
19      yhat = b + w * x_train_tensor
20
21      # Step 2 - Computes the loss
22      # We are using ALL data points, so this is BATCH gradient
23      # descent. How wrong is our model? That's the error!
24      error = (yhat - y_train_tensor)
25      # It is a regression, so it computes mean squared error (MSE)
26      loss = (error ** 2).mean()
27
28      # Step 3 - Computes gradients for both "b" and "w" parameters
29      loss.backward()
30
31      # Step 4 - Updates parameters using gradients and
32      # the learning rate. No more manual update!
33      # with torch.no_grad():
34      #     b -= lr * b.grad
35      #     w -= lr * w.grad
36      optimizer.step()                                       ②
37
38      # No more telling Pytorch to let gradients go!
39      # b.grad.zero_()
40      # w.grad.zero_()
```

```
41        optimizer.zero_grad()                              ③
42
43 print(b, w)
```

① Defining an optimizer

② New "Step 4 - Updating Parameters" using the optimizer

③ New "gradient zeroing" using the optimizer

Let's inspect our two parameters just to make sure everything is still working fine:

Output

```
tensor([1.0235], device='cuda:0', requires_grad=True)
tensor([1.9690], device='cuda:0', requires_grad=True)
```

Cool! We've *optimized* the **optimization** process :-) What's left?

Loss

We now tackle the **loss computation**. As expected, PyTorch has us covered once again. There are many loss functions to choose from, depending on the task at hand. Since ours is a regression, we are using the **mean squared error** (MSE) as loss, and thus we need PyTorch's nn.MSELoss():

```
# Defines an MSE loss function
loss_fn = nn.MSELoss(reduction='mean')
loss_fn
```

Output

```
MSELoss()
```

Notice that nn.MSELoss() **is NOT the loss function itself**: We do not pass *predictions* and *labels* to it! Instead, as you can see, it **returns another function**, which we called loss_fn: *That* is the **actual loss function**. So, we can pass a prediction and a label to it and get the corresponding loss value:

98 | Chapter 1: A Simple Regression Problem

```
# This is a random example to illustrate the loss function
predictions = torch.tensor(0.5, 1.0)
labels = torch.tensor(2.0, 1.3)
loss_fn(predictions, labels)
```

Output

```
tensor(1.1700)
```

> Moreover, you can also specify a **reduction method** to be applied; that is, **how do you want to aggregate the errors for individual points?** You can average them (`reduction="mean"`) or simply sum them up (`reduction="sum"`). In our example, we use the typical `mean` reduction to compute **MSE**. If we had used `sum` as reduction, we would actually be computing **SSE** (sum of squared errors).

> Technically speaking, `nn.MSELoss()` is a **higher-order function**. If you're not familiar with the concept, I will explain it briefly in Chapter 2.

We then **use** the created loss function in the code below, at line 29, to compute the loss, given our **predictions** and our **labels**:

Notebook Cell 1.8 - PyTorch's loss in action: no more manual loss computation!

```
 1  # Sets learning rate - this is "eta" ~ the "n"-like
 2  # Greek letter
 3  lr = 0.1
 4
 5  # Step 0 - Initializes parameters "b" and "w" randomly
 6  torch.manual_seed(42)
 7  b = torch.randn(1, requires_grad=True, \
 8                  dtype=torch.float, device=device)
 9  w = torch.randn(1, requires_grad=True, \
10                  dtype=torch.float, device=device)
11
12  # Defines an SGD optimizer to update the parameters
13  optimizer = optim.SGD([b, w], lr=lr)
14
15  # Defines an MSE loss function
16  loss_fn = nn.MSELoss(reduction='mean')                    ①
17
18  # Defines number of epochs
19  n_epochs = 1000
20
21  for epoch in range(n_epochs):
22      # Step 1 - Computes model's predicted output - forward pass
23      yhat = b + w * x_train_tensor
24
25      # Step 2 - Computes the loss
26      # No more manual loss!
27      # error = (yhat - y_train_tensor)
28      # loss = (error ** 2).mean()
29      loss = loss_fn(yhat, y_train_tensor)                  ②
30
31      # Step 3 - Computes gradients for both "b" and "w" parameters
32      loss.backward()
33
34      # Step 4 - Updates parameters using gradients and
35      # the learning rate
36      optimizer.step()
37      optimizer.zero_grad()
38
39  print(b, w)
```

① Defining a loss function

② New "Step 2 - Computing Loss" using `loss_fn()`

Output

```
tensor([1.0235], device='cuda:0', requires_grad=True)
tensor([1.9690], device='cuda:0', requires_grad=True)
```

Let's take a look at the **loss value** at the end of training...

```
loss
```

Output

```
tensor(0.0080, device='cuda:0', grad_fn=<MeanBackward0>)
```

What if we wanted to have it as a *Numpy* array? I guess we could just use `numpy()` again, right? (And `cpu()` as well, since our *loss* is in the `cuda` device.)

```
loss.cpu().numpy()
```

Output

```
RuntimeError                Traceback (most recent call last)
<ipython-input-43-58c76a7bac74> in <module>
----> 1 loss.cpu().numpy()

RuntimeError: Can't call numpy() on Variable that requires
grad. Use var.detach().numpy() instead.
```

What happened here? Unlike our *data tensors*, the **loss tensor** is actually computing gradients; to use `numpy()`, we need to `detach()` the tensor from the computation graph first:

```
loss.detach().cpu().numpy()
```

Output

```
array(0.00804466, dtype=float32)
```

This seems like **a lot of work**; there must be an easier way! And there is one, indeed: We can use `item()`, for **tensors with a single element**, or `tolist()` otherwise (it still returns a scalar if there is only *one* element, though).

```
print(loss.item(), loss.tolist())
```

Output

```
0.008044655434787273 0.008044655434787273
```

At this point, there's only one piece of code left to change: the **predictions**. It is then time to introduce PyTorch's way of implementing a...

Model

In PyTorch, a **model** is represented by a regular **Python class** that inherits from the `Module` class.

> **IMPORTANT**: Are you comfortable with **object-oriented programming (OOP)** concepts like *classes, constructors, methods, instances,* and *attributes*?
>
> If you're *unsure* about any of these terms, I'd **strongly recommend** you follow tutorials like Real Python's "Object-Oriented Programming (OOP) in Python 3"[48] and "Supercharge Your Classes With Python super()"[49] before proceeding.
>
> Having a good understanding of **OOP is key** to benefitting the most from PyTorch's capabilities.

So, assuming you're already comfortable with OOP, let's dive into developing a **model** in PyTorch.

The most fundamental methods a **model class** needs to implement are:

- __init__(self): **It defines the parts that make up the model**—in our case, two *parameters*, **b** and **w**.

  > You are **not** limited to defining **parameters**, though. **Models can contain other models as their attributes** as well, so you can easily nest them. We'll see an example of this shortly as well.
  >
  > Besides, **do not forget** to include **super().__init__()** to execute the __init__() method of the **parent class** (nn.Module) before your own.

- forward(self, x): It performs the **actual computation**; that is, it **outputs a prediction**, given the input **x**.

  > It may seem weird but, whenever using your model to make predictions, you should **NOT call the** forward(x) **method!**
  >
  > You should **call the whole model instead**, as in **model(x)**, to perform a forward pass and output predictions.
  >
  > The reason is, the call to the whole model involves *extra steps*, namely, handling **forward** and **backward hooks**. If you don't use **hooks** (and we don't use any right now), both calls are equivalent.
  >
  > **Hooks** are a very useful mechanism that allows retrieving intermediate values in deeper models. We'll get to them in the second volume of the series.

Let's build a proper (yet simple) model for our regression task. It should look like this:

Notebook Cell 1.9 - Building our "Manual" model, creating parameter by parameter!

```
1  class ManualLinearRegression(nn.Module):
2      def __init__(self):
3          super().__init__()
4          # To make "b" and "w" real parameters of the model,
5          # we need to wrap them with nn.Parameter
6          self.b = nn.Parameter(torch.randn(1,
7                                            requires_grad=True,
8                                            dtype=torch.float))
9          self.w = nn.Parameter(torch.randn(1,
10                                           requires_grad=True,
11                                           dtype=torch.float))
12
13     def forward(self, x):
14         # Computes the outputs / predictions
15         return self.b + self.w * x
```

Parameters

In the __init__() method, we define our **two parameters**, **b** and **w**, using the Parameter class, to tell PyTorch that these **tensors**, which are **attributes** of the ManualLinearRegression class, should be considered **parameters of the model** the class represents.

Why should we care about that? By doing so, we can use our model's parameters() method to retrieve **an iterator over the model's parameters**, including parameters of **nested models**. Then we can use it to feed our *optimizer* (instead of building a list of parameters ourselves!).

```
torch.manual_seed(42)
# Creates a "dummy" instance of our ManualLinearRegression model
dummy = ManualLinearRegression()
list(dummy.parameters())
```

Output

```
[Parameter containing:
 tensor([0.3367], requires_grad=True), Parameter containing:
 tensor([0.1288], requires_grad=True)]
```

state_dict

Moreover, we can get the **current values of all parameters** using our model's state_dict() method.

```
dummy.state_dict()
```

Output

```
OrderedDict([('b', tensor([0.3367])), ('w', tensor([0.1288]))])
```

The state_dict() of a given model is simply a Python dictionary that **maps each attribute / parameter to its corresponding tensor**. But only **learnable** parameters are included, as its purpose is to keep track of parameters that are going to be updated by the **optimizer**.

By the way, the **optimizer** itself has a state_dict() too, which contains its internal state, as well as other hyper-parameters. Let's take a quick look at it:

```
optimizer.state_dict()
```

Output

```
{'state': {},
 'param_groups': [{'lr': 0.1,
   'momentum': 0,
   'dampening': 0,
   'weight_decay': 0,
   'nesterov': False,
   'params': [140535747664704, 140535747688560]}]}
```

"What do we need this for?"

It turns out, *state dictionaries* can also be used for **checkpointing** a model, as we will see in Chapter 2.

Device

IMPORTANT: We need to **send our model to the same device where the data is**. If our data is made of GPU tensors, our model must "live" inside the GPU as well.

If we were to send our dummy model to a device, it would look like this:

```
torch.manual_seed(42)
# Creates a "dummy" instance of our ManualLinearRegression model
# and sends it to the device
dummy = ManualLinearRegression().to(device)
```

Forward Pass

The **forward pass** is the moment when the model **makes predictions**.

Remember: You should make predictions calling `model(x)`.

DO NOT call `model.forward(x)`!

Otherwise, your model's *hooks* will not work (if you have them).

We can use all these handy methods to change our code, which should be looking like this:

Notebook Cell 1.10 - PyTorch's model in action: no more manual prediction / forward step!

```
1  # Sets learning rate - this is "eta" ~ the "n"-like
2  # Greek letter
3  lr = 0.1
4
5  # Step 0 - Initializes parameters "b" and "w" randomly
6  torch.manual_seed(42)
7  # Now we can create a model and send it at once to the device
8  model = ManualLinearRegression().to(device)          ①
9
10 # Defines an SGD optimizer to update the parameters
11 # (now retrieved directly from the model)
12 optimizer = optim.SGD(model.parameters(), lr=lr)
13
14 # Defines an MSE loss function
15 loss_fn = nn.MSELoss(reduction='mean')
16
17 # Defines number of epochs
18 n_epochs = 1000
19
20 for epoch in range(n_epochs):
21     model.train() # What is this?!?                  ②
22
23     # Step 1 - Computes model's predicted output - forward pass
24     # No more manual prediction!
25     yhat = model(x_train_tensor)                     ③
26
27     # Step 2 - Computes the loss
28     loss = loss_fn(yhat, y_train_tensor)
29
30     # Step 3 - Computes gradients for both "b" and "w" parameters
31     loss.backward()
32
33     # Step 4 - Updates parameters using gradients and
34     # the learning rate
35     optimizer.step()
36     optimizer.zero_grad()
37
38 # We can also inspect its parameters using its state_dict
39 print(model.state_dict())
```

① Instantiating a model

② What **IS** this?!?

③ New "Step 1 - Forward Pass" using a model

Now, the printed statements will look like this—final values for parameters **b** and **w** are still the same, so everything is OK :-)

Output

```
OrderedDict([('b', tensor([1.0235], device='cuda:0')),
('w', tensor([1.9690], device='cuda:0'))])
```

train

I hope you noticed one particular statement in the code (line 21), to which I assigned a comment **"What is this?!?"**—model.train().

> In PyTorch, models have a train() method, which, somewhat disappointingly, **does NOT perform a training step**. Its only purpose is to **set the model to training mode**.
>
> Why is this important? Some models may use mechanisms like dropout, for instance, which have **distinct behaviors during training and evaluation** phases.

It is good practice to call model.train() in the training loop. It is also possible to set a model to evaluation mode, but this is a topic for the next chapter.

Nested Models

In our model, we *manually* created *two parameters* to perform a linear regression. What if, instead of defining individual parameters, we use PyTorch's Linear model?

We are implementing a *single-feature linear regression*, *one input* and *one output*, so the corresponding linear model would look like this:

```
linear = nn.Linear(1, 1)
linear
```

Output

```
Linear(in_features=1, out_features=1, bias=True)
```

Do we still have our **b** and **w** parameters? Sure, we do:

```
linear.state_dict()
```

Output

```
OrderedDict([('weight', tensor([[-0.2191]])),
('bias', tensor([0.2018]))])
```

So, our former parameter *b* is the **bias**, and our former parameter *w* is the **weight** (your values will be different since I haven't set up a random seed for this example).

Now, let's use PyTorch's `Linear` model as an **attribute** of our own, thus creating a **nested model**.

> 💡 You are **not** limited to defining parameters, though; **models can contain other models as their attributes** as well, so you can easily nest them. We'll see an example of this shortly.

Even though this clearly is a contrived example, since we are pretty much *wrapping the underlying model without adding anything useful* (or, at all!) to it, it illustrates the concept well.

Notebook Cell 1.11 - Building a model using PyTorch's Linear model

```python
class MyLinearRegression(nn.Module):
    def __init__(self):
        super().__init__()
        # Instead of our custom parameters, we use a Linear model
        # with a single input and a single output
        self.linear = nn.Linear(1, 1)

    def forward(self, x):
        # Now it only makes a call
        self.linear(x)
```

In the `__init__()` method, we create an **attribute** that contains our **nested Linear model**.

In the `forward()` method, we **call the nested model itself** to perform the forward pass (**notice, we are *not* calling** `self.linear.forward(x)!`).

Now, if we call the `parameters()` method of this model, **PyTorch will figure out the parameters of its attributes recursively**.

```
torch.manual_seed(42)
dummy = MyLinearRegression().to(device)
list(dummy.parameters())
```

Output

```
[Parameter containing:
 tensor([[0.7645]], device='cuda:0', requires_grad=True),
 Parameter containing:
 tensor([0.8300], device='cuda:0', requires_grad=True)]
```

You can also add extra `Linear` attributes, and, even if you don't use them at all in the forward pass, they will **still** be listed under `parameters()`.

If you prefer, you can also use `state_dict()` to get the parameter values, together with their names:

```
dummy.state_dict()
```

Output

```
OrderedDict([('linear.weight',
              tensor([[0.7645]], device='cuda:0')),
             ('linear.bias',
              tensor([0.8300], device='cuda:0'))])
```

Notice that both *bias* and *weight* have a **prefix** with the **attribute name**: *linear*, from the `self.linear` in the `__init__()` method.

Sequential Models

Our model was simple enough. You may be thinking: *"Why even bother to build a class for it?!"* Well, you have a point...

For **straightforward models** that use **a series of built-in PyTorch models** (like `Linear`), where the output of one is sequentially fed as an input to the next, we can use a, er... `Sequential` model :-)

In our case, we would build a sequential model with a single argument; that is, the `Linear` model we used to train our linear regression. The model would look like this:

Notebook Cell 1.12 - Building a model using PyTorch's Sequential model

```
1 torch.manual_seed(42)
2 # Alternatively, you can use a Sequential model
3 model = nn.Sequential(nn.Linear(1, 1)).to(device)
4
5 model.state_dict()
```

Output

```
OrderedDict([('0.weight', tensor([[0.7645]], device='cuda:0')),
             ('0.bias', tensor([0.8300], device='cuda:0'))])
```

Simple enough, right?

We've been talking about **models inside other models**. This may get confusing real quick, so let's follow convention and call any *internal* model a **layer**.

Layers

A Linear model can be seen as a **layer** in a neural network.

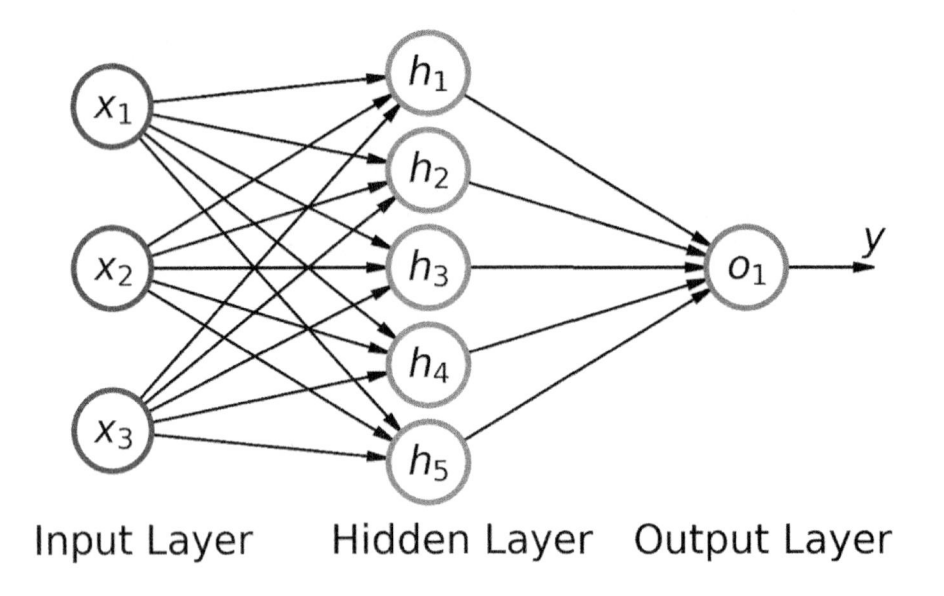

Figure 1.8 - Layers of a neural network

In the figure above, the **hidden layer** would be nn.Linear(3, 5) (since it takes three inputs—from the input layer—and generates five outputs), and the **output layer** would be nn.Linear(5, 1) (since it takes five inputs—the outputs from the hidden layer—and generates a single output).

If we use Sequential() to build it; it looks like this:

```
torch.manual_seed(42)
# Building the model from the figure above
model = nn.Sequential(nn.Linear(3, 5), nn.Linear(5, 1)).to(device)

model.state_dict()
```

Output

```
OrderedDict([
 ('0.weight',
   tensor([[ 0.4414,  0.4792, -0.1353],
           [ 0.5304, -0.1265,  0.1165],
           [-0.2811,  0.3391,  0.5090],
           [-0.4236,  0.5018,  0.1081],
           [ 0.4266,  0.0782,  0.2784]],
          device='cuda:0')),
 ('0.bias',
   tensor([-0.0815,  0.4451,  0.0853, -0.2695,  0.1472],
          device='cuda:0')),
 ('1.weight',
   tensor([[-0.2060, -0.0524, -0.1816,  0.2967, -0.3530]],
          device='cuda:0')),
 ('1.bias',
   tensor([-0.2062], device='cuda:0'))])
```

Since this sequential model **does not have attribute names**, state_dict() uses **numeric prefixes**.

You can also use a model's add_module() method to **name** the layers:

```
torch.manual_seed(42)
# Building the model from the figure above
model = nn.Sequential()
model.add_module('layer1', nn.Linear(3, 5))
model.add_module('layer2', nn.Linear(5, 1))
model.to(device)
```

Output

```
Sequential(
  (layer1): Linear(in_features=3, out_features=5, bias=True)
  (layer2): Linear(in_features=5, out_features=1, bias=True)
)
```

There are **MANY** different layers that can be used in PyTorch:

- Convolution Layers
- Pooling Layers
- Padding Layers
- Non-linear Activations
- Normalization Layers
- Recurrent Layers
- Transformer Layers
- Linear Layers
- Dropout Layers
- Sparse Layers (embeddings)
- Vision Layers
- DataParallel Layers (multi-GPU)
- Flatten Layer

So far, we have just used a `Linear` layer. In the next volume of the series, we'll use many others, like convolution, pooling, padding, flatten, dropout, and non-linear activations.

Putting It All Together

We've covered a lot of ground so far, from coding a **linear regression in *Numpy* using gradient descent** to transforming it into a **PyTorch model**, step-by-step.

It is time to put it all together and organize our code into **three** fundamental parts, namely:

- **data preparation** (*not* data generation!)
- **model configuration**
- **model training**

Let's tackle these three parts, in order.

Data Preparation

There hasn't been much data preparation up to this point, to be honest. After generating our data points in **Notebook Cell 1.1**, the only preparation step performed so far has been transforming *Numpy* arrays into PyTorch tensors, as in **Notebook Cell 1.3**, which is reproduced below:

Define - Data Preparation V0

```
1 %%writefile data_preparation/v0.py
2
3 device = 'cuda' if torch.cuda.is_available() else 'cpu'
4
5 # Our data was in Numpy arrays, but we need to transform them
6 # into PyTorch's Tensors and then send them to the
7 # chosen device
8 x_train_tensor = torch.as_tensor(x_train).float().to(device)
9 y_train_tensor = torch.as_tensor(y_train).float().to(device)
```

Run - Data Preparation V0

```
%run -i data_preparation/v0.py
```

This part will get much more interesting in the next chapter when we get to use `Dataset` and `DataLoader` classes :-)

> *"What's the purpose of saving cells to these files?"*

We know we have to run the **full sequence** to **train a model**: data preparation, model configuration, and model training. In Chapter 2, we'll *gradually improve* each of these parts, *versioning* them inside each corresponding folder. So, **saving them to files** allows us to **run** a full sequence using **different versions without having to duplicate code**.

Let's say we start improving **model configuration** (and we will do exactly that in Chapter 2), but the other two parts are still the same; how do we run the full sequence?

Putting It All Together | 115

We use **magic**, just like that:

```
%run -i data_preparation/v0.py
%run -i model_configuration/v1.py
%run -i model_training/v0.py
```

Since we're using the -i option, it works exactly as if we had copied the code from the files into a cell and executed it.

> ### Jupyter's *Magic* Commands
>
> You probably noticed the somewhat unusual %%writefile and %run commands above. These are built-in magic commands.[50] A magic is a kind of shortcut that extends a notebook's capabilities.
>
> We are using the following two magics to better organize our code:
>
> - **%%writefile**[51]: As its name says, it writes the contents of the cell to a file, but it **does not run it**, so we need to use yet another magic.
>
> - **%run**[52]: It runs the named file inside the notebook as a program—but **independent of the rest of the notebook**, so we need to use the -i option to make all variables available, from both the notebook and the file (technically speaking, the file is executed in IPython's namespace).
>
> In a nutshell, a cell containing one of our three fundamental parts will be written to a versioned file inside the folder corresponding to that part.
>
> In the example above, we write the cell to the **data_preparation** folder, name it **v0.py**, and then execute it using the %run -i magic.

Model Configuration

We have seen plenty of this part: from defining parameters *b* and *w* manually, then wrapping them up using the Module class, to using **layers** in a Sequential model. We have also defined a **loss function** and an **optimizer** for our particular **linear regression** model.

For the purpose of organizing our code, we'll include the following elements in the **model configuration** part:

- a **model**
- a **loss function** (which needs to be chosen according to your model)
- an **optimizer** (although some people may disagree with this choice, it makes it easier to further organize the code)

Most of the corresponding code can be found in **Notebook Cell 1.10**, lines 1-15, but we'll replace the `ManualLinearRegression` model with the `Sequential` model from **Notebook Cell 1.12**:

Define - Model Configuration V0

```
1  %%writefile model_configuration/v0.py
2
3  # This is redundant now, but it won't be when we introduce
4  # Datasets...
5  device = 'cuda' if torch.cuda.is_available() else 'cpu'
6
7  # Sets learning rate - this is "eta" ~ the "n"-like Greek letter
8  lr = 0.1
9
10 torch.manual_seed(42)
11 # Now we can create a model and send it at once to the device
12 model = nn.Sequential(nn.Linear(1, 1)).to(device)
13
14 # Defines an SGD optimizer to update the parameters
15 # (now retrieved directly from the model)
16 optimizer = optim.SGD(model.parameters(), lr=lr)
17
18 # Defines an MSE loss function
19 loss_fn = nn.MSELoss(reduction='mean')
```

Run - Model Configuration V0

```
%run -i model_configuration/v0.py
```

Model Training

This is the last part, where the *actual training* takes place. It loops over the **gradient descent steps** we saw at the beginning of this chapter:

- Step 1: compute **model's predictions**
- Step 2: compute the **loss**
- Step 3: compute the **gradients**
- Step 4: update the **parameters**

This sequence is repeated over and over until the **number of epochs** is reached. The corresponding code for this part also comes from **Notebook Cell 1.10**, lines 17-36.

> *"What happened to the random initialization step?"*

Since we are not manually creating parameters anymore, the initialization is handled **inside each layer** during model creation.

Define - Model Training V0

```
1  %%writefile model_training/v0.py
2  
3  # Defines number of epochs
4  n_epochs = 1000
5  
6  for epoch in range(n_epochs):
7      # Sets model to TRAIN mode
8      model.train()
9  
10     # Step 1 - Computes model's predicted output - forward pass
11     yhat = model(x_train_tensor)
12  
13     # Step 2 - Computes the loss
14     loss = loss_fn(yhat, y_train_tensor)
15  
16     # Step 3 - Computes gradients for both "b" and "w" parameters
17     loss.backward()
18  
19     # Step 4 - Updates parameters using gradients and
20     # the learning rate
21     optimizer.step()
22     optimizer.zero_grad()
```

Run - Model Training V0

```
%run -i model_training/v0.py
```

One last check to make sure we have everything right:

```
print(model.state_dict())
```

Output

```
OrderedDict([('0.weight', tensor([[1.9690]], device='cuda:0')),
('0.bias', tensor([1.0235], device='cuda:0'))])
```

Now, take a close, hard look at the code **inside the training loop.**

Ready? I have a question for you then…

"Would this code **change** if we were using a **different optimizer**, or **loss**, or even **model**?"

Before I give you the answer, let me address something else that may be on your mind: "*What is the point of all this?*"

Well, in the next chapter we'll get fancier, using more of PyTorch's classes (like `Dataset` and `DataLoader`) to further refine our **data preparation step**, and we'll also try to **reduce boilerplate code** to a minimum. So, splitting our code into three logical parts will allow us to better handle these improvements.

And here is the **answer: NO**, the code inside the loop **would not change**.

I guess you figured out which **boilerplate** I was referring to, right?

Recap

First of all, **congratulations** are in order: You have successfully implemented a **fully functioning model** and **training loop** in PyTorch!

We have covered a lot of ground in this first chapter:

- implementing a linear regression in *Numpy* using **gradient descent**
- creating **tensors** in PyTorch, sending them to a **device**, and making **parameters** out of them
- understanding PyTorch's main feature, **autograd**, to perform automatic differentiation using its associated properties and methods, like backward(), grad, zero_(), and no_grad()
- visualizing the **dynamic computation graph** associated with a sequence of operations
- creating an **optimizer** to simultaneously update multiple parameters, using its step() and zero_grad() methods
- creating a **loss function** using PyTorch's corresponding higher-order function (more on that topic in the next chapter)
- understanding PyTorch's Module class and creating your own **models**, implementing __init__() and forward() methods, and making use of its built-in parameters() and state_dict() methods
- transforming the original *Numpy* implementation into a **PyTorch** one using the elements above
- realizing the importance of including model.train() inside the **training loop** (never forget that!)
- implementing **nested** and **sequential** models using PyTorch's **layers**
- putting it all together into neatly organized code divided into **three distinct parts**: data preparation, model configuration, and model training

You are now ready for the next chapter. We'll see **more** of PyTorch's capabilities, and we'll **further develop our training loop** so it can be used for different problems and models. You'll be building your *own, small draft of a library* for training deep learning models.

[39] https://github.com/dvgodoy/PyTorchStepByStep/blob/master/Chapter01.ipynb
[40] https://colab.research.google.com/github/dvgodoy/PyTorchStepByStep/blob/master/Chapter01.ipynb

[41] https://en.wikipedia.org/wiki/Gaussian_noise

[42] https://bit.ly/2XZXjnk

[43] https://bit.ly/3fjCSHR

[44] https://bit.ly/2Y0lhPn

[45] https://pytorch.org/docs/stable/notes/randomness.html

[46] https://twitter.com/alecrad

[47] http://cs231n.stanford.edu/

[48] https://realpython.com/python3-object-oriented-programming/

[49] https://realpython.com/python-super/

[50] https://ipython.readthedocs.io/en/stable/interactive/magics.html

[51] https://bit.ly/30GH0vO

[52] https://bit.ly/3g1eQCm

Chapter 2
Rethinking the Training Loop

Spoilers

In this chapter, we will:

- build a **function** to perform **training steps**
- implement our **own dataset class**
- use **data loaders** to **generate mini-batches**
- build a **function** to perform **mini-batch gradient descent**
- **evaluate** our model
- integrate **TensorBoard** to monitor model training
- **save / checkpoint** our model to disk
- **load** our model from disk to **resume training** or to **deploy**

Jupyter Notebook

The Jupyter notebook corresponding to Chapter 2[53] is part of the official *Deep Learning with PyTorch Step-by-Step* repository on GitHub. You can also run it directly in **Google Colab**[54].

If you're using a *local installation*, open your terminal or Anaconda prompt and navigate to the PyTorchStepByStep folder you cloned from GitHub. Then, *activate* the pytorchbook environment and run jupyter notebook:

```
$ conda activate pytorchbook

(pytorchbook)$ jupyter notebook
```

If you're using Jupyter's default settings, http://localhost:8888/notebooks/Chapter02.ipynb should open Chapter 2's notebook. If not, just click on Chapter02.ipynb on your Jupyter's home page.

Imports

For the sake of organization, all libraries needed throughout the code used in any given chapter are imported at its very beginning. For this chapter, we'll need the following imports:

```python
import numpy as np
from sklearn.linear_model import LinearRegression

import torch
import torch.optim as optim
import torch.nn as nn
from torch.utils.data import Dataset, TensorDataset, DataLoader
from torch.utils.data.dataset import random_split
from torch.utils.tensorboard import SummaryWriter

import matplotlib.pyplot as plt
%matplotlib inline
plt.style.use('fivethirtyeight')
```

Rethinking the Training Loop

We finished the previous chapter with an important question:

> *"Would the code inside the training loop **change** if we were using a different **optimizer**, or **loss**, or even **model**?"*

The answer: **NO**.

But we did not actually elaborate on it in the previous chapter, so let's do so now.

The model training involves looping over **the four gradient descent steps** (or **one training step**, for that matter), and those are always the same, regardless of which **model**, **loss**, or **optimizer** we use (there may be exceptions to this, but it holds true for the scope of this book).

Let's take a look at the code once again:

Run - Data Generation & Preparation, Model Configuration

```
%run -i data_generation/simple_linear_regression.py
%run -i data_preparation/v0.py
%run -i model_configuration/v0.py
```

Run - Model Training V0

```
1  # %load model_training/v0.py
2
3  # Defines number of epochs
4  n_epochs = 1000
5
6  for epoch in range(n_epochs):
7      # Sets model to TRAIN mode
8      model.train()
9
10     # Step 1 - Computes model's predicted output - forward pass
11     # No more manual prediction!
12     yhat = model(x_train_tensor)
13
14     # Step 2 - Computes the loss
15     loss = loss_fn(yhat, y_train_tensor)
16
17     # Step 3 - Computes gradients for both "b" and "w" parameters
18     loss.backward()
19
20     # Step 4 - Updates parameters using gradients and
21     # the learning rate
22     optimizer.step()
23     optimizer.zero_grad()
```

```
print(model.state_dict())
```

Output

```
OrderedDict([('0.weight', tensor([[1.9690]], device='cuda:0')),
             ('0.bias', tensor([1.0235], device='cuda:0'))])
```

So, I guess we could say all these lines of code (7-23) **perform a training step**. For a given combination of **model**, **loss**, and **optimizer**, it takes the **features** and corresponding **labels** as arguments. Right?

How about **writing a function that takes a model, a loss, and an optimizer** and **returns another function that performs a training step**? The latter would then take the features and corresponding labels as arguments and return the corresponding loss.

❓ *"Wait; what?! A function that returns another function?"*

Sounds complicated, right? It is not as bad as it sounds, though; that's called a **higher-order function**, and it is very useful for reducing boilerplate.

If you're familiar with the concept of higher-order functions, feel free to skip the aside.

Higher-Order Functions

Although this is more of a *coding* topic, I believe it is necessary to have a good grasp on *how higher-order functions work* to fully benefit from Python's capabilities and make the best out of our code.

I will illustrate higher-order functions with an example so that you can gain a **working knowledge** of it, but I am not delving any deeper into the topic, as it is outside the scope of this book.

Let's say we'd like to build a **series of functions**, each performing an exponentiation to a given power. The code would look like this:

```
def square(x):
    return x ** 2

def cube(x):
    return x ** 3

def fourth_power(x):
    return x ** 4

# and so on and so forth...
```

Well, clearly there is a **higher structure** to this:

- **every function takes a single argument** *x*, which is the number we'd like to exponentiate
- **every function performs the same operation**, an exponentiation, but each function has a different exponent

One way of solving this is to **make the exponent an explicit argument**, just like the code below:

```
def generic_exponentiation(x, exponent):
    return x ** exponent
```

That's perfectly fine, and it works quite well. But it also requires that you *specify the exponent every time* you call the function. **There must be another way**! Of course, there is; that's the purpose of this section!

We need to **build another (higher-order) function to build those functions (square, cube, etc.)** for us. The (higher-order) function is just a **function builder**. But how do we do that?

First, let's build the "*skeleton*" of the functions we are trying to generate; they all **take a single argument x**, and **they all perform an exponentiation**, each using a different exponent.

Fine. It should look like this:

```
def skeleton_exponentiation(x):
    return x ** exponent
```

If you try **calling this function** with any x, say, skeleton_exponentiation(2), you'll get the following **error**:

```
skeleton_exponentiation(2)
```

Output

```
NameError: name 'exponent' is not defined
```

This is expected: Your "*skeleton*" function has **no idea what the variable exponent is**! And that's what the higher-order function is going to accomplish.

We "wrap" our skeleton function with a higher-order function (which will build the desired functions). Let's call it, rather unimaginatively, exponentiation_builder(). What are **its arguments**, if any? Well, we're trying to **tell our skeleton function what its exponent should be**, so let's start with that!

```
def exponentiation_builder(exponent):
    def skeleton_exponentiation(x):
        return x ** exponent

    return skeleton_exponentiation
```

Now I want you to take a look at the (outer) **return statement**. It is **not** returning a **value**; it is **returning the skeleton function** instead. This is a function builder after all: It should build (and return) functions.

What happens if we call this higher-order function with a given exponent, say, 2?

```
returned_function = exponentiation_builder(2)

returned_function
```

Output

```
<function __main__.exponentiation_builder.<locals>.skeleton_
exponentiation(x)>
```

The **result** is, as expected, a **function**! What does this function do? It should square its argument—let's check it out:

```
returned_function(5)
```

Output

```
25
```

And *voilà*! We have a function builder! We can use it to create as many exponentiation functions as we'd like:

```
square = exponentiation_builder(2)
cube = exponentiation_builder(3)
fourth_power = exponentiation_builder(4)

# and so on and so forth...
```

> *"How does this apply to the training loop?"* you may ask.

We'll be doing something similar to our training loop: The equivalent to the **exponent** argument of the higher-order function is the combination of **model**, **loss**, and **optimizer**. Every time we execute a training step for a different set of **features** and **labels**, which are the equivalent of the x argument in the skeleton function, we'll be using the same model, loss, and optimizer.

Training Step

The higher-order function that builds a training step function for us is taking, as already mentioned, the key elements of our training loop: **model**, **loss**, and **optimizer**. The actual training step function to be returned will have two arguments, namely, **features** and **labels**, and will return the corresponding **loss value**.

Apart from returning the loss value, the inner `perform_train_step_fn()` function below is exactly the same as the code inside the loop in **Model Training V0**. The code should look like this:

Helper Function #1

```
1  def make_train_step_fn(model, loss_fn, optimizer):
2      # Builds function that performs a step in the train loop
3      def perform_train_step_fn(x, y):
4          # Sets model to TRAIN mode
5          model.train()
6  
7          # Step 1 - Computes model's predictions - forward pass
8          yhat = model(x)
9          # Step 2 - Computes the loss
10         loss = loss_fn(yhat, y)
11         # Step 3 - Computes gradients for "b" and "w" parameters
12         loss.backward()
13         # Step 4 - Updates parameters using gradients and
14         # the learning rate
15         optimizer.step()
16         optimizer.zero_grad()
17  
18         # Returns the loss
19         return loss.item()
20  
21     # Returns the function that will be called inside the
22     # train loop
23     return perform_train_step_fn
```

Then we need to update our **model configuration** code (adding line 20 in the next snippet) to call this higher-order function to build a `train_step_fn()` function. But we need to run a data preparation script first.

Run - Data Preparation V0

```
%run -i data_preparation/v0.py
```

Define - Model Configuration V1

```
1  %%writefile model_configuration/v1.py
2
3  device = 'cuda' if torch.cuda.is_available() else 'cpu'
4
5  # Sets learning rate - this is "eta" ~ the "n"-like Greek letter
6  lr = 0.1
7
8  torch.manual_seed(42)
9  # Now we can create a model and send it at once to the device
10 model = nn.Sequential(nn.Linear(1, 1)).to(device)
11
12 # Defines an SGD optimizer to update the parameters
13 optimizer = optim.SGD(model.parameters(), lr=lr)
14
15 # Defines an MSE loss function
16 loss_fn = nn.MSELoss(reduction='mean')
17
18 # Creates the train_step function for our model, loss function
19 # and optimizer
20 train_step_fn = make_train_step_fn(model, loss_fn, optimizer)  ①
```

① Creating a function that performs a training step

Run - Model Configuration V1

```
%run -i model_configuration/v1.py
```

Let's check our `train_step_fn()` function out!

```
train_step_fn
```

Output

```
<function __main__.make_train_step_fn.<locals>\
.perform_train_step_fn(x, y)>
```

Looking good! Now we need to update our **model training** to replace the code inside the loop with a call to our newly created function.

Our code should look like this; see how **tiny** the training loop is now? Lots of **boilerplate** code is inside the `make_train_step_fn()` helper function now!

Define - Model Training V1

```
1  %%writefile model_training/v1.py
2
3  # Defines number of epochs
4  n_epochs = 1000
5
6  losses = []                                                    ②
7
8  # For each epoch...
9  for epoch in range(n_epochs):
10     # Performs one train step and returns the corresponding loss
11     loss = train_step_fn(x_train_tensor, y_train_tensor)  ①
12     losses.append(loss)                                    ②
```

① Performing one training step

② Keeping track of the training loss

Run - Model Training V1

```
%run -i model_training/v1.py
```

Besides getting rid of boilerplate code, there is another change introduced in the code. We keep track of the **loss** value now. Every epoch, we append the last computed loss to a list.

> "Adding to a list? This does not seem very cutting-edge..."

Indeed, it is not. But please bear with me, as we'll replace it with something nicer soon enough :-)

After updating two out of three fundamental parts, our current state of development is:

- **Data Preparation V0**
- **Model Configuration V1**
- **Model Training V1**

How do we check if our changes introduced any bugs? We can inspect our model's state_dict():

```
# Checks model's parameters
print(model.state_dict())
```

Output

```
OrderedDict([('0.weight', tensor([[1.9690]], device='cuda:0')),
('0.bias', tensor([1.0235], device='cuda:0'))])
```

Let's give our training loop a rest and focus on our **data** for a while. So far, we've simply used our *Numpy arrays* turned into **PyTorch tensors**. But we can do better; we can build a…

Dataset

In PyTorch, a **dataset** is represented by a regular **Python class** that inherits from the Dataset class. You can think of it as a **list of tuples**, each tuple corresponding to **one point (features, label)**.

The most fundamental methods it needs to implement are:

- __init__(self): This takes **whatever arguments** are needed to build a **list of tuples**—it may be the name of a CSV file that will be loaded and processed; it may be *two tensors*, one for features, another one for labels; or anything else, depending on the task at hand.

> There is **no need to load the whole dataset in the constructor method** (__init__()). If your **dataset is large** (tens of thousands of image files, for instance), loading it all at once would not be memory efficient. It is recommended to **load them on demand** (whenever __getitem__() is called).

- __getitem__(self, index): This allows the dataset to be **indexed** so that it can work **like a list** (dataset[i])—it must **return a tuple (features, label)** corresponding to the requested data point. We can either return the **corresponding slices** of our **pre-loaded** dataset or, as mentioned above, **load them on demand** (like in PyTorch's tutorial[55]).

- __len__(self): This should simply return the **size** of the whole dataset so, whenever it is sampled, its indexing is limited to the actual size.

Let's build a simple custom dataset that takes two tensors as arguments: one for the features, one for the labels. For any given index, our dataset class will return the corresponding slice of each of those tensors. It should look like this:

Notebook Cell 2.1 - Creating a custom dataset

```python
class CustomDataset(Dataset):
    def __init__(self, x_tensor, y_tensor):
        self.x = x_tensor
        self.y = y_tensor

    def __getitem__(self, index):
        return (self.x[index], self.y[index])

    def __len__(self):
        return len(self.x)

# Wait, is this a CPU tensor now? Why? Where is .to(device)?
x_train_tensor = torch.as_tensor(x_train).float()
y_train_tensor = torch.as_tensor(y_train).float()

train_data = CustomDataset(x_train_tensor, y_train_tensor)
print(train_data[0])
```

Output

```
(tensor([0.7713]), tensor([2.4745]))
```

> Did you notice we built our **training tensors** out of *Numpy* arrays, but we **did not send them to a device**? So, they are **CPU** tensors now! **Why**?
>
> We **don't want our whole training data to be loaded into GPU tensors**, as we have been doing in our example so far, because **this takes up space** in our precious **graphics card's RAM**.

TensorDataset

Once again, you may be thinking, *"Why go through all this trouble to wrap a couple of tensors in a class?"* And, once again, you do have a point... If a dataset is nothing more than a **couple of tensors**, we can use PyTorch's `TensorDataset` class, which will do pretty much the same thing as our custom dataset above.

Right now, the full-fledged **custom dataset class** may seem like a stretch, but we will use this structure repeatedly in later chapters. For now, let's enjoy the simplicity of the `TensorDataset` class :-)

Notebook Cell 2.2 - Creating a dataset from tensors

```
train_data = TensorDataset(x_train_tensor, y_train_tensor)
print(train_data[0])
```

Output

```
(tensor([0.7713]), tensor([2.4745]))
```

OK, fine, but then again, **why** are we building a dataset anyway? We're doing it because we want to use a...

DataLoader

Until now, we have used the **whole training data** at every training step. It has been **batch gradient descent** all along. This is fine for our *ridiculously small dataset*, sure, but if we want to get serious about all this, we **must** use **mini-batch** gradient descent. Thus, we need mini-batches. Thus, we need to **slice** our dataset accordingly. Do you want to do it **manually**?! Me neither!

So we use PyTorch's `DataLoader` class for this job. We tell it which **dataset** to use (the one we just built in the previous section), the desired **mini-batch size**, and if we'd like to **shuffle** it or not. That's it!

> **IMPORTANT**: in the absolute majority of cases, you **should** set `shuffle=True` for your **training set** to improve the performance of gradient descent. There are a few exceptions, though, like time series problems, where shuffling actually leads to data leakage.
>
> So, always ask yourself: "*Do I have a reason NOT to shuffle the data?*"
>
> "*What about the validation and test sets?*" There is **no need to shuffle** them since we are **not computing gradients** with them.

> There is more to a `DataLoader` than meets the eye—it is also possible to use it together with a **sampler** to fetch mini-batches that compensate for **imbalanced classes**, for instance. Too much to handle right now, but we will eventually get there.

Our **loader** will behave like an **iterator**, so we can **loop over it** and **fetch a different mini-batch** every time.

"*How do I choose my mini-batch size?*"

It is typical to use **powers of two** for mini-batch sizes, like 16, 32, 64, or 128, and **32** seems to be the choice of most people, Yann LeCun[56] included.

Some more-complex models may use even larger sizes, although sizes are usually constrained by hardware limitations (i.e., how many data points actually fit into memory).

In our example, we have only 80 training points, so I chose a mini-batch size of 16 to conveniently split the training set into five mini-batches.

Notebook Cell 2.3 - Building a data loader for our training data

```
train_loader = DataLoader(
    dataset=train_data,
    batch_size=16,
    shuffle=True,
)
```

To retrieve a mini-batch, one can simply run the command below—it will return a list containing two tensors, one for the features, another one for the labels:

```
next(iter(train_loader))
```

Output

```
[tensor([[0.1196],
         [0.1395],
         ...
         [0.8155],
         [0.5979]]), tensor([[1.3214],
         [1.3051],
         ...
         [2.6606],
         [2.0407]])]
```

"Why not use a list instead?"

If you call list(train_loader), you'll get, as a result, a list of five elements; that is, all five mini-batches. Then you could take the first element of that list to obtain a single mini-batch as in the example above. It would **defeat the purpose** of using the **iterable** provided by the **DataLoader**; that is, to **iterate** over the elements (mini-batches, in that case) **one at a time**.

To learn more about it, check RealPython's material on iterables[57] and iterators[58].

How does this change our code so far? Let's check it out!

First, we need to add both **Dataset** and **DataLoader** elements into our **data preparation** part of the code. Also, notice that we **do not** send our tensors to the device just yet (just like we did in **Notebook Cell 2.1**). It should look like this:

Define - Data Preparation V1

```
1  %%writefile data_preparation/v1.py
2
3  # Our data was in Numpy arrays, but we need to transform them
4  # into PyTorch's Tensors
5  x_train_tensor = torch.as_tensor(x_train).float()
6  y_train_tensor = torch.as_tensor(y_train).float()
7
8  # Builds Dataset
9  train_data = TensorDataset(x_train_tensor, y_train_tensor)   ①
10
11 # Builds DataLoader
12 train_loader = DataLoader(                                    ②
13     dataset=train_data,
14     batch_size=16,
15     shuffle=True,
16 )
```

① Building a dataset of tensors

② Building a data loader that yields mini-batches of size 16

Run - Data Preparation V1

```
%run -i data_preparation/v1.py
```

Next, we need to incorporate the **mini-batch** gradient descent logic into our **model training** part of the code. But we need to run the model configuration first.

Run - Model Configuration V1

```
%run -i model_configuration/v1.py
```

Define - Model Training V2

```
1  %%writefile model_training/v2.py
2
3  # Defines number of epochs
4  n_epochs = 1000
5
6  losses = []
7
8  # For each epoch...
9  for epoch in range(n_epochs):
10     # inner loop
11     mini_batch_losses = []                                    ④
12     for x_batch, y_batch in train_loader:                     ①
13         # the dataset "lives" in the CPU, so do our mini-batches
14         # therefore, we need to send those mini-batches to the
15         # device where the model "lives"
16         x_batch = x_batch.to(device)                          ②
17         y_batch = y_batch.to(device)                          ②
18
19         # Performs one train step and returns the
20         # corresponding loss for this mini-batch
21         mini_batch_loss = train_step_fn(x_batch, y_batch)     ③
22         mini_batch_losses.append(mini_batch_loss)             ④
23
24     # Computes average loss over all mini-batches
25     # That's the epoch loss
26     loss = np.mean(mini_batch_losses)                         ⑤
27
28     losses.append(loss)
```

① Mini-batch inner loop

② Sending one mini-batch to the device

③ Performing a training step

④ Keeping track of the loss inside each mini-batch

⑤ Averaging losses of mini-batches to get epoch's loss

Run - Model Training V2

```
%run -i model_training/v2.py
```

"Wow! What happened here?!"

It seems like a lot changed. Let's take a closer look, step by step:

- We added an **inner loop** to handle the **mini-batches** produced by the `DataLoader` (line 12).
- We sent **only one mini-batch to the device**, as opposed to sending the whole training set (lines 16 and 17).

> For larger datasets, **loading data on demand** (into a **CPU** tensor) inside `Dataset`'s `__getitem__()` method and then **sending all data points** that belong to the same **mini-batch at once to your GPU** (device) is the way to go to make the **best use of your graphics card's RAM**.
>
> Moreover, if you have **many GPUs** to train your model on, it is best to keep your dataset "device agnostic" and assign the batches to different GPUs during training.

- We performed a `train_step_fn()` on a mini-batch (line 21) and appended the corresponding loss to a list (line 22).
- After going through all mini-batches, that is, at the end of an **epoch**, we calculated the total loss for the epoch, which is the average loss over all mini-batches, appending the result to a list (lines 26 and 28).

> After another two updates, our current state of development is:
>
> - Data Preparation V1
> - Model Configuration V1
> - Model Training V2

Not so bad, right? So, it is time to check if our code still works well:

```
# Checks model's parameters
print(model.state_dict())
```

Output

```
OrderedDict([('0.weight', tensor([[1.9684]], device='cuda:0')),
('0.bias', tensor([1.0235], device='cuda:0'))])
```

Did you get *slightly different* values? Try running the whole pipeline again:

Full Pipeline

```
%run -i data_preparation/v1.py
%run -i model_configuration/v1.py
%run -i model_training/v2.py
```

Since the `DataLoader` draws random samples, executing other code between the last two steps of the pipeline may interfere with the reproducibility of the results.

Anyway, as long as your results are less than 0.01 far from mine for both weight and bias, your code is working fine :-)

Did you notice it is taking **longer** to train now? Can you guess **why**?

ANSWER: The training time is **longer** now because the inner loop is executed **five times** for each epoch (in our example, since we are using a mini-batch of size 16 and we have 80 training data points in total, we execute the inner loop 80 / 16 = 5 times). So, in total, we are calling the `train_step_fn()` a total of **5,000 times** now! No wonder it's taking longer!

Mini-Batch Inner Loop

From now on, it is very unlikely that you'll **ever** use **(full) batch gradient descent** again, both in this book or in real life :-) So, it makes sense to, once again, organize a piece of code that's going to be used repeatedly into its own function: the **mini-batch inner loop**!

The inner loop depends on **three elements**:

- the **device** where data is being sent
- a **data loader** to draw mini-batches from
- a **step function**, returning the corresponding loss

Taking these elements as inputs and using them to perform the inner loop, we'll end up with a function like this:

Helper Function #2

```
 1  def mini_batch(device, data_loader, step_fn):
 2      mini_batch_losses = []
 3      for x_batch, y_batch in data_loader:
 4          x_batch = x_batch.to(device)
 5          y_batch = y_batch.to(device)
 6
 7          mini_batch_loss = step_fn(x_batch, y_batch)
 8          mini_batch_losses.append(mini_batch_loss)
 9
10      loss = np.mean(mini_batch_losses)
11      return loss
```

In the last section, we realized that we were executing **five times more updates** (the `train_step_fn()` function) per epoch due to the *mini-batch inner loop*. Before, 1,000 epochs meant 1,000 updates. Now, we only need **200 epochs** to perform the same 1,000 updates.

What does our **training loop** look like now? It's **very** lean!

Run - Data Preparation V1, Model Configuration V1

```
%run -i data_preparation/v1.py
%run -i model_configuration/v1.py
```

Define - Model Training V3

```
1  %%writefile model_training/v3.py
2
3  # Defines number of epochs
4  n_epochs = 200
5
6  losses = []
7
8  for epoch in range(n_epochs):
9      # inner loop
10     loss = mini_batch(device, train_loader, train_step_fn)  ①
11     losses.append(loss)
```

① Performing mini-batch gradient descent

Run - Model Training V3

```
%run -i model_training/v3.py
```

After updating the model training part, our current state of development is:

- **Data Preparation V1**
- **Model Configuration V1**
- **Model Training V3**

Let's inspect the model's state:

```
# Checks model's parameters
print(model.state_dict())
```

Output

```
OrderedDict([('0.weight', tensor([[1.9687]], device='cuda:0')),
('0.bias', tensor([1.0236], device='cuda:0'))])
```

So far, we've focused on the **training data** only. We built a *dataset* and a *data loader* for it. We could do the same for the **validation** data, using the **split** we performed at the beginning of this book, or we could use `random_split()` instead.

Random Split

PyTorch's `random_split()` method is an easy and familiar way of performing a **training-validation split**.

So far, we've been using `x_train_tensor` and `y_train_tensor`, built out of the original split in *Numpy*, to build the **training dataset**. Now, we're going to be using the **full data** from *Numpy* (x and y) to build a PyTorch `Dataset` **first** and only then **split** the data using `random_split()`.

> Although there was a (funny) reasoning behind my choice of 42 as a random seed, I'll be using other numbers as seeds, mostly **odd numbers**, just because I like them better :-)

Then, for each subset of data, we'll build a corresponding `DataLoader`, so our code will look like this:

Define - Data Preparation V2

```
1  %%writefile data_preparation/v2.py
2
3  torch.manual_seed(13)
4
5  # Builds tensors from Numpy arrays BEFORE split
6  x_tensor = torch.as_tensor(x).float()                                    ①
7  y_tensor = torch.as_tensor(y).float()                                    ①
8
9  # Builds dataset containing ALL data points
10 dataset = TensorDataset(x_tensor, y_tensor)
11
12 # Performs the split
13 ratio = .8
14 n_total = len(dataset)
15 n_train = int(n_total * ratio)
16 n_val = n_total - n_train
17 train_data, val_data = random_split(dataset, [n_train, n_val])           ②
18
19 # Builds a loader of each set
20 train_loader = DataLoader(
21     dataset=train_data,
22     batch_size=16,
23     shuffle=True,
24 )
25 val_loader = DataLoader(dataset=val_data, batch_size=16)                  ③
```

① Making tensors out of the full dataset (before split)

② Performing train-validation split in PyTorch

③ Creating a data loader for the validation set

Run - Data Preparation V2

```
%run -i data_preparation/v2.py
```

Now that we have a **data loader** for our **validation set**, it makes sense to use it for the…

Evaluation

How can we **evaluate** the model? We can compute the **validation** loss; that is, how wrong the model's predictions are for **unseen data**.

First, we need to use the **model** to compute **predictions** and then use the **loss function** to compute the loss, given our predictions and the true labels. Sounds familiar? These are pretty much the **first two steps** of the **training step function** we built as **Helper Function #1**.

So, we can use that code as a starting point, getting rid of steps 3 and 4, and, most important, we need to **use the model's eval() method**. The only thing it does is **set the model to evaluation mode** (just like its `train()` counterpart did), so the model can adjust its behavior accordingly when it has to perform some operations, like dropout.

> *"Why is setting the mode so important?"*

As mentioned above, dropout (a regularization technique commonly used for reducing overfitting) is the main reason for it, since it requires the model to behave **differently** during training and evaluation. In a nutshell, dropout **randomly sets some weights to zero** during training.

> We'll get back to **dropout** in the second volume of the series.

What would happen if this behavior persisted outside of training time? You would end up with possibly **different predictions** for the **same input** since different weights would be set to zero every time you made a prediction. It would **ruin evaluation** and, if deployed, would also **ruin the confidence of the user**.

We **don't want that**, so we use `model.eval()` to prevent it!

Just like `make_train_step_fn()`, our new function, `make_val_step_fn()`, is a higher-order function. Its code looks like this:

Helper Function #3

```
1  def make_val_step_fn(model, loss_fn):
2      # Builds function that performs a step
3      # in the validation loop
4      def perform_val_step_fn(x, y):
5          # Sets model to EVAL mode
6          model.eval()        ①
7
8          # Step 1 - Computes our model's predicted output
9          # forward pass
10         yhat = model(x)
11         # Step 2 - Computes the loss
12         loss = loss_fn(yhat, y)
13         # There is no need to compute Steps 3 and 4,
14         # since we don't update parameters during evaluation
15         return loss.item()
16
17     return perform_val_step_fn
```

① Setting model to evaluation mode

And then, we update our **model configuration** code to include the creation of the corresponding function for the **validation step**.

Define - Model Configuration V2

```
1  %%writefile model_configuration/v2.py
2
3  device = 'cuda' if torch.cuda.is_available() else 'cpu'
4
5  # Sets learning rate - this is "eta" ~ the "n"-like Greek letter
6  lr = 0.1
7
8  torch.manual_seed(42)
9  # Now we can create a model and send it at once to the device
10 model = nn.Sequential(nn.Linear(1, 1)).to(device)
11
12 # Defines an SGD optimizer to update the parameters
13 optimizer = optim.SGD(model.parameters(), lr=lr)
14
15 # Defines an MSE loss function
16 loss_fn = nn.MSELoss(reduction='mean')
17
18 # Creates the train_step function for our model, loss function
19 # and optimizer
20 train_step_fn = make_train_step_fn(model, loss_fn, optimizer)
21
22 # Creates the val_step function for our model and loss function
23 val_step_fn = make_val_step_fn(model, loss_fn)  ①
```

① Creating a function that performs a validation step

Run - Model Configuration V2

```
%run -i model_configuration/v2.py
```

Finally, we need to change the training loop to include the **evaluation of our model**. The first step is to include another inner loop to handle the *mini-batches* that come from the *validation loader*, sending them to the same *device* as our model. Then, inside that inner loop, we use the *validation step function* to compute the loss.

> "Wait, this looks oddly familiar too..."

And indeed, it is—it is structurally the same as our **mini-batch function** (Helper Function #2). So let's use it once again!

There is just **one small, yet important** detail to consider: Remember no_grad()? We used it in Chapter 1 to avoid messing with PyTorch's dynamic computation graph during the (manual) update of the parameters. And it is making a comeback now—we need to use it to wrap our new validation's inner loop:

> torch.no_grad(): Even though it won't make a difference in our simple model, it is a **good practice** to **wrap the validation** inner loop with this **context manager**[59] **to disable any gradient computation** that you may inadvertently trigger—**gradients belong in training**, not in validation steps.

Now, our training loop should look like this:

Define - Model Training V4

```
1  %%writefile model_training/v4.py
2
3  # Defines number of epochs
4  n_epochs = 200
5
6  losses = []
7  val_losses = []                                              ③
8
9  for epoch in range(n_epochs):
10     # inner loop
11     loss = mini_batch(device, train_loader, train_step_fn)
12     losses.append(loss)
13
14     # VALIDATION - no gradients in validation!
15     with torch.no_grad():                                    ①
16         val_loss = mini_batch(device, val_loader, val_step_fn) ②
17         val_losses.append(val_loss)                          ③
```

① Using no_grad() as context manager to prevent gradient computation

② Performing a validation step

③ Keeping track of validation loss

Evaluation | 149

Run - Model Training V4

```
%run -i model_training/v4.py
```

After updating all parts, in sequence, our current state of development is:

- Data Preparation V2
- Model Configuration V2
- Model Training V4

Let's inspect the model's state:

```
# Checks model's parameters
print(model.state_dict())
```

Output

```
OrderedDict([('0.weight', tensor([[1.9419]], device='cuda:0')),
 ('0.bias', tensor([1.0244], device='cuda:0'))])
```

Plotting Losses

Let's take a look at both losses—**training** and **validation**.

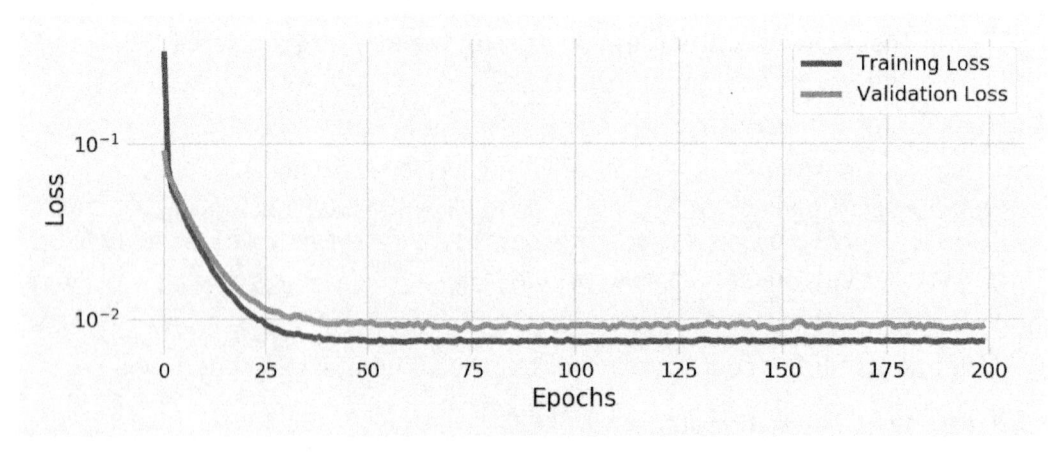

Figure 2.1 - Training and validation losses during training

Does your plot look different? Try running the whole pipeline again:

Full Pipeline

```
%run -i data_preparation/v2.py
%run -i model_configuration/v2.py
%run -i model_training/v4.py
```

And then plot the resulting losses one more time.

Cool, right? But, remember in the **training step** function, when I mentioned that adding losses to a list was not very **cutting-edge**? Time to fix that! To better visualize the training process, we can make use of…

TensorBoard

Yes, TensorBoard is *that* good! So good that we'll be using a tool from the competing framework, TensorFlow :-) Jokes aside, TensorBoard is a very useful tool, and PyTorch provides classes and methods so that we can integrate it with our model.

Running It Inside a Notebook

This section applies to both *Google Colab* and *local installation*.

If you are using a *local installation*, you can either run TensorBoard *inside* a notebook or *separately* (check the next section for instructions).

If you chose to follow this book using *Google Colab*, you'll **need** to run TensorBoard **inside a notebook**. Luckily, this is easily accomplished using some Jupyter **magics**.

If you are using *Binder*, this Jupyter **magic will not work**, for reasons that are beyond the scope of this section. More details on how to use TensorBoard with *Binder* can be found in the corresponding section below.

First, we need to load TensorBoard's *extension* for Jupyter:

Loading Extension

```
# Load the TensorBoard notebook extension
%load_ext tensorboard
```

Then, we *run* TensorBoard using the newly available magic:

Running TensorBoard

```
%tensorboard --logdir runs
```

The magic above tells TensorBoard to *look for logs* inside the folder specified by the `logdir` argument: `runs`. So, *there must be a* `runs` *folder in the same location as the notebook* you're using to train the model. To make things easier for you, I created a `runs` folder in the repository, so you get it out-of-the-box.

> If you get the error "**TypeError: Function expected**," please switch to a modern browser like Firefox or Chrome.

Your notebook will show TensorBoard inside a cell, just like this:

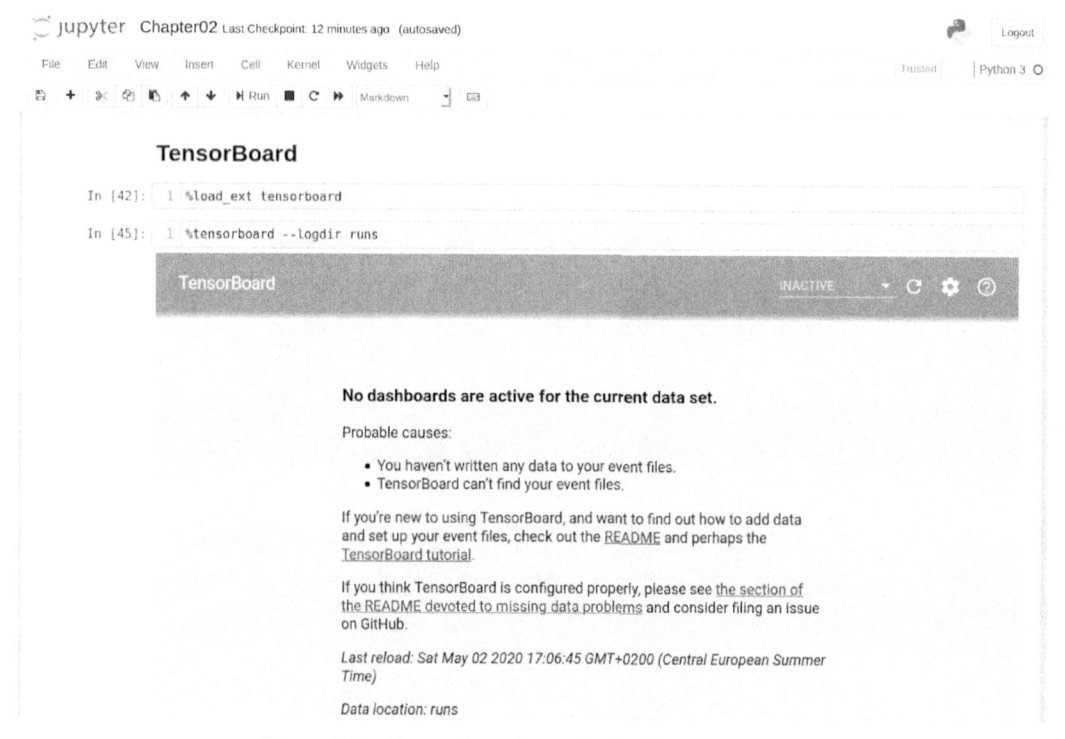

Figure 2.2 - TensorBoard running inside a notebook

152 | Chapter 2: Rethinking the Training Loop

It doesn't show you anything yet because it cannot find any data inside the runs folder, as we haven't sent anything there yet. It will be automatically updated when we send some data to it, so let's send some data to TensorBoard!

If you want to learn more about running TensorBoard inside a notebook, configuration options, and more, please check its official guide[60].

Running It Separately (Local Installation)

Assuming you've installed TensorBoard while following the **"Setup Guide"**, now you need to open a *new* terminal or Anaconda prompt, *navigate* to the PyTorchStepByStep folder you cloned from GitHub, and *activate* the pytorchbook environment:

Activating Environment

```
conda activate pytorchbook
```

Then you can run TensorBoard:

Running TensorBoard

```
(pytorchbook)$ tensorboard --logdir runs
```

The above command tells TensorBoard to *look for logs* inside the folder specified by the logdir argument: runs. So, *there must be a* runs *folder in the same location as the notebook* you're using to train the model. To make things easier, I created a runs folder in the repository, so you get it out-of-the-box. After running it, you'll see a message like this one (the version of TensorBoard may be different, though):

Output

```
TensorFlow installation not found - running with reduced
feature set.
Serving TensorBoard on localhost; to expose to the network,
use a proxy or pass --bind_all
TensorBoard 2.2.0 at http://localhost:6006/ (Press CTRL+C to quit)
```

You see, it "*complains*" about not finding TensorFlow :-) Nonetheless, it is up and running! If you throw the address http://localhost:6006/ at your favorite browser, you'll likely see something like this:

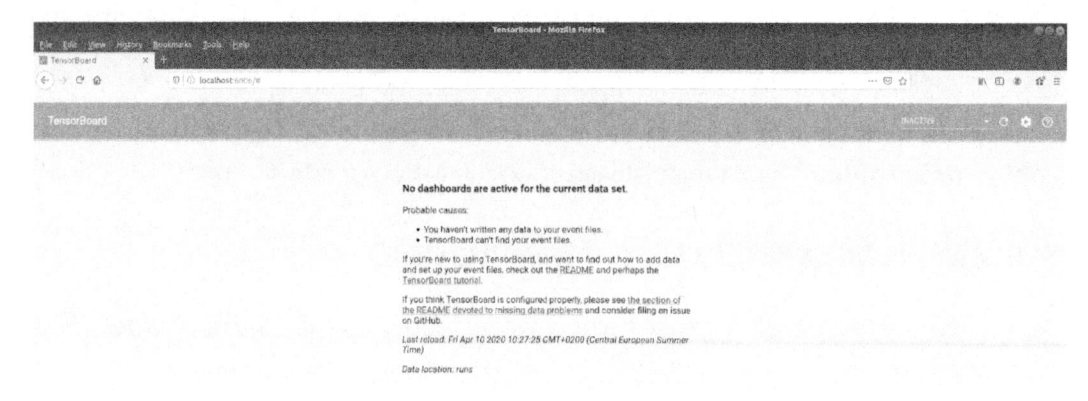

Figure 2.3 - Empty TensorBoard

It doesn't show you anything yet because it cannot find any data inside the runs folder, as we haven't sent anything there yet. It will be automatically updated when we send some data to it so, let's send some data to TensorBoard!

Running It Separately (Binder)

If you chose to follow this book using *Binder*, you'll **need** to run TensorBoard separately.

But you won't have to actually do much. Configuring TensorBoard for running inside Binder's environment is a bit *tricky* (it involves Jupyter's server extensions), so I took care of that for you :-)

Moreover, I've provided an **automatically generated link** that will **open a new tab** pointing to the TensorBoard instance running in your Binder environment.

The link looks like this (the actual URL is generated on the spot, this one is just a dummy):

Click here to open TensorBoard [https://notebooks.gesis.org/binder/jupyter/user/dvgodoy-pytorchstepbystep-xxxxxxxx/proxy/6006/]

The only downside is that the **folder** where TensorBoard will look for logs is **fixed**: runs.

SummaryWriter

It all starts with the creation of a SummaryWriter:

SummaryWriter

```
writer = SummaryWriter('runs/test')
```

Since we told TensorBoard to look for logs inside the runs folder, it makes sense to **actually log to that folder**. Moreover, to be able to *distinguish* between different experiments or models, we should also specify a sub-folder: test.

> If we do not specify any folder, TensorBoard will default to runs/CURRENT_DATETIME_HOSTNAME, which is not such a great name if you'll be looking for your experiment results in the future.
>
> So, it is recommended to **name it in a more meaningful way**, like runs/test or runs/simple_linear_regression. It will then create a sub-folder inside runs (the folder we specified when we started TensorBoard).
>
> Even better, you should name it in a meaningful way **and add datetime or a sequential number as a suffix**, like runs/test_001 or runs/test_20200502172130, to avoid writing data of multiple runs into the same folder (we'll see why this is bad in the "add_scalars" section below).

The summary writer implements several methods to allow us to send information to TensorBoard:

add_graph()	add_scalars()	add_scalar()
add_histogram()	add_images()	add_image()
add_figure()	add_video()	add_audio()
add_text()	add_embedding()	add_pr_curve()
add_custom_scalars()	add_mesh()	add_hparams()

It also implements two other methods for effectively writing data to disk:

- flush()
- close()

We'll be using the first two methods (add_graph() and add_scalars()) to send our

TensorBoard | 155

model's graph (not quite the same as the *dynamic computation graph* we drew using make_dot(), though), and, of course, both scalars: **training** and **validation losses**.

add_graph

Let's start with add_graph(): unfortunately, its documentation seems to be absent (as at the time of writing), and its default values for arguments lead you to believe you don't need to provide any inputs (input_to_model=None). What happens if we try it?

```
writer.add_graph(model)
```

We'll get an enormous **error message** that ends with:

Output

```
...
TypeError: 'NoneType' object is not iterable
```

So, we **do** need to send it some **inputs** together with our model. Let's fetch a mini-batch of data points from our train_loader and then pass it as input to add_graph():

Adding the Model's Graph

```
# Fetching a tuple of feature (dummy_x) and label (dummy_y)
dummy_x, dummy_y = next(iter(train_loader))

# Since our model was sent to device, we need to do the same
# with the data.
# Even here, both model and data need to be on the same device!
writer.add_graph(model, dummy_x.to(device))
```

If you open (or refresh) your browser (or re-run the cell containing the magic %tensorboard --logdir runs inside a notebook) to look at TensorBoard, it should look like this:

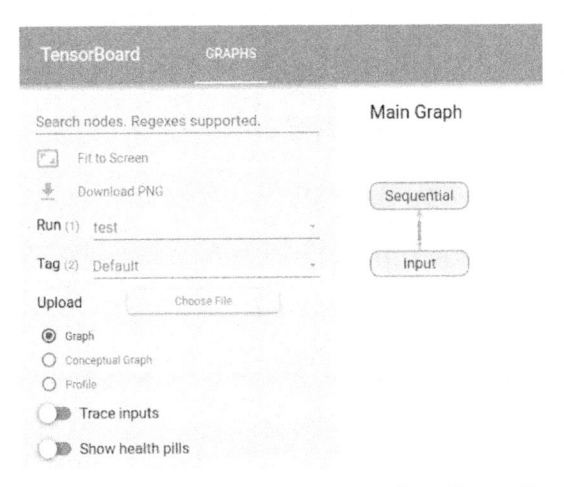

Figure 2.4 - Dynamic computation graph on TensorBoard

add_scalars

What about sending the **loss values** to TensorBoard? I'm on it! We can use the add_scalars() method to send multiple scalar values at once; it needs three arguments:

- **main_tag**: the parent name of the tags, or the "group tag," if you will
- **tag_scalar_dict**: the dictionary containing the key: value pairs for the scalars you want to keep track of (in our case, training and validation losses)
- **global_step**: step value; that is, the index you're associating with the values you're sending in the dictionary; the **epoch** comes to mind in our case, as losses are computed for each epoch

How does it translate into code? Let's check it out:

Adding Losses

```
writer.add_scalars(
    main_tag='loss',
    tag_scalar_dict={'training': loss,
                     'validation': val_loss},
    global_step=epoch
)
```

If you run the code above after performing the model training, it will just send both loss values computed for the last epoch (199). Your TensorBoard will look like this (don't forget to refresh it—it may take a while if you're running it on Google Colab):

Figure 2.5 - Scalars on TensorBoard

Not very useful, eh? We need to incorporate these elements into our **model configuration** and **model training** codes, which look like this now:

Run - Data Preparation V2

```
%run -i data_preparation/v2.py
```

Define - Model Configuration V3

```
1  %%writefile model_configuration/v3.py
2
3  device = 'cuda' if torch.cuda.is_available() else 'cpu'
4
5  # Sets learning rate - this is "eta" ~ the "n"-like Greek letter
6  lr = 0.1
7
8  torch.manual_seed(42)
9  # Now we can create a model and send it at once to the device
10 model = nn.Sequential(nn.Linear(1, 1)).to(device)
11
12 # Defines an SGD optimizer to update the parameters
13 optimizer = optim.SGD(model.parameters(), lr=lr)
14
15 # Defines an MSE loss function
16 loss_fn = nn.MSELoss(reduction='mean')
17
18 # Creates the train_step function for our model,
19 # loss function and optimizer
20 train_step_fn = make_train_step_fn(model, loss_fn, optimizer)
21
22 # Creates the val_step function for our model and loss function
23 val_step_fn = make_val_step_fn(model, loss_fn)
24
25 # Creates a Summary Writer to interface with TensorBoard
26 writer = SummaryWriter('runs/simple_linear_regression')  ①
27 # Fetches a single mini-batch so we can use add_graph
28 x_dummy, y_dummy = next(iter(train_loader))
29 writer.add_graph(model, x_dummy.to(device))
```

① Creating `SummaryWriter` to interface with TensorBoard

Run - Model Configuration V3

```
%run -i model_configuration/v3.py
```

Define - Model Training V5

```
 1  %%writefile model_training/v5.py
 2
 3  # Defines number of epochs
 4  n_epochs = 200
 5
 6  losses = []
 7  val_losses = []
 8
 9  for epoch in range(n_epochs):
10      # inner loop
11      loss = mini_batch(device, train_loader, train_step_fn)
12      losses.append(loss)
13
14      # VALIDATION - no gradients in validation!
15      with torch.no_grad():
16          val_loss = mini_batch(device, val_loader, val_step_fn)
17          val_losses.append(val_loss)
18
19      # Records both losses for each epoch under tag "loss"
20      writer.add_scalars(main_tag='loss',           ①
21                         tag_scalar_dict={
22                              'training': loss,
23                              'validation': val_loss},
24                         global_step=epoch)
25
26  # Closes the writer
27  writer.close()
```

① Sending losses to TensorBoard

Run - Model Training V5

```
%run -i model_training/v5.py
```

After the last update of both the model configuration and training parts, our current state of development is:

- **Data Preparation V2**
- **Model Configuration V3**
- **Model Training V5**

You probably noticed we **did not** throw the two lists (**losses** and **val_losses**) away. There is a reason for this, which will be clear in the next section.

Let's inspect the model's state:

```
# Checks model's parameters
print(model.state_dict())
```

Output

```
OrderedDict([('0.weight', tensor([[1.9448]], device='cuda:0')),
('0.bias', tensor([1.0295], device='cuda:0'))])
```

Now, let's inspect **TensorBoard**. You should see something like this:

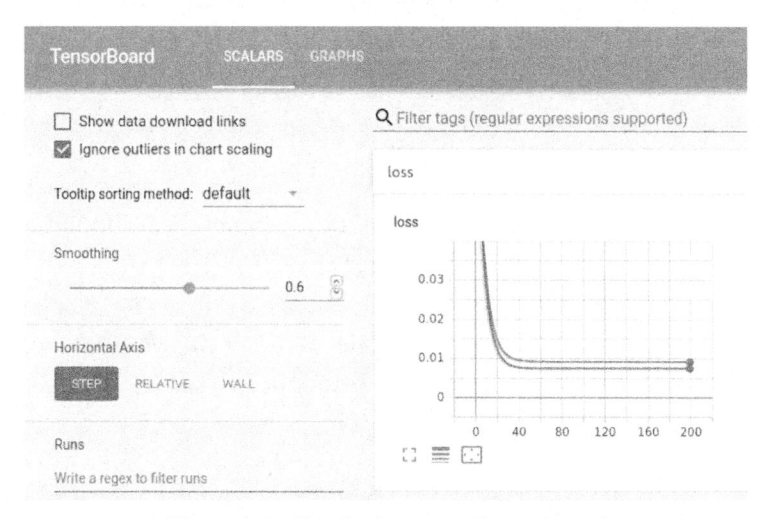

Figure 2.6 - Finally, losses on TensorBoard

This is the same plot we've built before using our lists and Matplotlib. If our model were large or complex enough to take at least a couple of minutes to train, we would be able to see the *evolution* of our losses in TensorBoard during training.

If, by any chance, you ended up with something like the weird plot below, don't worry just yet!

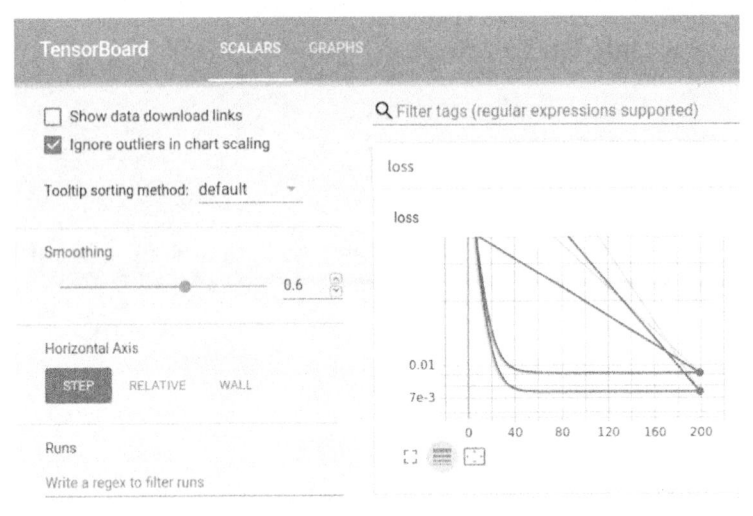

Figure 2.7 - Weird results on TensorBoard :P

Remember, I said writing the data of multiple runs into the same folder was bad? This is why...

Since we're writing data to the folder `runs/simple_linear_regression`, if we do not **change the name** of the folder (or **erase the data** there) before running the code a second time, TensorBoard gets somewhat confused, as you can guess from its output:

- *Found more than one graph event per run* (because we ran `add_graph()` more than once)

- *Found more than one "run metadata" event with tag step1* (because we ran `add_scalars()` more than once)

If you are using a local installation, you can see those messages in the **terminal window or Anaconda prompt** you used to run `tensorboard --log_dir=runs`.

So, you finished training your model, you inspected TensorBoard plots, and you're happy with the losses you got.

Congratulations! Your job is done; you successfully trained your model!

There is only **one more thing** you need to know, and that is how to handle...

Saving and Loading Models

Training a model successfully is great, no doubt about that, but not all models will train quickly, and **training may get interrupted** (computer crashing, timeout after 12 hours of continuous GPU usage on Google Colab, etc.). It would be a pity to have to start over, right?

So, it is important to be able to **checkpoint or save** our model, that is, save it to disk, in case we'd like to **restart training later** or **deploy it** as an application to **make predictions**.

Model State

To checkpoint a model, we basically have to **save its state** to a file so that it can be **loaded** back later—nothing special, actually.

What defines the **state of a model**?

- model.state_dict(): kinda obvious, right?
- optimizer.state_dict(): remember, optimizers have a state_dict() as well
- **losses**: after all, you should keep track of its evolution
- **epoch**: it is just a number, so why not? :-)
- **anything else you'd like to have restored later**

Saving

Now, we **wrap everything into a Python dictionary** and use torch.save() to dump it all into a file. Easy peasy! We have just **saved** our model to a file named model_checkpoint.pth.

Notebook Cell 2.4 - Saving checkpoint

```
checkpoint = {'epoch': n_epochs,
              'model_state_dict': model.state_dict(),
              'optimizer_state_dict': optimizer.state_dict(),
              'loss': losses,
              'val_loss': val_losses}

torch.save(checkpoint, 'model_checkpoint.pth')
```

The procedure is exactly the **same**, whether you are **checkpointing a partially trained model** to resume training later or **saving a fully trained model** to deploy and make predictions.

OK, what about **loading** it back? In that case, it will be a **bit different**, depending on what you're doing.

Resuming Training

If we're starting fresh (as if we had just turned on the computer and started Jupyter), we have to **set the stage** before actually loading the model. This means we need to **load the data** and **configure the model**.

Luckily, we have code for that already: **Data Preparation V2** and **Model Configuration V3**:

Notebook Cell 2.5

```
%run -i data_preparation/v2.py
%run -i model_configuration/v3.py
```

Let's double-check that we do have an **untrained model**:

```
print(model.state_dict())
```

Output

```
OrderedDict([('0.weight', tensor([[0.7645]], device='cuda:0')),
('0.bias', tensor([0.8300], device='cuda:0'))])
```

Now we are **ready** to load the model back, which is easy:

- load the dictionary back using `torch.load()`
- load **model** and **optimizer** state dictionaries back using the `load_state_dict()` method
- load everything else into their corresponding variables

Notebook Cell 2.6 - Loading checkpoint to resume training

```
checkpoint = torch.load('model_checkpoint.pth')

model.load_state_dict(checkpoint['model_state_dict'])
optimizer.load_state_dict(checkpoint['optimizer_state_dict'])

saved_epoch = checkpoint['epoch']
saved_losses = checkpoint['loss']
saved_val_losses = checkpoint['val_loss']

model.train() # always use TRAIN for resuming training ①
```

① Never forget to set the mode!

```
print(model.state_dict())
```

Output

```
OrderedDict([('0.weight', tensor([[1.9448]], device='cuda:0')),
('0.bias', tensor([1.0295], device='cuda:0'))])
```

Cool, we recovered our **model's state**, and we can **resume training**.

> After **loading a model to resume training**, make sure you **ALWAYS** set it to **training mode**:
>
> `model.train()`
>
> In our example, this is going to be redundant because our `train_step_fn()` function already does it. But it is important to pick up the habit of **setting the mode** of the model accordingly.

Next, we can run **Model Training V5** to train it for another 200 epochs.

> *"Why 200 more epochs? Can't I choose a different number?"*

Well, you could, but you'd have to change the code in **Model Training V5**. This clearly **isn't** ideal, but we will make our model training code more flexible very soon, so please bear with me for now.

Notebook Cell 2.7

```
%run -i model_training/v5.py
```

What does the model look like after training another 200 epochs?

```
print(model.state_dict())
```

Output

```
OrderedDict([('0.weight', tensor([[1.9448]], device='cuda:0')),
('0.bias', tensor([1.0295], device='cuda:0'))])
```

Well, it didn't change at all, which is **no surprise**: The original model had **converged** already; that is, the loss was at a **minimum**. These extra epochs served an educational purpose only; they did not improve the model. But, since we are at it, let's check the evolution of the losses, **before** and **after** checkpointing:

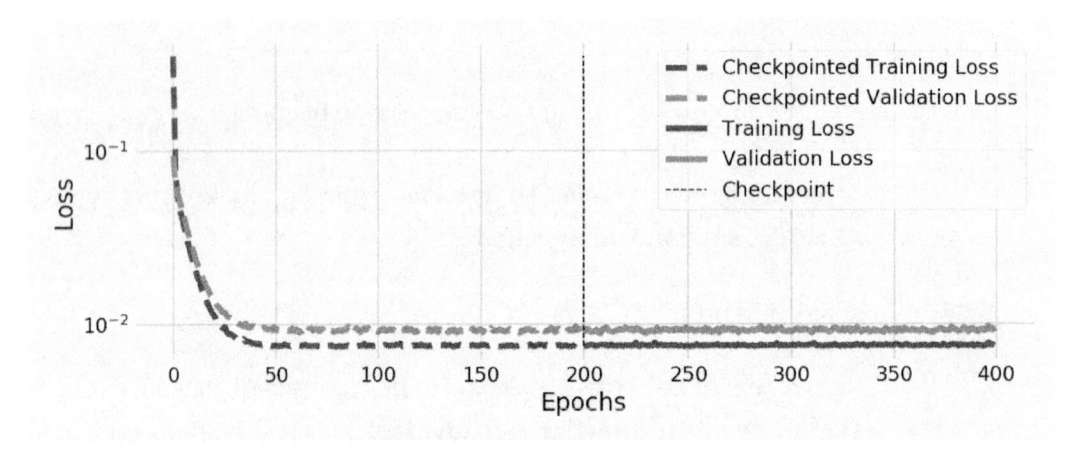

Figure 2.8 - Losses, before and after resuming training

Clearly, the loss was already at a minimum before the checkpoint, so nothing has changed!

It turns out, the model we saved to disk was a **fully trained model**, so we can use it for…

Deploying / Making Predictions

Again, if we're starting fresh (as if we had just turned on the computer and started Jupyter), we have to **set the stage** before actually loading the model. But, this time, we **only** need to **configure the model**:

Notebook Cell 2.8

```
%run -i model_configuration/v3.py
```

Once again, we have an **untrained model** at this point. The loading procedure is simpler, though:

- load the dictionary back using `torch.load()`
- load **model** state dictionary back using its method `load_state_dict()`

Since the model is **fully trained**, we don't need to load the optimizer or anything else.

Notebook Cell 2.9 - Loading a fully trained model to make predictions

```
checkpoint = torch.load('model_checkpoint.pth')

model.load_state_dict(checkpoint['model_state_dict'])

print(model.state_dict())
```

Output

```
OrderedDict([('0.weight', tensor([[1.9448]], device='cuda:0')),
('0.bias', tensor([1.0295], device='cuda:0'))])
```

After recovering our **model's state**, we can finally use it to **make predictions** for **new inputs**:

Notebook Cell 2.10

```
new_inputs = torch.tensor([[.20], [.34], [.57]])

model.eval() # always use EVAL for fully trained models! ①
model(new_inputs.to(device))
```

① Never forget to set the mode!

Output

```
tensor([[1.4185],
        [1.6908],
        [2.1381]], device='cuda:0', grad_fn=<AddmmBackward>)
```

Since **Model Configuration V3** created a model and sent it automatically to our **device**, we need to do the same with our **new inputs**.

> After **loading a fully trained model for deployment / to make predictions**, make sure you **ALWAYS** set it to **evaluation mode**:
>
> `model.eval()`

Congratulations, you "*deployed*" your first model :-)

Setting the Model's Mode

I know, I am probably a bit obsessive about this, but here we go one more time:

> After loading the model, **DO NOT FORGET** to **SET THE MODE**:
> - **checkpointing**: `model.train()`
> - **deploying / making predictions**: `model.eval()`

Putting It All Together

We have **updated** each of the three **fundamental parts** of our code at least twice. It is time to put it all together to get an overall view of what we have achieved so far.

Behold your pipeline: **Data Preparation V2**, **Model Configuration V3**, and **Model Training V5**!

Run - Data Preparation V2

```python
# %load data_preparation/v2.py

torch.manual_seed(13)

# Builds tensors from Numpy arrays BEFORE split
x_tensor = torch.as_tensor(x).float()
y_tensor = torch.as_tensor(y).float()

# Builds dataset containing ALL data points
dataset = TensorDataset(x_tensor, y_tensor)

# Performs the split
ratio = .8
n_total = len(dataset)
n_train = int(n_total * ratio)
n_val = n_total - n_train
train_data, val_data = random_split(dataset, [n_train, n_val])
# Builds a loader of each set
train_loader = DataLoader(
    dataset=train_data,
    batch_size=16,
    shuffle=True,
)
val_loader = DataLoader(dataset=val_data, batch_size=16)
```

Run - Model Configuration V3

```
1  # %load model_configuration/v3.py
2
3  device = 'cuda' if torch.cuda.is_available() else 'cpu'
4
5  # Sets learning rate - this is "eta" ~ the "n"-like Greek letter
6  lr = 0.1
7
8  torch.manual_seed(42)
9  # Now we can create a model and send it at once to the device
10 model = nn.Sequential(nn.Linear(1, 1)).to(device)
11
12 # Defines an SGD optimizer to update the parameters
13 optimizer = optim.SGD(model.parameters(), lr=lr)
14
15 # Defines an MSE loss function
16 loss_fn = nn.MSELoss(reduction='mean')
17
18 # Creates the train_step function for our model,
19 # loss function and optimizer
20 train_step_fn = make_train_step_fn(model, loss_fn, optimizer)
21
22 # Creates the val_step function for our model and loss function
23 val_step_fn = make_val_step_fn(model, loss_fn)
24
25 # Creates a Summary Writer to interface with TensorBoard
26 writer = SummaryWriter('runs/simple_linear_regression')
27 # Fetches a single mini-batch so we can use add_graph
28 x_dummy, y_dummy = next(iter(train_loader))
29 writer.add_graph(model, x_dummy.to(device))
```

Run - Model Training V5

```python
1  # %load model_training/v5.py
2
3  # Defines number of epochs
4  n_epochs = 200
5
6  losses = []
7  val_losses = []
8
9  for epoch in range(n_epochs):
10     # inner loop
11     loss = mini_batch(device, train_loader, train_step_fn)
12     losses.append(loss)
13
14     # VALIDATION - no gradients in validation!
15     with torch.no_grad():
16         val_loss = mini_batch(device, val_loader, val_step_fn)
17         val_losses.append(val_loss)
18
19     # Records both losses for each epoch under tag "loss"
20     writer.add_scalars(main_tag='loss',
21                        tag_scalar_dict={
22                             'training': loss,
23                             'validation': val_loss},
24                        global_step=epoch)
25
26 # Closes the writer
27 writer.close()
```

```python
print(model.state_dict())
```

Output

```
OrderedDict([('0.weight', tensor([[1.9440]], device='cuda:0')),
('0.bias', tensor([1.0249], device='cuda:0'))])
```

This is the **general structure** you'll use *over and over again* for **training PyTorch models**.

Sure, a **different dataset and problem** will require a **different model and loss function**, and you may want to try a different optimizer and a cycling learning rate (we'll get to that later, in the second volume of the series), but the rest is likely to remain exactly the same.

Recap

We have covered a lot of ground in this chapter:

- writing a **higher-order function** that builds functions to perform **training steps**
- understanding PyTorch's `Dataset` and `TensorDataset` classes, implementing its `__init__()`, `__getitem__()`, and `__len__()` methods
- using PyTorch's `DataLoader` class to **generate mini-batches** out of a dataset
- modifying our **training loop** to incorporate **mini-batch gradient descent** logic
- writing a **helper function** to handle the **mini-batch inner loop**
- using PyTorch's `random_split()` method to generate training and validation datasets
- writing a **higher-order function** that builds functions to perform **validation steps**
- realizing the **importance** of including `model.eval()` inside the **validation loop**
- remembering the purpose of `no_grad()` and using it to **prevent** any kind of **gradient computation during validation**
- using `SummaryWriter` to **interface** with *TensorBoard* for logging
- adding a graph representing our model to **TensorBoard**
- sending **scalars** to *TensorBoard* to track the **evolution of training and validation losses**
- **saving / checkpointing** and **loading** models to and from disk to allow **resuming model training** or **deployment**
- realizing the importance of **setting the mode** of the model: `train()` or `eval()`, for **checkpointing** or **deploying** for prediction, respectively

172 | Chapter 2: Rethinking the Training Loop

Congratulations! You now possess the necessary **knowledge** and **tools** to tackle more interesting (and complex!) problems using PyTorch. We'll put them to good use in the next chapters.

[53] https://github.com/dvgodoy/PyTorchStepByStep/blob/master/Chapter02.ipynb

[54] https://colab.research.google.com/github/dvgodoy/PyTorchStepByStep/blob/master/Chapter02.ipynb

[55] https://bit.ly/3jJtJeT

[56] https://bit.ly/37vJVdG

[57] https://bit.ly/39u1tbo

[58] https://bit.ly/39ovRUx

[59] https://www.geeksforgeeks.org/context-manager-in-python/

[60] https://www.tensorflow.org/tensorboard/tensorboard_in_notebooks

Chapter 2.1
Going Classy

Spoilers

In this chapter, we will:

- define a **class** to handle **model training**
- implement the **constructor** method
- understand the difference between **public**, **protected**, and **private** methods of a class
- **integrate the code** we've developed so far into our class
- **instantiate** our class and use it to run a **classy** pipeline

Jupyter Notebook

The Jupyter notebook corresponding to Chapter 2.1[61] is part of the official *Deep Learning with PyTorch Step-by-Step* repository on GitHub. You can also run it directly in **Google Colab**[62].

If you're using a *local installation*, open your terminal or Anaconda prompt and navigate to the `PyTorchStepByStep` folder you cloned from GitHub. Then, *activate* the `pytorchbook` environment and run `jupyter notebook`:

```
$ conda activate pytorchbook

(pytorchbook)$ jupyter notebook
```

If you're using Jupyter's default settings, `http://localhost:8888/notebooks/Chapter02.1.ipynb` should open Chapter 2.1's notebook. If not, just click on `Chapter02.1.ipynb` on your Jupyter's home page.

Imports

For the sake of organization, all libraries needed throughout the code used in any given chapter are imported at its very beginning. For this chapter, we'll need the following imports:

```
import numpy as np
import datetime

import torch
import torch.optim as optim
import torch.nn as nn
import torch.functional as F
from torch.utils.data import DataLoader, TensorDataset, random_split
from torch.utils.tensorboard import SummaryWriter

import matplotlib.pyplot as plt
%matplotlib inline
plt.style.use('fivethirtyeight')
```

Going Classy

So far, the %%writefile magic has helped us to organize the code into three distinct parts: *data preparation*, *model configuration*, and *model training*. At the end of Chapter 2, though, we bumped into some of its **limitations**, like being unable to choose a different number of epochs without having to **edit** the model training code.

Clearly, this situation is **not** ideal. We need to do better. We need to **go classy**; that is, we need to build a **class** to handle the **model training** part.

> I am assuming you have a *working knowledge* of **object-oriented programming (OOP)** in order to benefit the most from this chapter. If that's not the case, and if you didn't do it in Chapter 1, now is the time to follow tutorials like Real Python's "Object-Oriented Programming (OOP) in Python 3"[63] and "Supercharge Your Classes With Python super()."[64]

The Class

Let's start by defining our class with a rather unoriginal name: StepByStep. We're starting it from scratch: Either we don't specify a parent class, or we inherit it from the fundamental object class. I personally prefer the latter, so our class definition looks like this:

```python
# A completely empty (and useless) class
class StepByStep(object):
    pass
```

Boring, right? Let's make it more interesting.

The Constructor

"From where do we start building a class?"

That would be the **constructor**, the __init__(self) method that we've already seen a couple of times when handling both **model** and **dataset** classes.

The constructor **defines the parts that make up the class**. These parts are the **attributes** of the class. Typical attributes include:

- **arguments** provided by the user
- **placeholders** for other objects that are not available at the moment of creation (pretty much like *delayed* arguments)
- **variables** we may want to keep track of
- **functions** that are dynamically built using some of the arguments and **higher-order functions**

Let's see how each of these applies to our problem.

Arguments

Let's start with the **arguments**, the part that **needs to be specified by the user**. At the beginning of Chapter 2, we asked ourselves: "Would the code inside the training loop **change** if we were using a **different optimizer**, or **loss**, or even **model**?" The answer was and still is, **no, it wouldn't change**.

So, these **three** elements, **optimizer**, **loss**, and **model**, will be our main **arguments**. The user **needs** to specify these; we can't figure them out on our own.

But there is one more piece of information needed: the **device** to be used for training the model. Instead of asking the user to supply it, we'll *automatically check* if there is a GPU available and fall back to a CPU if there isn't. But we still want to give the user a chance to use a different device (whatever the reason may be); thus, we add a very simple method (conveniently named to()) that allows the user to specify a device.

Our constructor (__init__()) method will initially look like this:

```python
class StepByStep(object):
    def __init__(self, model, loss_fn, optimizer):
        # Here we define the attributes of our class
        # We start by storing the arguments as attributes
        # to use later
        self.model = model
        self.loss_fn = loss_fn
        self.optimizer = optimizer
        self.device = 'cuda' if torch.cuda.is_available() else 'cpu'
        # Let's send the model to the specified device right away
        self.model.to(self.device)

    def to(self, device):
        # This method allows the user to specify a different device
        # It sets the corresponding attribute (to be used later in
        # the mini-batches) and sends the model to the device
        try:
            self.device = device
            self.model.to(self.device)
        except RuntimeError:
            self.device = ('cuda' if torch.cuda.is_available()
                           else 'cpu')
            print(f"Couldn't send it to {device}, \
                sending it to {self.device} instead.")
            self.model.to(self.device)
```

Placeholders

Next, let's tackle the **placeholders** or *delayed arguments*. We expect the user to **eventually** provide **some** of these, as they are *not necessarily required*. There are another three elements that fall into that category: **train and validation data loaders** and a **summary writer** to interface with TensorBoard.

We need to append the following code to the constructor method above (I am not reproducing the rest of the method here for the sake of simplicity; in the Jupyter notebook you'll find the full code):

```python
# These attributes are defined here, but since they are
# not available at the moment of creation, we keep them None
self.train_loader = None
self.val_loader = None
self.writer = None
```

The **train data loader** is obviously required. How could we possibly train a model without it?

> *"Why don't we make the train data loader an **argument** then?"*

Conceptually speaking, the data loader (and the dataset it contains) is **not** part of the model. It is the **input** we use to train the model. Since we **can** specify a model without it, it shouldn't be made an argument of our class.

In other words, our `StepByStep` class is **defined by a particular combination of arguments** (model, loss function, and optimizer), which can then be used to perform model training on any (compatible) dataset.

The **validation data loader** is not required (although it is recommended), and the **summary writer** is definitely optional.

The class should implement **methods** to allow the user to supply those at a later time (both methods should be placed *inside* the `StepByStep` class, after the constructor method):

```python
def set_loaders(self, train_loader, val_loader=None):
    # This method allows the user to define which train_loader
    # (and val_loader, optionally) to use
    # Both loaders are then assigned to attributes of the class
    # So they can be referred to later
    self.train_loader = train_loader
    self.val_loader = val_loader

def set_tensorboard(self, name, folder='runs'):
    # This method allows the user to create a SummaryWriter to
    # interface with TensorBoard
    suffix = datetime.datetime.now().strftime('%Y%m%d%H%M%S')
    self.writer = SummaryWriter(f'{folder}/{name}_{suffix}')
```

> *"Why do we need to specify a default value to the* `val_loader`*? Its placeholder value is already* None*."*

Since the validation loader is **optional**, setting a **default value** for a particular argument in the method's definition frees the user from having to provide that argument when calling the method. The best default value, in our case, is the same value we chose when specifying the placeholder for the validation loader: None.

Variables

Then, there are **variables** we may want to keep track of. Typical examples are the **number of epochs**, and the training and validation **losses**. These variables are likely to be computed and updated internally by the class.

We need to **append the following code to the constructor** method (like we did with the placeholders):

```
# These attributes are going to be computed internally
self.losses = []
self.val_losses = []
self.total_epochs = 0
```

> *"Can't we just set these variables whenever we use them for the first time?"*

Yes, we could, and we would probably get away with it just fine since our class is quite simple. As classes grow more complex, though, it may lead to problems. So, it is **best practice** to **define all attributes of a class in the constructor method**.

Functions

For convenience, sometimes it is useful to create **attributes** that are **functions**, which will be called somewhere else inside the class. In our case, we can create both `train_step_fn()` and `val_step_fn()` using the higher-order functions we defined in Chapter 2 (Helper Functions #1 and #3, respectively). Both of them take a model, a loss function, and an optimizer as arguments, and all of those are already known attributes of our `StepByStep` class at construction time.

The code below will be the last addition to our constructor method (once again, as we did with the placeholders):

```
        # Creates the train_step function for our model,
        # loss function and optimizer
        # Note: there are NO ARGS there! It makes use of the class
        # attributes directly
        self.train_step_fn = self._make_train_step_fn()
        # Creates the val_step function for our model and loss
        self.val_step_fn = self._make_val_step_fn()
```

If you have patched together the pieces of code above, your code should look like this:

StepByStep Class

```
class StepByStep(object):
    def __init__(self, model, loss_fn, optimizer):
        # Here we define the attributes of our class
        # We start by storing the arguments as attributes
        # to use them later
        self.model = model
        self.loss_fn = loss_fn
        self.optimizer = optimizer
        self.device = 'cuda' if torch.cuda.is_available() else 'cpu'
        # Let's send the model to the specified device right away
        self.model.to(self.device)

        # These attributes are defined here, but since they are
        # not available at the moment of creation, we keep them None
        self.train_loader = None
        self.val_loader = None
        self.writer = None

        # These attributes are going to be computed internally
        self.losses = []
        self.val_losses = []
        self.total_epochs = 0

        # Creates the train_step function for our model,
        # loss function and optimizer
        # Note: there are NO ARGS there! It makes use of the class
        # attributes directly
        self.train_step_fn = self._make_train_step_fn()
```

```python
        # Creates the val_step function for our model and loss
        self.val_step_fn = self._make_val_step_fn()

    def to(self, device):
        # This method allows the user to specify a different device
        # It sets the corresponding attribute (to be used later in
        # the mini-batches) and sends the model to the device
        try:
            self.device = device
            self.model.to(self.device)
        except RuntimeError:
            self.device = ('cuda' if torch.cuda.is_available()
                           else 'cpu')
            print(f"Couldn't send it to {device}, \
                sending it to {self.device} instead.")
            self.model.to(self.device)

    def set_loaders(self, train_loader, val_loader=None):
        # This method allows the user to define which train_loader
        # (and val_loader, optionally) to use
        # Both loaders are then assigned to attributes of the class
        # So they can be referred to later
        self.train_loader = train_loader
        self.val_loader = val_loader

    def set_tensorboard(self, name, folder='runs'):
        # This method allows the user to create a SummaryWriter to
        # interface with TensorBoard
        suffix = datetime.datetime.now().strftime('%Y%m%d%H%M%S')
        self.writer = SummaryWriter(f'{folder}/{name}_{suffix}')
```

Sure, we are still missing both _make_train_step_fn() and _make_val_step_fn() functions. Both are pretty much the same as before, except that they refer to the class attributes self.model, self.loss_fn, and self.optimizer, instead of taking them as arguments. They look like this now:

Step Methods

```python
def _make_train_step_fn(self):
    # This method does not need ARGS... it can use directly
    # the attributes: self.model, self.loss_fn and self.optimizer
```

Going Classy | 181

```python
    # Builds function that performs a step in the train loop
    def perform_train_step_fn(x, y):
        # Sets model to TRAIN mode
        self.model.train()

        # Step 1 - Computes model's predicted output - forward pass
        yhat = self.model(x)
        # Step 2 - Computes the loss
        loss = self.loss_fn(yhat, y)
        # Step 3 - Computes gradients for "b" and "w" parameters
        loss.backward()
        # Step 4 - Updates parameters using gradients and the
        # learning rate
        self.optimizer.step()
        self.optimizer.zero_grad()

        # Returns the loss
        return loss.item()

    # Returns the function that will be called inside the train loop
    return perform_train_step_fn

def _make_val_step_fn(self):
    # Builds function that performs a step in the validation loop
    def perform_val_step_fn(x, y):
        # Sets model to EVAL mode
        self.model.eval()

        # Step 1 - Computes model's predicted output - forward pass
        yhat = self.model(x)
        # Step 2 - Computes the loss
        loss = self.loss_fn(yhat, y)
        # There is no need to compute Steps 3 and 4,
        # since we don't update parameters during evaluation
        return loss.item()

    return perform_val_step_fn
```

> *"Why do these methods have an underscore as a prefix? How is this different than the double underscore in the __init__() method?"*

Methods, _methods, and __methods

Some programming languages, like Java, have three kinds of methods: public, protected, and private. **Public methods** are the kind you're most familiar with: They can be **called by the user**.

Protected methods, on the other hand, **shouldn't** be called by the user—they are supposed to be called either **internally** or by the **child class** (the child class can call a protected method from its parent class).

Finally, **private methods** are supposed to be called **exclusively internally**. They should be invisible even to a child class.

These rules are strictly enforced in Java, but **Python** takes a more relaxed approach: **All methods are public**, meaning you can call whatever method you want. But you can **suggest** the appropriate usage by **prefixing the method name** with a **single underscore** (for **protected methods**) or a **double underscore** (for **private methods**). This way, the user is aware of the programmer's intention.

In our example, both _make_train_step_fn() and _make_val_step_fn() are defined as **protected methods**. I expect users **not to call them directly**, but if someone decides to define a class that inherits from StepByStep, they **should feel entitled** to do so.

In order to make the **additions** to our code **visually simpler**; that is, without having to *replicate the full class* every time I introduce a new method, I am resorting to something that **shouldn't be used in regular circumstances**: setattr.[65]

```
# ATTENTION! Using SETATTR for educational purposes only :-)
setattr(StepByStep, '_make_train_step_fn', _make_train_step_fn)
setattr(StepByStep, '_make_val_step_fn', _make_val_step_fn)
```

> ⚠ Using setattr is a **hack**, I can't stress this enough! **Please don't use setattr in your regular code.**

setattr

The `setattr` function sets the value of the specified attribute of a given object. But **methods** are also **attributes**, so we can use this function to "attach" a method to an existing class and to all its existing instances in one go!

Yes, this is a hack! No, you should not use it in your regular code! Using `setattr` to build a class by appending methods to it incrementally serves educational purposes only.

To illustrate how it works and why it may be dangerous, I will show you a little example. Let's create a simple `Dog` class, which takes only the dog's name as argument:

```python
class Dog(object):
    def __init__(self, name):
        self.name = name
```

Next, let's **instantiate** our class; that is, we are *creating* a dog. Let's call it Rex. Its name is going to be stored in the `name` attribute:

```python
rex = Dog('Rex')
print(rex.name)
```

Output

```
Rex
```

Then, let's create a `bark()` function that takes an **instance of Dog** as argument:

```python
def bark(dog):
    print('{} barks: "Woof!"'.format(dog.name))
```

Sure enough, we can call this function to make Rex bark:

```
bark(rex)
```

Output

```
Rex barks: "Woof!"
```

But that's **not** what we want. We want our dogs to be able to bark out of the box! So we will use `setattr` to give dogs the ability to bark. There is **one thing we need to change**, though, and that's the function's argument. Since we want the bark function to be a method of the `Dog` class itself, the **argument** needs to be the **method's own instance**: `self`.

```
def bark(self):
    print('{} barks: "Woof!"'.format(self.name))
setattr(Dog, 'bark', bark)
```

Does it work? Let's create a new dog:

```
fido = Dog('Fido')
fido.bark()
```

Output

```
Fido barks: "Woof!"
```

Of course it works! Not only new dogs can bark now, but **all dogs can bark**:

```
rex.bark()
```

Output

```
Rex barks: "Woof!"
```

> See? We effectively **modified the underlying Dog class** and **all its instances** at once! It looks very cool, sure. And it can wreak havoc too!

Instead of creating an attribute or method directly in the class, as we've been doing so far, it is possible to use `setattr` to create them dynamically. In our `StepByStep` class, the last two lines of code created two methods in the class, each having the same name of the function used to create the method.

OK, but there are still some parts missing in order to perform model training. Let's keep adding more methods.

Training Methods

The next method we need to add corresponds to the **Helper Function #2** in Chapter 2: the **mini-batch loop**. We need to **change it** a bit, though; there, both the **data loader** and the **step function** were arguments. This is not the case anymore since we have both of them as attributes: `self.train_loader` and `self.train_step_fn`, for training; `self.val_loader` and `self.val_step_fn`, for validation. The only thing this method needs to know is if it is handling training or validation data.

The code should look like this:

Mini-Batch

```
1  def _mini_batch(self, validation=False):
2      # The mini-batch can be used with both loaders
3      # The argument `validation` defines which loader and
4      # corresponding step function are going to be used
5      if validation:
6          data_loader = self.val_loader
7          step_fn = self.val_step_fn
8      else:
9          data_loader = self.train_loader
10         step_fn = self.train_step_fn
11
12     if data_loader is None:
13         return None
14
15     # Once the data loader and step function are set, this is the
16     # same mini-batch loop we had before
17     mini_batch_losses = []
18     for x_batch, y_batch in data_loader:
19         x_batch = x_batch.to(self.device)
20         y_batch = y_batch.to(self.device)
21
22         mini_batch_loss = step_fn(x_batch, y_batch)
23         mini_batch_losses.append(mini_batch_loss)
24
25     loss = np.mean(mini_batch_losses)
26
27     return loss
28
29 setattr(StepByStep, '_mini_batch', _mini_batch)
```

Moreover, if the user decides **not** to provide a validation loader, it will retain its initial **None** value from the constructor method. If that's the case, we don't have a corresponding loss to compute, and it returns **None** instead (line 13 in the snippet above).

What's left to do? The **training loop**, of course! This is similar to our **Model Training V5** in Chapter 2, but we can make it more flexible, taking the **number of epochs** and

Going Classy | 187

the **random seed** as arguments.

This solves the issue we faced in Chapter 2, when we *had* to train for another 200 epochs after loading a checkpoint, just because it was *hard-coded* into the training loop. Well, not anymore!

Moreover, we need to ensure the **reproducibility of the training loop**. We already set up seeds to ensure the reproducibility of the *random split* (data preparation) and the *model initialization* (model configuration). So far, we have been running the full pipeline in order, so the training loop yielded the same results every time. Now, to gain flexibility without compromising reproducibility, we need to set yet another random seed.

We're building a method to take care of seed-setting only, following PyTorch's guidelines on reproducibility[66]:

Seeds

```
def set_seed(self, seed=42):
    torch.backends.cudnn.deterministic = True
    torch.backends.cudnn.benchmark = False
    torch.manual_seed(seed)
    np.random.seed(seed)

setattr(StepByStep, 'set_seed', set_seed)
```

It is also time to use the variables we defined as attributes in the constructor method: `self.total_epochs`, `self.losses`, and `self.val_losses`. All of them are being updated inside the training loop.

Training Loop

```python
def train(self, n_epochs, seed=42):
    # To ensure reproducibility of the training process
    self.set_seed(seed)

    for epoch in range(n_epochs):
        # Keeps track of the number of epochs
        # by updating the corresponding attribute
        self.total_epochs += 1

        # inner loop
        # Performs training using mini-batches
        loss = self._mini_batch(validation=False)
        self.losses.append(loss)

        # VALIDATION
        # no gradients in validation!
        with torch.no_grad():
            # Performs evaluation using mini-batches
            val_loss = self._mini_batch(validation=True)
            self.val_losses.append(val_loss)

        # If a SummaryWriter has been set...
        if self.writer:
            scalars = {'training': loss}
            if val_loss is not None:
                scalars.update({'validation': val_loss})
            # Records both losses for each epoch under tag "loss"
            self.writer.add_scalars(main_tag='loss',
                                    tag_scalar_dict=scalars,
                                    global_step=epoch)

    if self.writer:
        # Flushes the writer
        self.writer.flush()

setattr(StepByStep, 'train', train)
```

Did you notice this function **does not return anything**? It doesn't need to! Instead of returning values, it simply updates several class attributes: self.losses, self.val_losses, and self.total_epochs.

The current state of development of our StepByStep class already allows us to train a model fully. Now, let's give our class the ability to save and load models as well.

Saving and Loading Models

Most of the code here is exactly the same as the code we had in Chapter 2. The only difference is that we use the class' attributes instead of local variables.

The methods for saving and loading checkpoints should look like this now:

Saving

```python
def save_checkpoint(self, filename):
    # Builds dictionary with all elements for resuming training
    checkpoint = {
        'epoch': self.total_epochs,
        'model_state_dict': self.model.state_dict(),
        'optimizer_state_dict': self.optimizer.state_dict(),
        'loss': self.losses,
        'val_loss': self.val_losses
    }
    torch.save(checkpoint, filename)

setattr(StepByStep, 'save_checkpoint', save_checkpoint)
```

Loading

```python
def load_checkpoint(self, filename):
    # Loads dictionary
    checkpoint = torch.load(filename)
    # Restore state for model and optimizer
    self.model.load_state_dict(checkpoint['model_state_dict'])
    self.optimizer.load_state_dict(
        checkpoint['optimizer_state_dict']
    )
    self.total_epochs = checkpoint['epoch']
    self.losses = checkpoint['loss']
    self.val_losses = checkpoint['val_loss']
    self.model.train() # always use TRAIN for resuming training

setattr(StepByStep, 'load_checkpoint', load_checkpoint)
```

Notice that the model is set to **training mode** after loading the checkpoint.

What about making predictions? To make it easier for the user to make predictions for any new data points, we will be handling all the *Numpy* to PyTorch back and forth conversion inside the function.

Making Predictions

```
def predict(self, x):
    # Set it to evaluation mode for predictions
    self.model.eval()
    # Take a Numpy input and make it a float tensor
    x_tensor = torch.as_tensor(x).float()
    # Send input to device and use model for prediction
    y_hat_tensor = self.model(x_tensor.to(self.device))
    # Set it back to train mode
    self.model.train()
    # Detach it, bring it to CPU and back to Numpy
    return y_hat_tensor.detach().cpu().numpy()

setattr(StepByStep, 'predict', predict)
```

First, we set the model to **evaluation mode**, as it is required in order to make predictions. Then, we convert the x argument (assumed to be a *Numpy* array) to a float PyTorch tensor, send it to the configured device, and use the model to make a prediction.

Next, we set the model back to **training mode**. The last step includes detaching the tensor containing the predictions and making it a *Numpy* array to be returned to the user.

We have already covered most of what was developed in the previous chapters, except for a couple of visualization functions. Let's tackle them now.

Visualization Methods

Since we have kept track of both training and validation losses as attributes, let's build a simple plot for them:

Losses

```
def plot_losses(self):
    fig = plt.figure(figsize=(10, 4))
    plt.plot(self.losses, label='Training Loss', c='b')
    if self.val_loader:
        plt.plot(self.val_losses, label='Validation Loss', c='r')
    plt.yscale('log')
    plt.xlabel('Epochs')
    plt.ylabel('Loss')
    plt.legend()
    plt.tight_layout()
    return fig

setattr(StepByStep, 'plot_losses', plot_losses)
```

Finally, if both training loader and TensorBoard were already configured, we can use the former to fetch a single mini-batch and the latter to build the model graph in TensorBoard:

Model Graph

```
def add_graph(self):
    if self.train_loader and self.writer:
        # Fetches a single mini-batch so we can use add_graph
        x_dummy, y_dummy = next(iter(self.train_loader))
        self.writer.add_graph(self.model, x_dummy.to(self.device))

setattr(StepByStep, 'add_graph', add_graph)
```

The Full Code

If you'd like to check what the full code of the class looks like, you can see it in https://github.com/dvgodoy/PyTorchStepByStep/blob/master/stepbystep/v0.py or in the Jupyter notebook of this chapter.

We are **classy** now, so let's build a **classy pipeline** too!

Classy Pipeline

In Chapter 2, our pipeline was composed of three steps: **Data Preparation V2**, **Model Configuration V3**, and **Model Training V5**. The last step, model training, has already been integrated into our `StepByStep` class. Let's take a look at the other two steps.

But, first, let's generate our synthetic data once again.

Run - Data Generation

```
# Runs data generation - so we do not need to copy code here
%run -i data_generation/simple_linear_regression.py
```

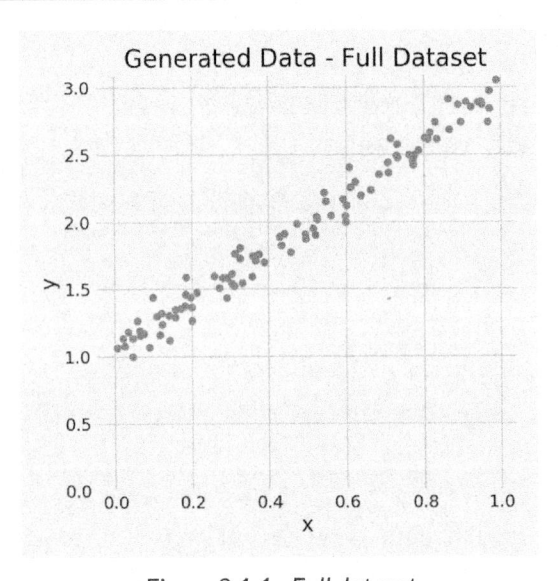

Figure 2.1.1 - Full dataset

Looks familiar, doesn't it?

The first part of the pipeline is the **data preparation**. It turns out, we can keep it exactly the way it was.

Run - Data Preparation V2

```
1  # %load data_preparation/v2.py
2
3  torch.manual_seed(13)
4
5  # Builds tensors from Numpy arrays BEFORE split
6  x_tensor = torch.as_tensor(x).float()
7  y_tensor = torch.as_tensor(y).float()
8
9  # Builds dataset containing ALL data points
10 dataset = TensorDataset(x_tensor, y_tensor)
11
12 # Performs the split
13 ratio = .8
14 n_total = len(dataset)
15 n_train = int(n_total * ratio)
16 n_val = n_total - n_train
17
18 train_data, val_data = random_split(dataset, [n_train, n_val])
19
20 # Builds a loader of each set
21 train_loader = DataLoader(
22     dataset=train_data,
23     batch_size=16,
24     shuffle=True
25 )
26 val_loader = DataLoader(dataset=val_data, batch_size=16)
```

Next in line is the **model configuration**. Some of its code got integrated into our class already: both `train_step_fn()` and `val_step_fn()` functions, the `SummaryWriter`, and adding the model graph.

So, we strip the model configuration code down to its bare minimum; that is, we keep only the elements we need to pass as **arguments** to our `StepByStep` class: **model**, **loss function**, and **optimizer**. Notice that we do not send the model to the device at this point anymore since that is going to be handled by our class' constructor.

Define - Model Configuration V4

```
1  %%writefile model_configuration/v4.py
2
3  # Sets learning rate - this is "eta" ~ the "n"-like Greek letter
4  lr = 0.1
5
6  torch.manual_seed(42)
7  # Now we can create a model
8  model = nn.Sequential(nn.Linear(1, 1))
9
10 # Defines an SGD optimizer to update the parameters
11 # (now retrieved directly from the model)
12 optimizer = optim.SGD(model.parameters(), lr=lr)
13
14 # Defines an MSE loss function
15 loss_fn = nn.MSELoss(reduction='mean')
```

Run - Model Configuration V4

```
%run -i model_configuration/v4.py
```

Let's inspect the randomly initialized parameters of our model:

```
print(model.state_dict())
```

Output

```
OrderedDict([('0.weight', tensor([[0.7645]])),
             ('0.bias', tensor([0.8300]))])
```

These are **CPU tensors**, since our model wasn't sent anywhere (yet).

And now the **fun** begins: Let's put our StepByStep class to good use and **train our model**.

Model Training

We start by **instantiating** the StepByStep class with the corresponding arguments. Next, we set its loaders using the appropriately named method set_loaders(). Then, we set up an interface with TensorBoard and name our experiment **classy** (what else could it be?!).

Notebook Cell 2.1.1

```
1 sbs = StepByStep(model, loss_fn, optimizer)
2 sbs.set_loaders(train_loader, val_loader)
3 sbs.set_tensorboard('classy')
```

One important thing to notice is that the model attribute of the sbs object is **the same object** as the model variable created in the model configuration. It is **not a copy**! We can easily verify this:

```
print(sbs.model == model)
print(sbs.model)
```

Output

```
True
Sequential(
  (0): Linear(in_features=1, out_features=1, bias=True)
)
```

As expected, the equality holds. If we print the model itself, we get our simple **one input-one output** model.

Let's **train the model** now, using the same 200 epochs as before:

Notebook Cell 2.1.2

```
1 sbs.train(n_epochs=200)
```

Done! It is trained! Really? Really! Let's check it out:

```
print(model.state_dict()) # remember, model == sbs.model
print(sbs.total_epochs)
```

Output

```
OrderedDict([('0.weight', tensor([[1.9414]], device='cuda:0')),
            ('0.bias', tensor([1.0233], device='cuda:0'))])
200
```

Our class sent the model to the available device (a GPU, in this case), and now the model's parameters are **GPU tensors**.

The weights of our trained model are quite close to the ones we got in Chapter 2. They are slightly different, though, because we are now using yet another *random seed* before starting the training loop. The total number of epochs was tracked by the total_epochs attribute, as expected.

Let's take a look at the losses:

```
fig = sbs.plot_losses()
```

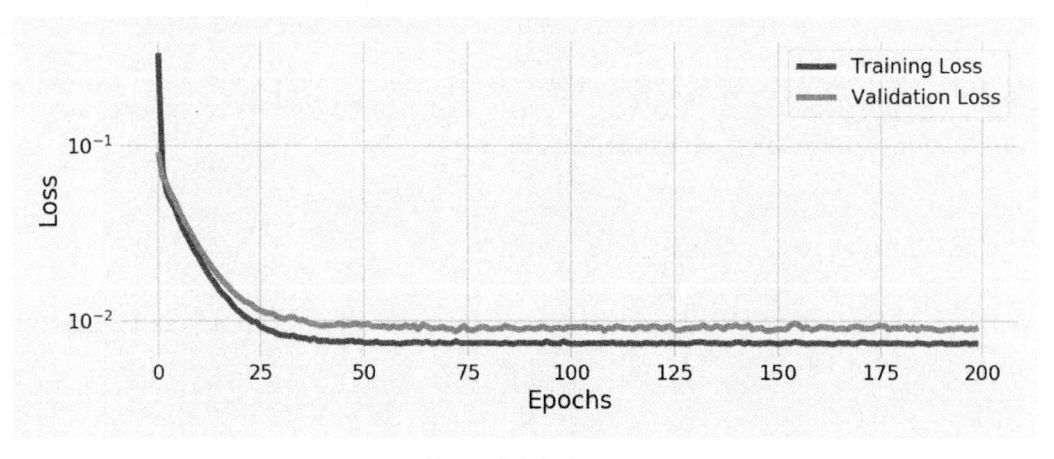

Figure 2.1.2 - Losses

Again, no surprises here; what about making predictions for new, never seen before data points?

Making Predictions

Let's make up some data points for our feature *x*, and shape them as a single-column matrix:

```
new_data = np.array([.5, .3, .7]).reshape(-1, 1)
```

Output

```
array([[0.5],
       [0.3],
       [0.7]])
```

Since the *Numpy* array to PyTorch tensor conversion is already handled by the `predict()` method, we can call the method right away, passing the array as its argument:

```
predictions = sbs.predict(new_data)
predictions
```

Output

```
array([[1.9939734],
       [1.6056864],
       [2.3822603]], dtype=float32)
```

And now we have predictions! Easy, right?

What if, instead of making predictions, we wanted to **checkpoint** the model to resume training later?

Checkpointing

That's a no-brainer—the `save_checkpoint()` method handles the state dictionaries for us and saves them to a file:

Notebook Cell 2.1.3

```
sbs.save_checkpoint('model_checkpoint.pth')
```

Resuming Training

Remember, when we did this in Chapter 2 we had to **set the stage**, loading the data and configuring the model, before actually loading the model. We still need to do this, but we are now using the latest version of **model configuration**:

Run - Model Configuration V4

```
%run -i model_configuration/v4.py
```

Let's double-check that we do have an **untrained model**:

```
print(model.state_dict())
```

Output

```
OrderedDict([('0.weight', tensor([[0.7645]], device='cuda:0')),
             ('0.bias', tensor([0.8300], device='cuda:0'))])
```

Good, same as before! Besides, the model configuration has created the **three elements** we need to pass as **arguments** to **instantiate** our StepByStep class:

Notebook Cell 2.1.4

```
new_sbs = StepByStep(model, loss_fn, optimizer)
```

Next, let's **load the trained model** back using the `load_checkpoint()` method and then inspect the model's weights:

Notebook Cell 2.1.5

```
new_sbs.load_checkpoint('model_checkpoint.pth')
print(model.state_dict())
```

Output

```
OrderedDict([('0.weight', tensor([[1.9414]], device='cuda:0')),
            ('0.bias', tensor([1.0233], device='cuda:0'))])
```

Great, these are the weights of our trained model. Let's **train it a bit further**.

In Chapter 2, we could only train it for another 200 epochs since the number of epochs was hard-coded. Not anymore! Thanks to our StepByStep class, we have the flexibility to train the model for as many epochs as we please.

But we are still missing one thing ... the data! First, we need to **set the data loader(s)**, and then we can train our model for another, say, 50 epochs.

Notebook Cell 2.1.6

```
new_sbs.set_loaders(train_loader, val_loader)
new_sbs.train(n_epochs=50)
```

Let's take a look at the losses:

```
fig = new_sbs.plot_losses()
```

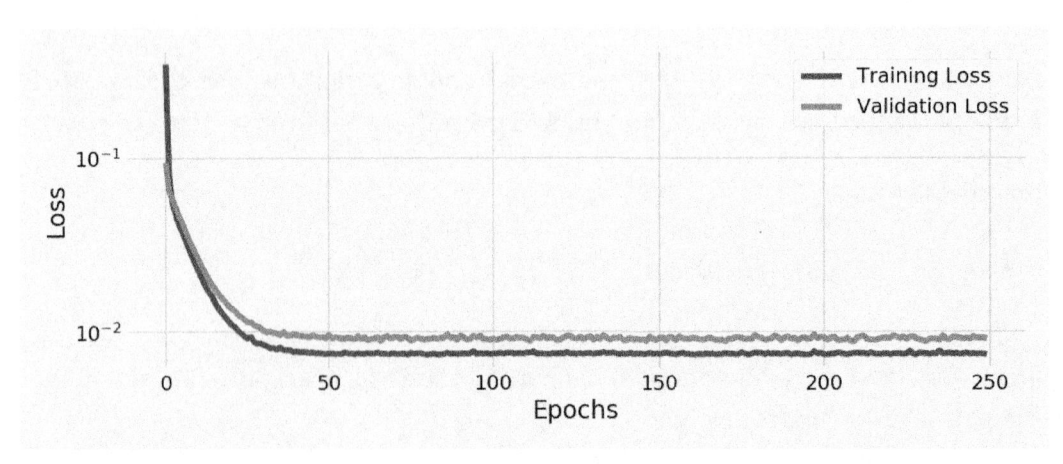

Figure 2.1.3 - More losses!

We have loss values over 250 epochs now. The losses for the first 200 epochs were loaded from the checkpoint, and the losses for the last 50 epochs were computed after training was resumed. Once again, as in Chapter 2, the overall levels of the losses didn't change much.

If the losses haven't changed, it means the training loss was at a **minimum** already. So, we expect the **weights to remain unchanged**. Let's check it out:

```
print(sbs.model.state_dict())
```

Output

```
OrderedDict([('0.weight', tensor([[1.9414]], device='cuda:0')),
('0.bias', tensor([1.0233], device='cuda:0'))])
```

No changes, indeed.

Putting It All Together

In this chapter, we have heavily modified the training pipeline. Even though the data preparation part was left *unchanged*, the model configuration part was reduced to its bare minimum, and the model training part was fully integrated into the StepByStep class. In other words, our pipeline went **classy**!

Run - Data Preparation V2

```python
1  # %load data_preparation/v2.py
2
3  torch.manual_seed(13)
4
5  # Builds tensors from Numpy arrays BEFORE split
6  x_tensor = torch.as_tensor(x).float()
7  y_tensor = torch.as_tensor(y).float()
8
9  # Builds dataset containing ALL data points
10 dataset = TensorDataset(x_tensor, y_tensor)
11
12 # Performs the split
13 ratio = .8
14 n_total = len(dataset)
15 n_train = int(n_total * ratio)
16 n_val = n_total - n_train
17
18 train_data, val_data = random_split(dataset, [n_train, n_val])
19
20 # Builds a loader of each set
21 train_loader = DataLoader(
22     dataset=train_data,
23     batch_size=16,
24     shuffle=True
25 )
26 val_loader = DataLoader(dataset=val_data, batch_size=16)
```

Run - Model Configuration V4

```python
# %load model_configuration/v4.py

# Sets learning rate - this is "eta" ~ the "n"-like Greek letter
lr = 0.1

torch.manual_seed(42)
# Now we can create a model
model = nn.Sequential(nn.Linear(1, 1))

# Defines an SGD optimizer to update the parameters
# (now retrieved directly from the model)
optimizer = optim.SGD(model.parameters(), lr=lr)

# Defines an MSE loss function
loss_fn = nn.MSELoss(reduction='mean')
```

Run - Model Training

```python
n_epochs = 200

sbs = StepByStep(model, loss_fn, optimizer)
sbs.set_loaders(train_loader, val_loader)
sbs.set_tensorboard('classy')
sbs.train(n_epochs=n_epochs)
```

```python
print(model.state_dict())
```

Output

```
OrderedDict([('0.weight', tensor([[1.9414]], device='cuda:0')),
             ('0.bias', tensor([1.0233], device='cuda:0'))])
```

Recap

In this chapter, we've revisited and reimplemented many methods. This is what we've covered:

- defining our `StepByStep` **class**
- understanding the purpose of the **constructor** (`__init__()`) method
- defining the **arguments** of the constructor method
- defining **class' attributes** to store *arguments*, *placeholders*, and *variables* we need to keep track of
- defining **functions as attributes**, using higher-order functions and the class' attributes to build functions that perform training and validation steps
- understanding the **difference** between **public**, **protected**, and **private methods**, and Python's "relaxed" approach to it
- creating methods to set **data loaders** and **TensorBoard** integration
- (re)implementing **training** methods: `_mini_batch()` and `train()`
- implementing **saving** and **loading** methods: `save_checkpoint()` and `load_checkpoint()`
- implementing a method for **making predictions** that takes care of all boilerplate code regarding *Numpy*-to-PyTorch conversion and back
- implementing methods to **plot losses** and add the **model's graph** to TensorBoard
- **instantiating** our `StepByStep` class and running a **classy** pipeline: configuring the model, loading the data, training the model, making predictions, checkpointing, and resuming training. The whole nine yards!

Congratulations! You have developed a **fully functioning class** that implements all methods relevant to model training and evaluation. From now on, we'll use it over and over again to tackle different tasks and models. Next stop: classification!

[61] https://github.com/dvgodoy/PyTorchStepByStep/blob/master/Chapter02.1.ipynb
[62] https://colab.research.google.com/github/dvgodoy/PyTorchStepByStep/blob/master/Chapter02.1.ipynb
[63] https://realpython.com/python3-object-oriented-programming/
[64] https://realpython.com/python-super/
[65] https://www.w3schools.com/python/ref_func_setattr.asp
[66] https://pytorch.org/docs/stable/notes/randomness.html

Chapter 3
A Simple Classification Problem

Spoilers

In this chapter, we will:

- build a model for **binary classification**
- understand the concept of **logits** and how it is related to **probabilities**
- use **binary cross-entropy loss** to train a model
- use the loss function to handle **imbalanced datasets**
- understand the concepts of **decision boundary** and **separability**
- learn how the **choice of a classification threshold** impacts evaluation metrics
- build **ROC** and **precision-recall** curves

Jupyter Notebook

The Jupyter notebook corresponding to Chapter 3[67] is part of the official *Deep Learning with PyTorch Step-by-Step* repository on GitHub. You can also run it directly in **Google Colab**[68].

If you're using a *local installation*, open your terminal or Anaconda prompt and navigate to the PyTorchStepByStep folder you cloned from GitHub. Then, *activate* the pytorchbook environment and run jupyter notebook:

```
$ conda activate pytorchbook

(pytorchbook)$ jupyter notebook
```

If you're using Jupyter's default settings, http://localhost:8888/notebooks/Chapter03.ipynb should open Chapter 3's notebook. If not, just click on Chapter03.ipynb on your Jupyter's home page.

Imports

For the sake of organization, all libraries needed throughout the code used in any given chapter are imported at its very beginning. For this chapter, we'll need the following imports:

```
import numpy as np

import torch
import torch.optim as optim
import torch.nn as nn
import torch.functional as F
from torch.utils.data import DataLoader, TensorDataset

from sklearn.datasets import make_moons
from sklearn.preprocessing import StandardScaler
from sklearn.model_selection import train_test_split
from sklearn.metrics import confusion_matrix, roc_curve, \
precision_recall_curve, auc

from stepbystep.v0 import StepByStep
```

A Simple Classification Problem

It is time to handle a different **class** of problems: **classification problems** (pun intended). In a classification problem, we're trying to predict **which class a data point belongs to**.

Let's say we have **two classes** of points: They are either **red** or **blue**. These are the **labels (y)** of the points. Sure enough, we need to assign **numeric values** to them. We could assign **zero** to **red** and **one** to **blue**. The class associated with **zero** is the **negative class**, while **one** corresponds to the **positive class**.

In a nutshell, for **binary classification**, we have:

Color	Value	Class
Red	0	Negative
Blue	1	Positive

> **IMPORTANT**: In a classification model, the **output** is the predicted probability of the **positive class**. In our case, the model will predict the *probability of a point being blue*.

The choice of *which class is positive* and *which class is negative* **does not** affect model performance. If we reverse the mapping, making *red the positive class*, the only difference would be that the model would predict the *probability of a point being red*. But, since **both probabilities have to add up to one**, we could easily convert between them, so the **models are equivalent**.

Instead of defining a model first and *then* generating synthetic data for it, we'll do it the other way around.

Data Generation

Let's make the data a *bit* more interesting by using **two features (x_1 and x_2)** this time. We'll use Scikit-Learn's `make_moons()` to generate a **toy dataset with 100 data points**. We will also add some *Gaussian noise* and set a *random seed* to ensure reproducibility.

Data Generation

```
1 X, y = make_moons(n_samples=100, noise=0.3, random_state=0)
```

Then, we'll perform the **train-validation split** using Scikit-Learn's `train_test_split()` for convenience (we'll get back to *splitting indices* later):

Train-validation Split

```
1 X_train, X_val, y_train, y_val = train_test_split(
2     X,
3     y,
4     test_size=.2,
5     random_state=13
6 )
```

Remember, the split should **always** be the **first thing** you do—no pre-processing, no transformations, **nothing happens before the split**.

Next, we'll **standardize the features** using Scikit-Learn's `StandardScaler`:

Feature Standardization

```
1  sc = StandardScaler()
2  sc.fit(X_train)
3
4  X_train = sc.transform(X_train)
5  X_val = sc.transform(X_val)
```

> ⚠ Remember, you should use **only the training set** to fit the `StandardScaler`, and then use its `transform()` method to apply the pre-processing step to **all datasets**: training, validation, and test. Otherwise, you'll be **leaking** information from the validation and / or test sets to your model!

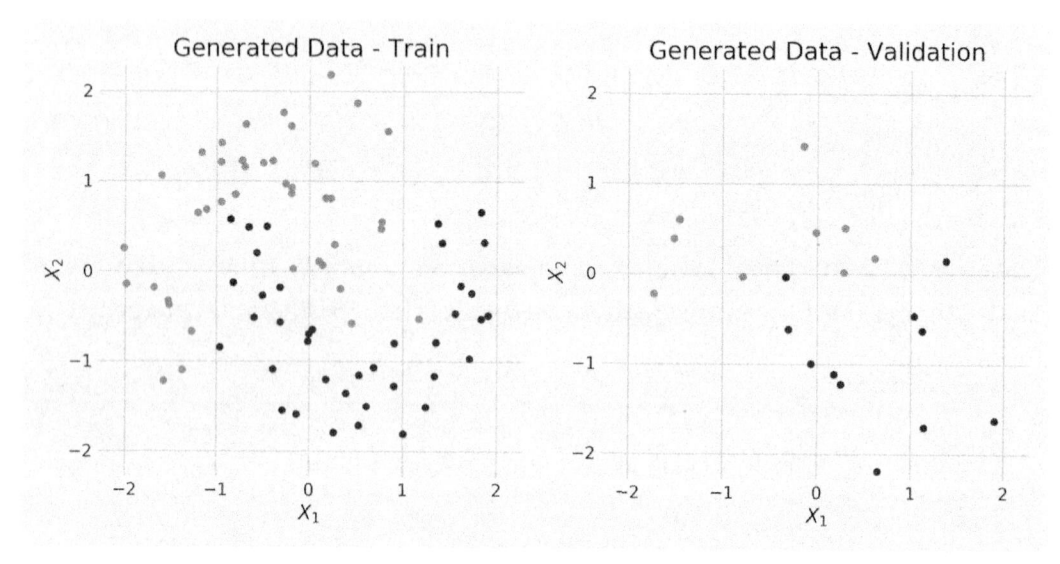

Figure 3.1 - Moons dataset

Data Preparation

Hopefully, this step feels familiar to you already! As usual, the data preparation step converts *Numpy* arrays into PyTorch tensors, builds `TensorDatasets` for them, and creates the corresponding *data loaders*.

Data Preparation

```
 1 torch.manual_seed(13)
 2
 3 # Builds tensors from Numpy arrays
 4 x_train_tensor = torch.as_tensor(X_train).float()
 5 y_train_tensor = torch.as_tensor(y_train.reshape(-1, 1)).float()
 6
 7 x_val_tensor = torch.as_tensor(X_val).float()
 8 y_val_tensor = torch.as_tensor(y_val.reshape(-1, 1)).float()
 9
10 # Builds dataset containing ALL data points
11 train_dataset = TensorDataset(x_train_tensor, y_train_tensor)
12 val_dataset = TensorDataset(x_val_tensor, y_val_tensor)
13
14 # Builds a loader of each set
15 train_loader = DataLoader(
16     dataset=train_dataset,
17     batch_size=16,
18     shuffle=True
19 )
20 val_loader = DataLoader(dataset=val_dataset, batch_size=16)
```

There are **80 data points** (N = 80) in our training set. We have **two features**, x_1 and x_2, and the **labels (y)** are either **zero (red)** or **one (blue)**. We have a dataset; now we need a...

Model

Given a **classification problem**, one of the more straightforward models is the **logistic regression**. But, instead of simply *presenting* it and using it right away, I am going to **build up to it**. The rationale behind this approach is twofold: First, it will make clear why this algorithm is called logistic *regression* if it is used for classification; second, you'll get a **clear understanding of what a** *logit* **is**.

Well, since it is called logistic **regression**, I would say that **linear regression** is a good starting point. What would a linear regression model with two features look like?

$$y = b + w_1 x_1 + w_2 x_2 + \epsilon$$

Equation 3.1 - A linear regression model with two features

There is one obvious **problem** with the model above: Our **labels (y)** are **discrete**; that is, they are either **zero** or **one**; no other value is allowed. We need to **change the model slightly** to adapt it to our purposes.

> "What if we assign the **positive** outputs to **one** and the **negative** outputs to **zero**?"

Makes sense, right? We're already calling them **positive** and **negative** classes anyway; why not put their names to good use? Our model would look like this:

$$y = \begin{cases} 1, & \text{if } b + w_1 x_1 + w_2 x_2 \geq 0 \\ 0, & \text{if } b + w_1 x_1 + w_2 x_2 < 0 \end{cases}$$

Equation 3.2 - Mapping a linear regression model to **discrete labels**

Logits

To make our lives easier, let's give the right-hand side of the equation above a name: **logit (z)**.

$$z = b + w_1 x_1 + w_2 x_2$$

Equation 3.3 - Computing **logits**

The equation above is strikingly similar to the original **linear regression model**, but we're calling the resulting value **z**, or **logit**, instead of **y**, or **label**.

> "Does it mean a **logit** is the same as **linear regression**?"

Not quite—there is one **fundamental difference** between them: There is **no error term (epsilon)** in Equation 3.3.

> "If there is no error term, where does the **uncertainty** come from?"

I am glad you asked :-) That's the role of the **probability**: Instead of assigning a data point to a **discrete label (zero or one)**, we'll compute the **probability of a data point's belonging to the positive class**.

Probabilities

If a data point has a **logit** that equals **zero**, it is exactly at the decision boundary since it is neither positive nor negative. For the sake of completeness, we assigned it to the **positive class**, but this assignment has **maximum uncertainty**, right? So, the corresponding **probability needs to be 0.5** (50%), since it could go either way.

Following this reasoning, we would like to have **large *positive* logit values** assigned to *higher* **probabilities** (of being in the positive class) and **large *negative* logit values** assigned to *lower* **probabilities** (of being in the positive class).

For *really large* positive and negative **logit values (z)**, we would like to have:

$$P(y = 1) \approx 1.0, \text{ if } z \gg 0$$
$$P(y = 1) = 0.5, \text{ if } z = 0$$
$$P(y = 1) \approx 0.0, \text{ if } z \ll 0$$

Equation 3.4 - Probabilities assigned to different logit values (z)

We still need to figure out a **function** that maps **logit values** into **probabilities**. We'll get there soon enough, but first, we need to talk about…

Odds Ratio

"What are the odds?!"

This is a colloquial expression meaning something very unlikely has happened. But **odds** do not have to refer to an unlikely event or a slim chance. The odds of getting **heads** in a (fair) coin flip are 1 to 1 since there is a 50% chance of success and a 50% chance of failure.

Let's imagine we are betting on the winner of the World Cup final. There are two countries: **A** and **B**. Country **A** is the **favorite**: It has a 75% chance of winning. So, Country **B** has only a 25% chance of winning. If you bet on Country **A**, your chances of winning—that is, your **odds (in favor)**—are **3 to 1** (75 to 25). If you decide to test your luck and bet on Country **B**, your chances of winning—that is, your **odds (in favor)**—are **1 to 3** (25 to 75), or **0.33 to 1**.

The **odds ratio** is given by the **ratio** between the **probability of success** (*p*) and the **probability of failure** (*q*):

$$\text{odds ratio}(p) = \frac{p}{q} = \frac{p}{1-p}$$

Equation 3.5 - Odds ratio

In code, our `odds_ratio()` function looks like this:

```
def odds_ratio(prob):
    return prob / (1 - prob)

p = .75
q = 1 - p
odds_ratio(p), odds_ratio(q)
```

Output

```
(3.0, 0.3333333333333333)
```

We can also **plot** the resulting **odds ratios** for probabilities ranging from 1% to 99%. The *red dots* correspond to the probabilities of 25% (*q*), 50%, and 75% (*p*).

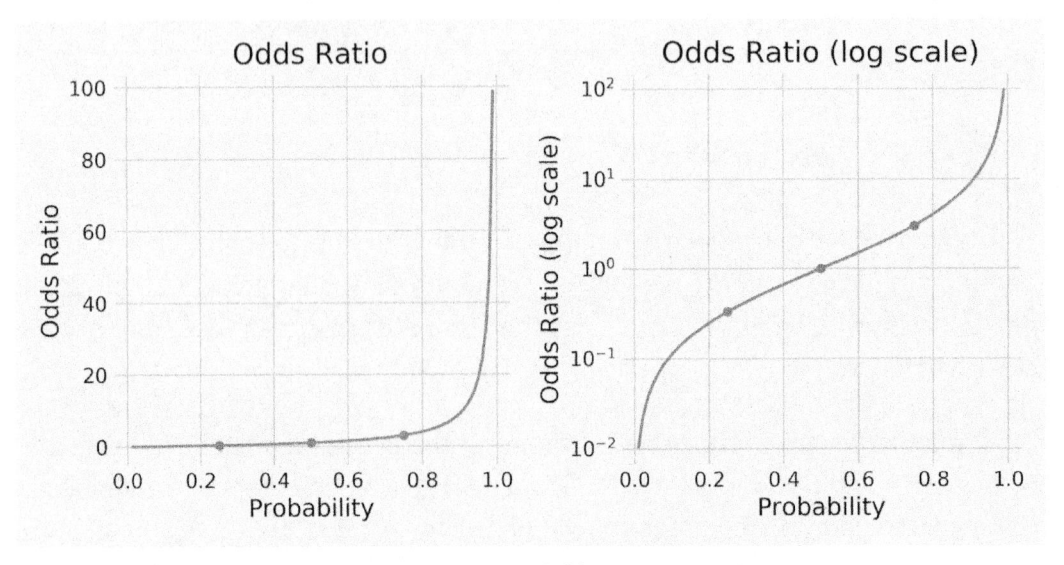

Figure 3.2 - Odds ratio

Clearly, the odds ratios (left plot) are **not symmetrical**. But, in a **log scale** (right plot), **they are**. This serves us very well since we're looking for a **symmetrical function** that maps **logit values** into **probabilities**.

> ❓ *"Why does it need to be symmetrical?"*

If the function **weren't** symmetrical, different choices for the **positive class** would produce models that were **not** equivalent. But, using a symmetrical function, we could train **two equivalent models** using the **same dataset**, just flipping the classes:

- **Blue Model** (the positive class (y=1) corresponds to **blue** points)
    - Data Point #1: P(y=1) = P(blue) = .83 (which is the same as P(red) = .17)
- **Red Model** (the positive class (y=1) corresponds to **red** points)
    - Data Point #1: P(y=1) = P(red) = .17 (which is the same as P(blue) = .83)

Log Odds Ratio

By taking the **logarithm** of the **odds ratio**, the function is not only **symmetrical**, but also maps **probabilities** into **real numbers**, instead of only the positive ones:

$$\text{log odds ratio}(p) = \log\left(\frac{p}{1-p}\right)$$

Equation 3.6 - Log odds ratio

In code, our `log_odds_ratio()` function looks like this:

```
def log_odds_ratio(prob):
    return np.log(odds_ratio(prob))

p = .75
q = 1 - p
log_odds_ratio(p), log_odds_ratio(q)
```

Output

```
(1.0986122886681098, -1.0986122886681098)
```

As expected, **probabilities that add up to 100%** (like 75% and 25%) correspond to **log odds ratios** that are the **same in absolute value**. Let's plot it:

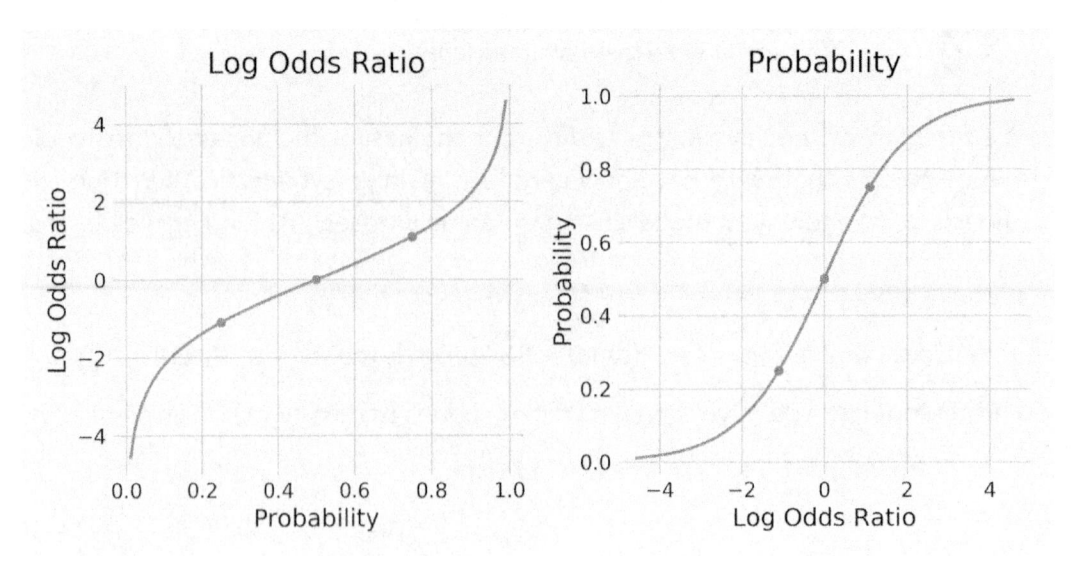

Figure 3.3 - Log odds ratio and probability

On the left, **each probability maps into a log odds ratio**. The *red dots* correspond to probabilities of 25%, 50%, and 75%, the same as before.

If we **flip** the horizontal and vertical axes (right plot), we are **inverting the function**, thus mapping **each log odds ratio into a probability**. That's the function we were looking for!

Does its shape look familiar? Wait for it...

From Logits to Probabilities

In the previous section, we were trying to **map logit values into probabilities**, and we've just found out, graphically, a function that **maps log odds ratios into probabilities**.

Clearly, our **logits are log odds ratios** :-) Sure, drawing conclusions like this is not very scientific, but the purpose of this exercise is to illustrate how the results of a regression, represented by the **logits (z)**, get to be mapped into probabilities.

214 | Chapter 3: A Simple Classification Problem

So, here's what we arrived at:

$$b + w_1 x_1 + w_2 x_2 = z = \log\left(\frac{p}{1-p}\right)$$

$$e^{b+w_1 x_1 + w_2 x_2} = e^z = \frac{p}{1-p}$$

Equation 3.7 - Regression, logits, and log odds ratios

Let's work this equation out a bit, inverting, rearranging, and simplifying some terms to **isolate p**:

$$\frac{1}{e^z} = \frac{1-p}{p}$$

$$e^{-z} = \frac{1}{p} - 1$$

$$1 + e^{-z} = \frac{1}{p}$$

$$p = \frac{1}{1 + e^{-z}}$$

Equation 3.8 - From logits (z) to probabilities (p)

Does it look familiar? That's a **sigmoid function**! It is the **inverse of the log odds ratio**.

$$p = \sigma(z) = \frac{1}{1 + e^{-z}}$$

Equation 3.9 - Sigmoid function

Sigmoid Function

```
def sigmoid(z):
    return 1 / (1 + np.exp(-z))

p = .75
q = 1 - p
sigmoid(log_odds_ratio(p)), sigmoid(log_odds_ratio(q))
```

Output

```
(0.75, 0.25)
```

Sigmoid

There is no need to implement our own sigmoid function, though. PyTorch provides two different ways of using a **sigmoid**: `torch.sigmoid()` and `nn.Sigmoid`.

The first one is a simple **function**, like the one above, but takes a tensor as input and returns another tensor:

```
torch.sigmoid(torch.tensor(1.0986)), torch.sigmoid(torch.tensor(-1.0986))
```

Output

```
(tensor(0.7500), tensor(0.2500))
```

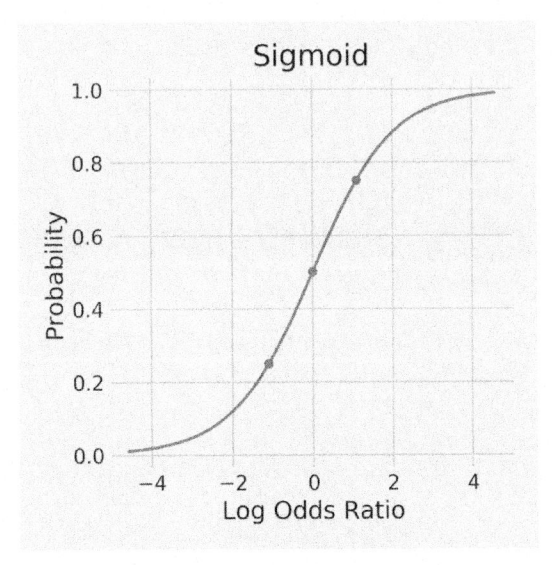

Figure 3.4 - Sigmoid function

The second one is a full-fledged **class** inherited from nn.Module. It is, for all intents and purposes, a **model on its own**. It is quite a simple and straightforward model: It **only** implements a forward() method, which, surprise, surprise, calls torch.sigmoid().

> *"Why do you need a model for a sigmoid function?"*

Remember, models can be used as **layers** of another, larger model. That's exactly what we're going to do with the **sigmoid class**.

Logistic Regression

Given **two features**, x_1 and x_2, the model will fit a **linear regression** such that its outputs are **logits (z)**, which are then converted into **probabilities** using a **sigmoid function**.

$$P(y = 1) = \sigma(z) = \sigma(b + w_1 x_1 + w_2 x_2)$$

Equation 3.10 - Logistic regression

A picture is worth a thousand words, so let's visualize it:

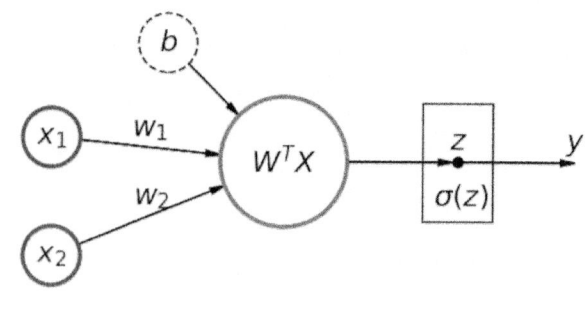

Input Layer   Output Layer   Sigmoid

Figure 3.5 - The (second) simplest of all neural networks

We can think of the **logistic regression** as the **second simplest neural network possible**. It is pretty much the **same as the linear regression**, but with a **sigmoid** applied to the results of the output layer (z).

> ## Sigmoid, nonlinearities, and activation functions
>
> The sigmoid function is **nonlinear**. It can be used to map **logits** into **probabilities**, as we've just figured out. But this **is not** its only purpose!
>
> **Nonlinear functions play a fundamental role** in neural networks. We know these nonlinearities by their usual name: **activation functions**.
>
> The sigmoid is the "biologically-inspired" and first activation function to be used back in the old days. It was followed by the hyperbolic-tangent (TanH) and, more recently, by the rectified linear unit (ReLU) and the whole family of functions it spawned.
>
> Moreover, there would be **no neural networks without a nonlinear function**. Have you ever wondered *what would happen to a neural network*, no matter how many layers deep, **if all its activation functions were removed**?
>
> I will get back to this topic in the next volume of the series, but I will spoil the answer now: The network would be **equivalent to linear regression**. True story!

A Note on Notation

So far, we've handled either **one feature** (up to Chapter 2) or **two features** (this chapter). It has allowed us to spell equations out, listing all terms.

But the number of features will soon increase *quickly* when we tackle **images as inputs** in the second volume of the series. So we need to agree on notation for **vectorized features**. Actually, I already used it in Figure 3.5 above.

The vectorized representations of the **weights (W)** and **features (X)** are:

$$W = \begin{bmatrix} b \\ w_1 \\ w_2 \end{bmatrix}_{(3 \times 1)} ; X = \begin{bmatrix} 1 \\ x_1 \\ x_2 \end{bmatrix}_{(3 \times 1)}$$

I will always place the dimensions below the vectors to make it more clear.

The **logits (z)**, as shown in Figure 3.5, are given by the expression below:

$$z = W^T X = \begin{bmatrix} - & w^T & - \end{bmatrix}_{(1 \times 3)} \begin{bmatrix} 1 \\ x_1 \\ x_2 \end{bmatrix}_{(3 \times 1)} = \begin{bmatrix} b & w_1 & w_2 \end{bmatrix}_{(1 \times 3)} \begin{bmatrix} 1 \\ x_1 \\ x_2 \end{bmatrix}_{(3 \times 1)}$$

$$= b + w_1 x_1 + w_2 x_2$$

From now on, instead of using the final and *long* expression, we'll use the first and more concise one.

Now let's use the Sequential model to build our logistic regression in PyTorch:

```
torch.manual_seed(42)
model1 = nn.Sequential()
model1.add_module('linear', nn.Linear(2, 1))
model1.add_module('sigmoid', nn.Sigmoid())
print(model1.state_dict())
```

Model | 219

Output

```
OrderedDict([('linear.weight', tensor([[0.5406, 0.5869]])),
             ('linear.bias', tensor([-0.1657]))])
```

Did you notice that state_dict() contains parameters from the linear layer only? Even though the model has a second sigmoid layer, this layer does not contain any parameters since it does not need to learn anything: The sigmoid function will be the same regardless of which model it is a part of.

Loss

We already have a model, and now we need to define an appropriate **loss** for it. A **binary classification** problem calls for the **binary cross-entropy (BCE) loss**, sometimes known as **log loss**.

The **BCE loss** requires the **predicted probabilities**, as returned by the **sigmoid function**, and the **true labels (y)** for its computation. For each data point *i* in the training set, it starts by computing the **error** corresponding to the point's **true class**.

If the data point belongs to the **positive class (y=1)**, we would like our model to **predict a probability close to one**, right? A **perfect one** would result in the **logarithm of one**, which is **zero**. It makes sense; a perfect prediction means zero loss. It goes like this:

$$y_i = 1 \Rightarrow \text{error}_i = \log(P(y_i = 1))$$

Equation 3.11 - Error for a data point in the positive class

What if the data point belongs to the **negative class (y=0)**? Then we **cannot** simply use the predicted probability. Why not? Because the model outputs the probability of a point's belonging to the *positive*, not the *negative*, class. Luckily, the latter can be easily computed:

$$P(y_i = 0) = 1 - P(y_i = 1)$$

Equation 3.12 - Probability of a data point's belonging to the negative class

And thus, the **error** associated with a data point's belonging to the **negative class** goes like this:

$$y_i = 0 \Rightarrow \text{error}_i = \log(1 - P(y_i = 1))$$

Equation 3.13 - Error for a data point in the negative class

Once all errors are computed, they are **aggregated into a loss value**. For the binary-cross entropy loss, we simply take the **average of the errors** and **invert its sign**.

$$\text{BCE}(y) = -\frac{1}{(N_{\text{pos}} + N_{\text{neg}})} \left[\sum_{i=1}^{N_{\text{pos}}} \log(P(y_i = 1)) + \sum_{i=1}^{N_{\text{neg}}} \log(1 - P(y_i = 1)) \right]$$

Equation 3.14 - Binary Cross-Entropy formula, the intuitive way

Let's assume we have two dummy data points, one for each class. Then, let's pretend our model made predictions for them: 0.9 and 0.2. The predictions are not bad since it predicts a 90% probability of being positive for an actual positive, and only 20% of being positive for an actual negative. How does this look in code? Here it is:

```python
dummy_labels = torch.tensor([1.0, 0.0])
dummy_predictions = torch.tensor([.9, .2])

# Positive class (labels == 1)
positive_pred = dummy_predictions[dummy_labels == 1]
first_summation = torch.log(positive_pred).sum()
# Negative class (labels == 0)
negative_pred = dummy_predictions[dummy_labels == 0]
second_summation = torch.log(1 - negative_pred).sum()
# n_total = n_pos + n_neg
n_total = dummy_labels.size(0)

loss = -(first_summation + second_summation) / n_total
loss
```

Output

```
tensor(0.1643)
```

The first summation adds up the errors corresponding to the points in the positive class. The second summation adds up the errors corresponding to the points in the negative class. I believe the **formula above** is quite **straightforward** and **easy to understand**. Unfortunately, it is usually *skipped* over, and only its equivalent is presented:

$$\text{BCE}(y) = -\frac{1}{N}\sum_{i=1}^{N}[y_i \log(P(y_i = 1)) + (1 - y_i)\log(1 - P(y_i = 1))]$$

Equation 3.15 - Binary Cross-Entropy formula, the clever way

The formula above is a *clever way* of computing the loss in a single expression, sure, but the split of positive and negative points is less obvious. If you pause for a minute, you'll realize that points in the **positive class (y=1)** have their **second term equal zero**, while points in the **negative class (y=0)** have their **first term equal zero**.

Let's see how it looks in code:

```
summation = torch.sum(
    dummy_labels * torch.log(dummy_predictions) +
    (1 - dummy_labels) * torch.log(1 - dummy_predictions)
)
loss = -summation / n_total
loss
```

Output

```
tensor(0.1643)
```

Of course, we got the same loss (0.1643) as before.

For a *very* detailed explanation of the rationale behind this loss function, make sure to check my post: "Understanding binary cross-entropy / log loss: a visual explanation."[69]

BCELoss

Sure enough, PyTorch implements the *binary cross-entropy loss*, nn.BCELoss(). Just like its regression counterpart, nn.MSELoss(), introduced in Chapter 1, it is a *higher-order function* that **returns the actual loss function**.

222 | Chapter 3: A Simple Classification Problem

The **nn.BCELoss()** higher-order function takes two **optional** arguments (the others are deprecated, and you can safely ignore them):

- **reduction**: It takes either **mean**, **sum**, or **none**. The default **mean** corresponds to our **Equation 3.15** above. As expected, **sum** will return the sum of the errors, instead of the average. The last option, **none**, corresponds to the **unreduced** form; that is, it returns the full **array of errors**.
- **weight**: The default is **none**, meaning every data point has equal weight. If supplied, it needs to be a tensor with a size equal to the number of elements in a mini-batch, representing the weights assigned to each element in the batch. In other words, this argument allows you to assign different weights to each element of the current batch, based on its position. So, the **first element** would have a given weight, the **second element** would have a different weight, and so on, **regardless of the actual class of that particular data point**. Sounds confusing? Weird? Yes, this is weird; I think so too. Of course, this is not useless or a mistake, but the proper usage of this argument is a more advanced topic and outside the scope of this book.

> ⚠️ This argument **DOES NOT** help with weighting imbalanced datasets! We'll see how to handle that shortly.

We'll be sticking with the default arguments, corresponding to Equation 3.15 above.

```
loss_fn = nn.BCELoss(reduction='mean')

loss_fn
```

Output

```
BCELoss()
```

As expected, nn.BCELoss() returned another function; that is, the actual loss function. The latter takes both predictions and labels to compute the loss.

Loss | 223

> **IMPORTANT**: Make sure to pass the **predictions first** and then the **labels** to the loss function. The **order matters** in the implementation of this loss function, unlike with the mean squared error.

Let's check this out:

```
dummy_labels = torch.tensor([1.0, 0.0])
dummy_predictions = torch.tensor([.9, .2])

# RIGHT
right_loss = loss_fn(dummy_predictions, dummy_labels)

# WRONG
wrong_loss = loss_fn(dummy_labels, dummy_predictions)

print(right_loss, wrong_loss)
```

Output

```
tensor(0.1643) tensor(15.0000)
```

Clearly, the order matters. It matters because the nn.BCELoss() takes the logarithm of the probabilities, which is expected as the **first argument**. If we swap the arguments, it will yield different results. In Chapter 1, we followed the same convention when using nn.MSELoss()—**first predictions, then labels**—even though it wouldn't make any difference there.

So far, so good. But there is yet **another** binary cross-entropy loss available, and it is **very important** to know **when to use one or the other**, so you don't end up with an inconsistent combination of model and loss function. Moreover, you'll understand why I made such a fuss about the **logits**.

BCEWithLogitsLoss

The former loss function took probabilities as an argument (together with the labels, obviously). This loss function takes **logits** as an argument, instead of probabilities.

"What does that mean, in practical terms?"

It means you **should NOT add a sigmoid as the last layer of your model** when using this loss function. This loss combines both the **sigmoid layer and the former binary cross-entropy loss into one.**

> **IMPORTANT**: I can't stress this enough: You **must** use the **right combination of model and loss function**.
>
> **Option 1**: nn.Sigmoid as the **last** layer, meaning your model is producing **probabilities**, combined with the nn.BCELoss() function.
>
> **Option 2**: **No sigmoid** in the last layer, meaning your model is producing **logits**, combined with the nn.BCEWithLogitsLoss() function.
>
> Mixing nn.Sigmoid and nn.BCEWithLogitsLoss() is just **wrong**.
>
> Besides, **Option 2 is preferred** since it is numerically more stable than Option 1.

Now, let's take a closer look at the nn.BCEWithLogitsLoss() function. It is also a higher-order function, but it takes three **optional** arguments (the others are deprecated, and you can safely ignore them):

- reduction: It takes either mean, sum, or none, and it works just like in nn.BCELoss(). The default is **mean**.
- weight: This argument also works just like in nn.BCELoss(), and it is unlikely to be used.
- pos_weight: The weight of positive samples, it must be a tensor with length equal to the **number of labels associated with a data point** (the documentation refers to *classes*, instead of labels, which just makes everything even more confusing).

> To make it clear: In this chapter, we're dealing with a **single-label binary classification** (we have only **one label** per data point), and the **label is binary** (there are only two possible values for it, zero or one). If the label is **zero**, we say it belongs to the **negative class**. If the label is **one**, it belongs to the **positive class**.
>
> Please do not confuse the positive and negative classes of our single label with *c*, the so-called **class number** in the documentation. That *c* corresponds to the **number of different labels associated with a data point**. In our example, *c* = **1**.

> You *can* use this argument to handle **imbalanced datasets**, but there's more to it than meets the eye. We'll get back to it in the next sub-section.

Enough talking (or writing!): Let's see how to use this loss in code. We start by creating the loss function itself:

```
loss_fn_logits = nn.BCEWithLogitsLoss(reduction='mean')

loss_fn_logits
```

Output

```
BCEWithLogitsLoss()
```

Next, we use **logits** and **labels** to compute the loss. Following the same principle as before, **logits first, then labels**. To keep the example consistent, let's get the values of the logits corresponding to the probabilities we used before, 0.9 and 0.2, using our `log_odds_ratio()` function:

```
logit1 = log_odds_ratio(.9)
logit2 = log_odds_ratio(.2)

dummy_labels = torch.tensor([1.0, 0.0])
dummy_logits = torch.tensor([logit1, logit2])

print(dummy_logits)
```

Output

```
tensor([ 2.1972, -1.3863])
```

We have logits, and we have labels. Time to compute the loss:

```
loss = loss_fn_logits(dummy_logits, dummy_labels)
loss
```

Output

```
tensor(0.1643)
```

OK, we got the same result, as expected.

Imbalanced Dataset

In our dummy example with two data points, we had one of each class: positive and negative. The dataset was perfectly balanced. Let's create another dummy example but with an imbalance, adding **two extra data points belonging to the negative class**. For the sake of simplicity and to illustrate a *quirk* in the behavior of nn.BCEWithLogitsLoss(), I will give those two extra points the **same logits** as the other data point in the negative class. It looks like this:

```
dummy_imb_labels = torch.tensor([1.0, 0.0, 0.0, 0.0])
dummy_imb_logits = torch.tensor([logit1, logit2, logit2, logit2])
```

Clearly, this is an **imbalanced dataset**. There are **three times more** data points in the negative class than in the positive one. Now, let's turn to the pos_weight argument of nn.BCEWithLogitsLoss(). To compensate for the imbalance, one can set the weight to equal the ratio of negative to positive examples:

$$\text{pos\_weight} = \frac{\#\text{ points in negative class}}{\#\text{ points in positive class}}$$

In our imbalanced dummy example, the result would be 3.0. This way, every point in the *positive class* would have its corresponding **loss multiplied by three**. Since there is a **single label** for each data point (c = 1), the **tensor used as an argument for pos_weight** has only **one element**: tensor([3.0]). We could compute it like this:

```
n_neg = (dummy_imb_labels == 0).sum().float()
n_pos = (dummy_imb_labels == 1).sum().float()

pos_weight = (n_neg / n_pos).view(1,)
pos_weight
```

Output

```
tensor([3])
```

Now, let's create yet another loss function, including the pos_weight argument this time:

```
loss_fn_imb = nn.BCEWithLogitsLoss(
    reduction='mean',
    pos_weight=pos_weight
)
```

Then, we can use this **weighted** loss function to compute the loss for our **imbalanced dataset**. I guess one would expect the **same loss** as before; after all, this is a *weighted* loss. Right?

```
loss = loss_fn_imb(dummy_imb_logits, dummy_imb_labels)
loss
```

Output

```
tensor(0.2464)
```

Wrong! It was 0.1643 when we had two data points, one of each class. Now it is 0.2464, **even though we assigned a weight** to the positive class.

❓ *"Why is it different?"*

Well, it turns out, PyTorch **does not compute a weighted average**. Here's what you would expect from a weighted average:

$$\text{weighted average} = \frac{\text{pos\_weight} \sum_{i=1}^{N_{pos}} \text{loss}_i + \sum_{i=1}^{N_{neg}} \text{loss}_i}{\text{pos\_weight} N_{pos} + N_{neg}}$$

Equation 3.16 - Weighted average of losses

But this is what PyTorch does:

$$\text{BCEWithLogitsLoss} = \frac{\text{pos\_weight} \sum_{i=1}^{N_{pos}} \text{loss}_i + \sum_{i=1}^{N_{neg}} \text{loss}_i}{N_{pos} + N_{neg}}$$

Equation 3.17 - PyTorch's `BCEWithLogitsLoss`

See the difference in the denominator? Of course, if you **multiply the losses** of the positive examples **without multiplying their count (N_{pos})**, you'll end up with a number **larger than an actual weighted average**.

❓ *"What if I really want the weighted average?"*

It is not that hard, to be honest. Remember the `reduction` argument? If we set it to `sum`, our loss function will only return the **numerator** of the equation above. And then we can divide it by the weighted counts ourselves:

```
loss_fn_imb_sum = nn.BCEWithLogitsLoss(
    reduction='sum',
    pos_weight=pos_weight
)

loss = loss_fn_imb_sum(dummy_imb_logits, dummy_imb_labels)

loss = loss / (pos_weight * n_pos + n_neg)
loss
```

Output

```
tensor([0.1643])
```

There we go!

Model Configuration

In Chapter 2.1, we ended up with a *lean* "**Model Configuration**" section: We only need to define a **model**, an appropriate **loss function**, and an **optimizer**. Let's define a model that **produces logits** and use `nn.BCEWithLogitsLoss()` as the loss function. Since we have **two features**, and we are producing *logits* instead of probabilities, our model will have **one layer** and one layer alone: `Linear(2, 1)`. We will keep using the SGD optimizer with a learning rate of 0.1 for now.

This is what the model configuration looks like for our classification problem:

Model Configuration

```
 1 # Sets learning rate - this is "eta" ~ the "n"-like Greek letter
 2 lr = 0.1
 3
 4 torch.manual_seed(42)
 5 model = nn.Sequential()
 6 model.add_module('linear', nn.Linear(2, 1))
 7
 8 # Defines an SGD optimizer to update the parameters
 9 optimizer = optim.SGD(model.parameters(), lr=lr)
10
11 # Defines a BCE with logits loss function
12 loss_fn = nn.BCEWithLogitsLoss()
```

Model Training

Time to **train** our model! We can leverage the StepByStep class we built in Chapter 2.1 and use pretty much the same code as before:

Model Training

```
1 n_epochs = 100
2
3 sbs = StepByStep(model, loss_fn, optimizer)
4 sbs.set_loaders(train_loader, val_loader)
5 sbs.train(n_epochs)
```

```
fig = sbs.plot_losses()
```

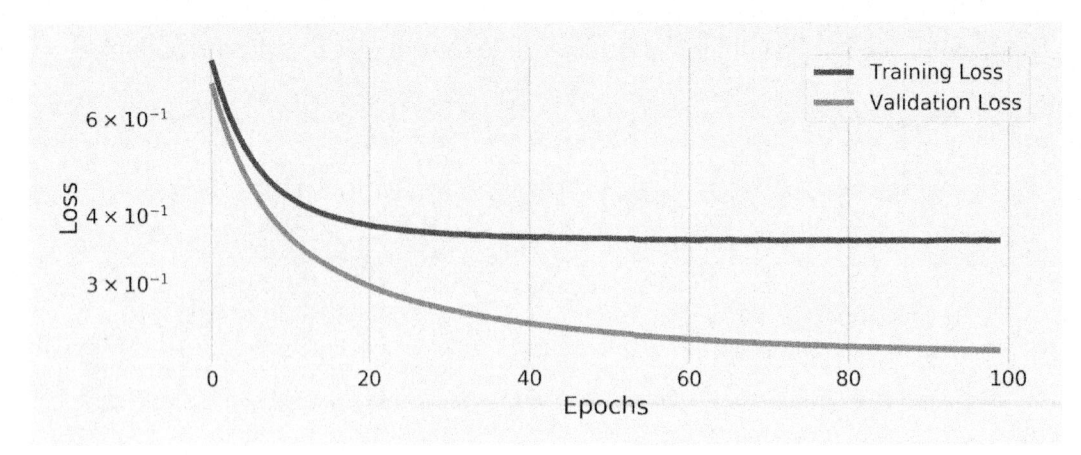

Figure 3.6 - Training and validation losses

> "Wait, there is something weird with this plot." you say.

You're right; the **validation loss** is **lower** than the **training loss**. Shouldn't it be the other way around?! Well, generally speaking, *YES*, it should, but you can learn more about situations where this *swap* happens at this great post: "Why is my validation loss lower than my training loss?" (*http://pyimg.co/kku35*). In our case, it is simply that the **validation set is easier** to classify: If you check Figure 3.1 at the beginning of the chapter, you'll notice that the red and blue points in the right plot (validation) are not as mixed up as the ones in the left plot (training).

Having settled that, it is time to inspect the model's trained parameters:

```
print(model.state_dict())
```

Output

```
OrderedDict([('linear.weight', tensor([[ 1.1822, -1.8684]], device
='cuda:0')),
            ('linear.bias', tensor([-0.0587], device='cuda:0'))])
```

Our model produced **logits**, right? So we can plug the weights above into the corresponding **logit equation** (Equation 3.3), and end up with:

$$z = b + w_1x_1 + w_2x_2$$
$$z = -0.0587 + 1.1822x_1 - 1.8684x_2$$

Equation 3.18 - Model's output

The value **z** above is the **output of our model**. It is a "*glorified* linear regression!" And this is a classification problem! How come?! Hold that thought; it will become more clear in the next section, "Decision Boundary".

But, before going down that road, I would like to use our model (and the StepByStep class) to **make predictions** for, say, the first four data points in our training set:

Making Predictions (Logits)

```
predictions = sbs.predict(x_train_tensor[:4])
predictions
```

Output

```
array([[ 0.20252657],
       [ 2.944347  ],
       [ 3.6948545 ],
       [-1.2356305 ]], dtype=float32)
```

Clearly, these are not probabilities, right? These are **logits**, as expected.

We can still get the corresponding probabilities, though.

> "*How do we go from logits to probabilities,*" you ask, just to make sure you got it right.

That's what the **sigmoid function** is good for.

Making Predictions (Probabilities)

```
probabilities = sigmoid(predictions)
probabilities
```

Output

```
array([[0.5504593 ],
       [0.94999564],
       [0.9757515 ],
       [0.22519748]], dtype=float32)
```

Now we're talking! These are the **probabilities**, given our model, of those four points being positive examples.

Lastly, we need to go from probabilities to classes. If the **probability is greater than or equal to a threshold**, it is a **positive** example. If it is **less than the threshold**, it is a **negative** example. Simple enough. The trivial choice of a **threshold** is **0.5**:

$$y = \begin{cases} 1, & \text{if } P(y=1) \geq 0.5 \\ 0, & \text{if } P(y=1) < 0.5 \end{cases}$$

Equation 3.19 - From probabilities to classes

But the probability itself is just the **sigmoid** function applied to the **logit (z)**:

$$y = \begin{cases} 1, & \text{if } \sigma(z) \geq 0.5 \\ 0, & \text{if } \sigma(z) < 0.5 \end{cases}$$

Equation 3.20 - From logits to classes, via sigmoid function

But the **sigmoid** function has a value of **0.5** only when the **logit (z)** has a value of zero:

$$y = \begin{cases} 1, & \text{if } z \geq 0 \\ 0, & \text{if } z < 0 \end{cases}$$

Equation 3.21 - From logits to classes, directly

Thus, if we don't care about the probabilities, we could use the **predictions (logits)** directly to get the **predicted classes** for the data points:

Making Predictions (Classes)

```
classes = (predictions >= 0).astype(np.int)
classes
```

Output

```
array([[1],
       [1],
       [1],
       [0]])
```

Clearly, the points where the **logits (z) equal zero** determine the **boundary** between **positive** and **negative** examples.

> ❓ *"Why 0.5? Can I choose a **different threshold**?"*

Sure, you can! **Different thresholds** will give you **different confusion matrices** and, therefore, **different metrics**, like accuracy, precision, and recall. We'll get back to that in the "Decision Boundary" section.

By the way, are you still *holding that thought* about the *"glorified linear regression?"* Good!

Decision Boundary

We have just figured out that whenever **z equals zero**, we are in the **decision boundary**. But z is given by a **linear combination** of features x_1 and x_2. If we work out some basic operations, we arrive at:

$$
\begin{aligned}
z = 0 &= b + w_1 x_1 + w_2 x_2 \\
-w_2 x_2 &= b + w_1 x_1 \\
x_2 &= -\frac{b}{w_2} - \frac{w_1}{w_2} x_1
\end{aligned}
$$

Equation 3.22 - Decision boundary for logistic regression with two features

Given our model (**b**, **w₁**, and **w₂**), for any value of the first feature (**x₁**), we can compute the corresponding value of the second feature (**x₂**) that sits **exactly at the**

decision boundary.

> Look at the expression in Equation 3.22: This is a **straight line**. It means the **decision boundary is a straight line**.

Let's plug the **weights** of our **trained model** into it:

$$x_2 = -\frac{0.0587}{1.8684} + \frac{1.1822}{1.8684}x_1$$
$$x_2 = -0.0314 + 0.6327x_1$$

An image is worth a thousand words, right? Let's plot it!

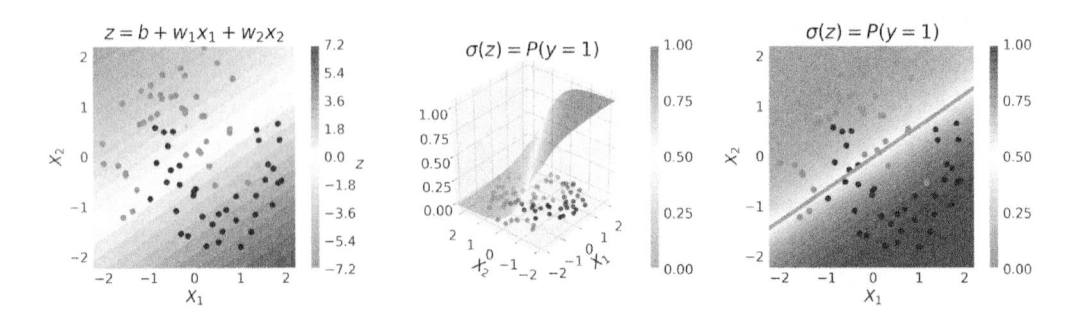

Figure 3.7 - Decision boundary

The figure above tells the whole story! It contains only **data points** from the **training set**. So, that's what the model "sees" when it is training. It will try to achieve the **best possible separation** between the two classes, depicted as **red** (negative class) and **blue** (positive class) points.

In the left plot, we have a **contour plot** (remember those from the loss surfaces in Chapter 0?) of the **logits (z)**.

In the center plot, we have a 3D plot of the **probabilities** resulting from **applying a sigmoid function** to the logits. You can even see the **shape** of the sigmoid function in 3D, approaching zero to the left and one to the right.

Finally, in the right plot, we have a **contour plot** of the **probabilities**, so it is the same as the center plot but without the cool 3D effect. Maybe it is not as cool, but it is surely easier to understand. **Darker blue (red) colors** mean **higher (lower) probabilities**, and we have the **decision boundary as a straight gray line**, corresponding to a **probability of 50%** (and a logit value of zero).

> A logistic regression always separates two classes with a straight line.

Our model produced a straight line that does quite a good job of separating red and blue points, right? Well, it was not *that* hard anyway, since the blue points were more concentrated on the bottom right corner, while the red points were mostly on the top left corner. In other words, the classes were quite **separable**.

> The more **separable** the **classes** are, the **lower** the **loss** will be.

Now we can make sense of the **validation loss**, being **lower** than the training loss. In the *validation set*, the classes are **more separable** than in the *training set*. The **decision boundary** obtained using the training set can do an *even better* job separating red and blue points. Let's check it out, plotting the **validation set** against the **same contour plots** as above:

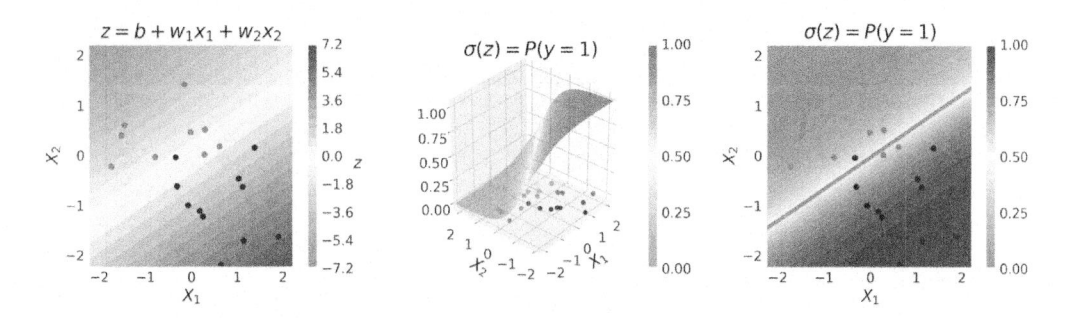

Figure 3.8 - Decision boundary (validation dataset)

See? Apart from three points, two red and one blue, which are *really* close to the decision boundary, the data points are correctly classified. **More separable, indeed.**

Are my data points separable?

That's the million-dollar question! In the example above, we can clearly see that data points in the validation set are **more separable** than those in the training set.

What happens if the points are **not separable at all**? Let's take a quick detour and look at another tiny dataset with 10 data points, seven red, three blue. The colors are the **labels (y)**, and each data point has a **single feature (x_1)**. We could plot them **along a line**; after all, we have only **one dimension**.

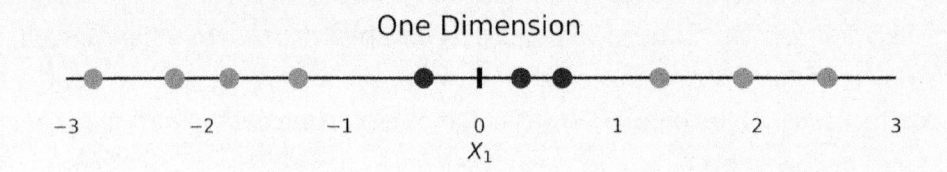

One Dimension

Can you **separate the blue points from the red ones with one straight line**? Obviously not—these points **are not separable** (in one dimension, that is).

Should we give up, then?

> *"Never give up, never surrender!"*
>
> Commander Taggart

If it doesn't work in one dimension, try using two! There is just one problem, though: Where does the other dimension come from? We can use a **trick** here: We apply a **function** to the **original dimension (feature)** and use the result as a **second dimension (feature)**. Quite simple, right?

For the tiny dataset at hand, we could try the **square function**:

$$X_2 = f(X_1) = X_1^2$$

What does it look like?

238 | Chapter 3: A Simple Classification Problem

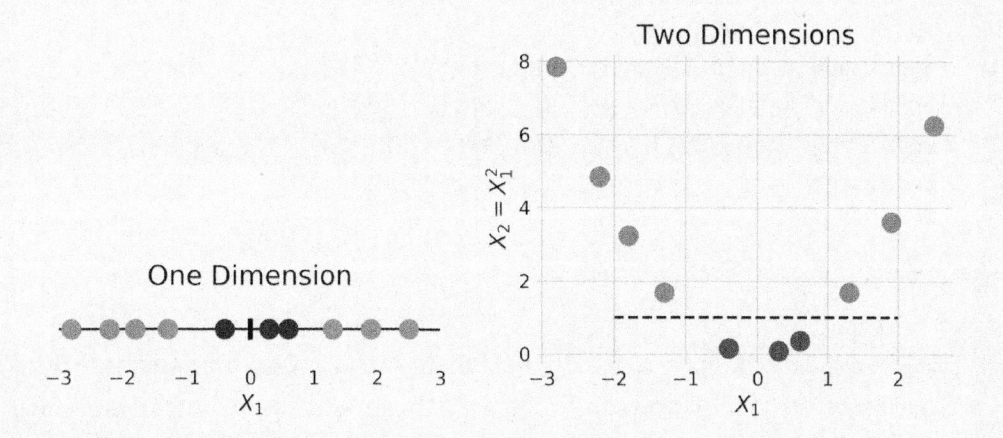

Back to the original question: "*Can you separate the blue points from the red ones with one straight line?*"

In two dimensions, that's a piece of cake!

The more dimensions, the more separable the points are.

It is beyond the scope of this book to explain *why* this trick works. The important thing is to **understand the general idea**: As the **number of dimensions increases**, there is **more and more empty space**. If the data points are farther apart, it is likely easier to separate them. In two dimensions, the decision boundary is a line. In three dimensions, it is a plane. In four dimensions and more, it is a hyper-plane (fancier wording for a plane you can't draw).

Have you heard of the **kernel trick** for support vector machines (SVMs)? That's pretty much what it does! The **kernel** is nothing but the **function** we use to create additional dimensions. The square function we used is a **polynomial**, so we used a **polynomial kernel**.

"*Why are we talking about SVMs in a deep learning book?*"

Excellent question! It turns out **neural networks** may also **increase the dimensionality**. That's what happens if you add a **hidden layer** with **more units** than the **number of features**. For instance:

Decision Boundary | **239**

```
model = nn.Sequential()
model.add_module('hidden', nn.Linear(2, 10))
model.add_module('activation', nn.ReLU())
model.add_module('output', nn.Linear(10, 1))
model.add_module('sigmoid', nn.Sigmoid())

loss_fn = nn.BCELoss()
```

The model above increases dimensionality **from two dimensions** (two features) to **ten dimensions** and then uses those **ten dimensions to compute logits**. But it **only works if there is an activation function between the layers**.

I suppose you may have two questions right now: "Why is that?" and "What actually is an activation function?" Fair enough. But these are topics for the next volume of the series.

Classification Threshold

This section is **optional**. In it, I will dive deeper into using different thresholds for classification and how this affects the confusion matrix. I will explain the most common classification metrics: true and false positive rates, precision and recall, and accuracy. Finally, I will show you how these metrics can be combined to build ROC and Precision-Recall curves.

If you are already comfortable with these concepts, feel free to *skip* this section.

So far, we've been using the trivial threshold of 50% to classify our data points, given the probabilities predicted by our model. Let's dive a bit deeper into this and see the **effects of choosing different thresholds**. We'll be working on the data points in the **validation set**. There are only **20 data points** in it, so we can easily **keep track of all of them**.

First, let's compute the logits and corresponding probabilities:

Evaluation

```
logits_val = sbs.predict(X_val)
probabilities_val = sigmoid(logits_val).squeeze()
```

Then, let's **visualize the probabilities on a line**. It means we're going from the fancy contour plot to a **simpler plot**:

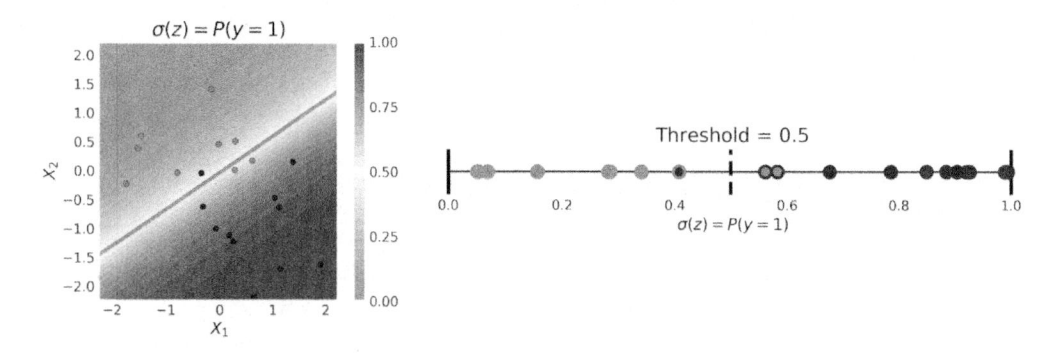

Figure 3.9 - Probabilities on a line

The left plot comes from Figure 3.8. It shows the **contour plot of the probabilities** and the **decision boundary as a straight gray line**. We place the data points **on a line**, according to their **predicted probabilities**. That's the plot on the right.

The **decision boundary** is shown as a **vertical dashed line** placed at the **chosen threshold** (0.5). Points to the **left** of the dashed line are **classified as red**, and therefore have **red edges around them**, while those to the **right** are **classified as blue**, and have **blue edges around them**.

The points are **filled with their actual color**, meaning that those with **distinct colors for edge and filling** are **misclassified**. In the figure above, we have **one blue point classified as red (left)** and **two red points classified as blue (right)**.

Now, let's make a *tiny* change to our plot to make it **more visually interesting**: We'll plot **blue (positive) points below the probability line** and **red (negative) points above the probability line**.

It looks like this:

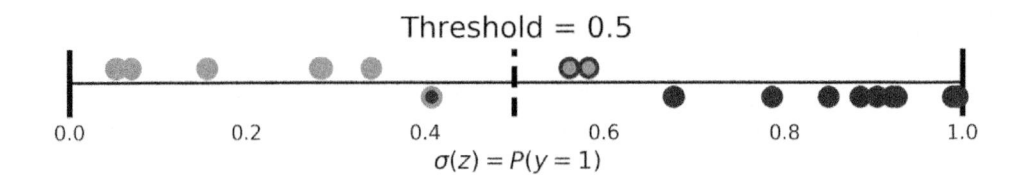

Figure 3.10 - Split probability line

"*Why is it more visually interesting?*" you ask.

Well, now **all correctly classified** and **all misclassified** points are in **different quadrants**. There is something else that **looks exactly like this**...

Confusion Matrix

Those quadrants have names: **true negative (TN)** and **false positive (FP)**, above the line, **false negative (FN)** and **true positive (TP)**, below the line.

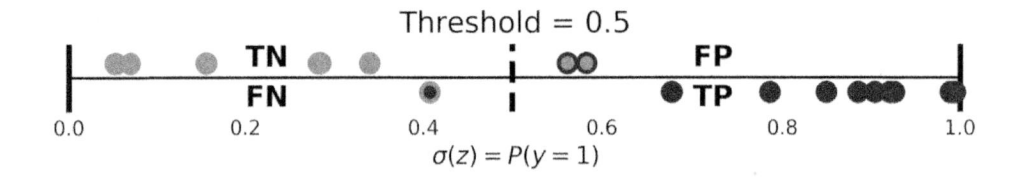

Figure 3.11 - Probability line as a confusion matrix

Points **above the line** are **actual negatives**, points **below the line** are **actual positives**.

Points to the **right of the threshold** are **classified as positive**, points to the **left of the threshold** are **classified as negative**.

Cool, right? Let's double-check it with Scikit-Learn's `confusion_matrix()` method:

```
cm_thresh50 = confusion_matrix(y_val, (probabilities_val >= 0.5))
cm_thresh50
```

Output

```
array([[ 7,  2],
       [ 1, 10]])
```

All 20 points in our validation set are accounted for. There are **three misclassified points**: one false negative and two false positives, just like in the figure above. I chose to move the **blue points (positive) below** the line to **match Scikit-Learn's convention for the confusion matrix**.

> Confusion matrices are already **confusing enough** on their own, but what's even **worse** is that you'll find all sorts of layouts around. Some people list positives first and negatives last. Some people even *flip* actuals and predicted classes, effectively transposing the confusion matrix. Make sure to always **check the layout** before drawing conclusions from matrices you see "in the wild."
>
> To make your life, and mine, simpler, I am just sticking with Scikit-Learn's convention throughout this book.

There is one more thing I hope you noticed already: **The confusion matrix depends on the threshold**. If you **shift the threshold** along the probability line, you'll end up **changing the number of points in each quadrant**.

> There are **many confusion matrices, one for each threshold**.

Moreover, **different confusion matrices** mean **different metrics**. We need the individual components of the confusion matrix, namely, TN, FP, FN, and TP, to construct those metrics. The function below *splits* the confusion matrix accordingly:

True and False Positives and Negatives

```
def split_cm(cm):
    # Actual negatives go in the top row, above probability line
    actual_negative = cm[0]
    # Predicted negatives go in the first column
    tn = actual_negative[0]
    # Predicted positives go in the second column
    fp = actual_negative[1]
    # Actual positives go in the bottow row, below probability line
    actual_positive = cm[1]
    # Predicted negatives go in the first column
    fn = actual_positive[0]
    # Predicted positives go in the second column
    tp = actual_positive[1]
    return tn, fp, fn, tp
```

Metrics

Starting with these four numbers, TN, FP, FN, and TP, you may construct **a ton of metrics**. We're focusing here on the most commonly used: **true and false positive rates** (TPR and FPR), **precision**, **recall**, and **accuracy**.

True and False Positive Rates

Let's start with the first two:

$$\text{TPR} = \frac{\text{TP}}{\text{TP} + \text{FN}} \qquad \text{FPR} = \frac{\text{FP}}{\text{FP} + \text{TN}}$$

For both of them, you **divide one value on the right column (positive)** by the **sum of the corresponding row**. So, the **true positive rate** is computed by dividing the value on the **bottom right** by the sum of the **bottom row**. Similarly, the **false positive rate** is computed by dividing the value on the **top right** by the sum of the **top row**. Fine, but what do they mean?

The **true positive rate** tells you, from **all points you *know* to be positive, how many your model got right**. In our example, we **know** there are **11 positive** examples. Our model **got ten right**. The **TPR** is 10 out of 11, or roughly 91%. There is yet another name for this metric: **recall**. Makes sense, right? From all the positive examples, how many does your model **recall**?

> 💡 If **false negatives** are bad for your application, you need to **focus on improving the TPR (recall)** metric of your model.

> ℹ️ When is a false negative *really* bad? Take airport security screening, for example, where **positive means the existence of a threat**. False positives are common: You have nothing to hide, and still, your bag will eventually be more thoroughly inspected due to the extreme sensitivity of the machinery. A **false negative** means that the machine **failed to detect an actual threat**. I don't have to explain why this is **bad**.

The **false positive rate** tells you, from **all points you *know* to be negative, how many your model got wrong**. In our example, we **know** there are **nine negative** examples. Our model **got two wrong**. The **FPR** is 2 out of 9, or roughly 22%.

> 💡 If **false positives** are bad for your application, you need to **focus on reducing the FPR** metric of your model.

> ℹ️ When is a false positive *really* bad? Take an investment decision, for example, where **positive means a profitable investment**. False negatives are missed opportunities: They seemed like bad investments, but they weren't. You did not make a profit, but you didn't sustain any losses either. A **false positive** means that you chose to invest but ended up **losing your money**.

We can use the function below to compute both metrics, given a confusion matrix:

True and False Positive Rates

```python
def tpr_fpr(cm):
    tn, fp, fn, tp = split_cm(cm)
    
    tpr = tp / (tp + fn)
    fpr = fp / (fp + tn)
    
    return tpr, fpr
```

```
tpr_fpr(cm_thresh50)
```

Output

```
(0.9090909090909091, 0.2222222222222222)
```

The trade-off between TPR and FPR

As always, there is a *trade-off* between the two metrics.

Let's say **false negatives** are bad for our application, and we want to **improve TPR**. Here is one quick idea: Let's make a model that **only predicts the positive class**, using a **threshold of zero**. We get **no false negatives whatsoever** (because there aren't any negatives in the first place). Our **TPR is 100%**. Awesome, right?

Wrong! If all points are predicted to be positive, **every negative example will be a false positive, and there are no true negatives**. Our **FPR is 100% too**.

There is no free lunch: The model is useless.

What if **false positives** are the problem instead? We would like to **reduce FPR**. Another *brilliant* idea comes to mind: Let's make a model that **only predicts the negative class**, using a **threshold of one**. We get **no false positives whatsoever** (because there aren't any positives in the first place). Our **FPR is 0%**. Mission accomplished, right?

Guess what? Wrong again! If all points are predicted to be negative, **every positive example will be a false negative, and there are no true positives**. Our **TPR is 0% too**.

It turns out, you cannot have the cake and eat it too.

Precision and Recall

Moving on to the next pair of metrics, we have:

$$\text{Recall} = \frac{TP}{TP + FN} \qquad \text{Precision} = \frac{TP}{TP + FP}$$

We can *skip* the **recall** because, as I mentioned above, it is the **same as TPR**: from all the positive examples, how many does your model **recall**?

What about **precision**? We compute it in the **right column (positive) only**. We divide the value on the **bottom right** by the sum of the **right column**. Its meaning is somewhat complementary to that of recall: From **all points classified as positive by your model**, how many did it get right? In our example, the **model classified 12 points as positive**. The model **got 10 right**. The **precision** is 10 out of 12, or roughly 83%.

> If **false positives** are bad for your application, you need to **focus on improving the precision** metric of your model.

We can use the function below to compute both metrics, given a confusion matrix:

Precision and Recall

```
def precision_recall(cm):
    tn, fp, fn, tp = split_cm(cm)

    precision = tp / (tp + fp)
    recall = tp / (tp + fn)

    return precision, recall
```

```
precision_recall(cm_thresh50)
```

Output

```
(0.8333333333333334, 0.9090909090909091)
```

Classification Threshold | 247

The trade-off between precision and recall

Here, too, there is no free lunch. The trade-off is a bit different, though.

Let's say **false negatives** are bad for our application, and we want to **improve recall**. Once again, let's make a model that **only predicts the positive class**, using a **threshold of zero**. We get **no false negatives whatsoever** (because there aren't any negatives in the first place). Our **recall is 100%**. Now you're probably waiting for the bad news, right?

If all points are predicted to be positive, **every negative example will be a false positive**. The **precision** is exactly the **proportion of positive samples in the dataset**.

What if **false positives** are the problem instead? We would like to **increase precision**. It's time to make a model that **only predicts the negative class** by using a **threshold of one**. We get **no false positives whatsoever** (because there aren't any positives in the first place). Our **precision is 100%**.

Of course, this is too good to be true. If all points are predicted to be negative, **there are no true positives**. Our **recall is 0%**.

No free lunch, no cake, just another couple of useless models.

There is one metric left to explore.

Accuracy

This is the simplest and most intuitive of them all: how many times your model got it right, considering all data points. Totally straightforward!

$$\text{Accuracy} = \frac{TP+TN}{TP+TN+FP+FN}$$

In our example, the model got 17 points right out of a total of 20 data points. Its accuracy is 85%. Not bad, right? The higher the accuracy, the better, but it does not tell the whole story. If you have an imbalanced dataset, relying on accuracy can be misleading.

Let's say we have 1,000 data points: 990 points are negative, and only 10 are positive. Now, let's take that model that uses a threshold of one and **only predicts the negative class**. This way, we get **all 990 negative points right** at the cost of **ten false negatives**. This model's accuracy is **99%**. But the model is still useless because it will *never* get a positive example right.

Accuracy may be misleading because it does not involve a trade-off with another metric, like the previous ones.

Speaking of trade-offs...

Trade-offs and Curves

We already know there are trade-offs between true and false positive rates, as well as between precision and recall. We also know that there are many confusion matrices, one for each threshold. What if we combine these two pieces of information? I present to you the **receiver operating characteristic (ROC)** and **precision-recall (PR)** curves! Well, they are not curves *yet*, but they will be soon enough!

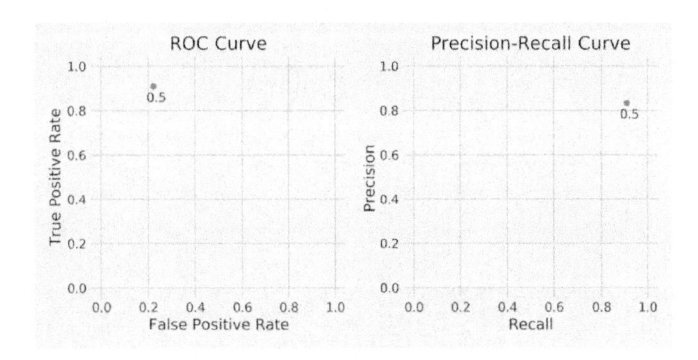

Figure 3.12 - Trade-offs for a threshold of 50%

We've already computed TPR (recall) (91%), FPR (22%), and precision (83%) for our model using the threshold of 50%. If we plot them, we'll get the figure above.

Time to try **different thresholds**.

Low Threshold

What about 30%? If the predicted probability is greater than or equal to 30%, we classify the data point as positive, and as negative otherwise. That's a very **loose** threshold since we don't require the model to be very confident to consider a data point to be positive. What can we expect from it? **More false positives, fewer false negatives**.

Classification Threshold | 249

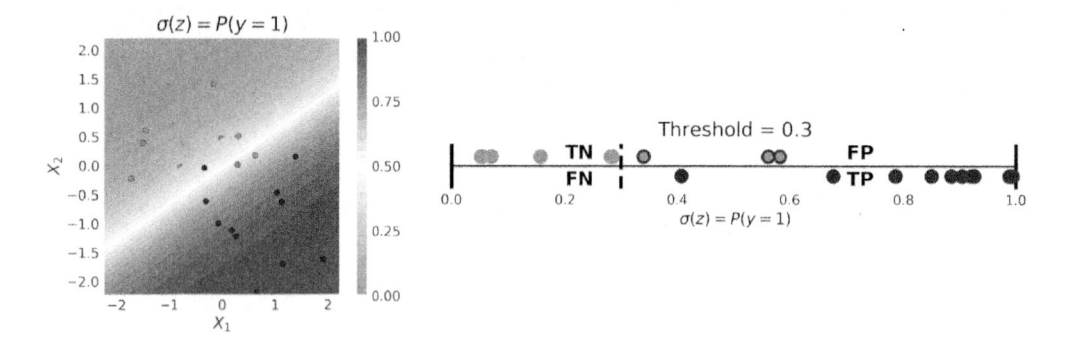

Figure 3.13 - Using a low threshold

You can see in the figure above that **lowering the threshold** (moving it to the left on the probability line) **turned one false negative into a true positive** (blue point close to 0.4), but it also **turned one true negative into a false positive** (red point close to 0.4).

Let's double-check it with Scikit-Learn's confusion matrix:

```
confusion_matrix(y_val, (probabilities_val >= 0.3))
```

Output

```
array([[ 6,  3],
       [ 0, 11]])
```

OK, now let's plot the corresponding metrics one more time:

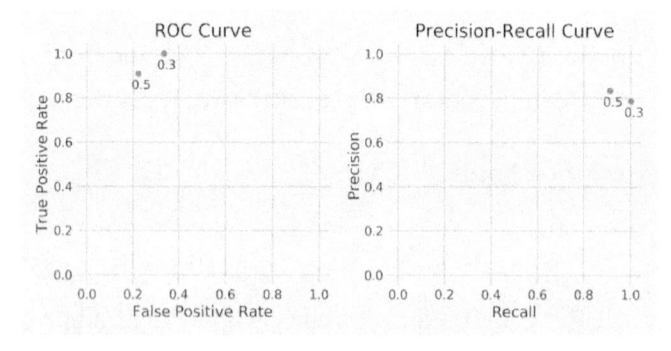

Figure 3.14 - Trade-offs for two different thresholds

Still not a curve, I know, but we can already learn something from these two points.

250 | Chapter 3: A Simple Classification Problem

> Lowering the threshold moves you to the right along both curves.

Let's move to the other side now.

High Threshold

What about 70%? If the predicted probability is greater than or equal to 70%, we classify the data point as positive, and as negative otherwise. That's a very **strict** threshold since we require the model to be very confident to consider a data point to be positive. What can we expect from it? **Fewer false positives, more false negatives**.

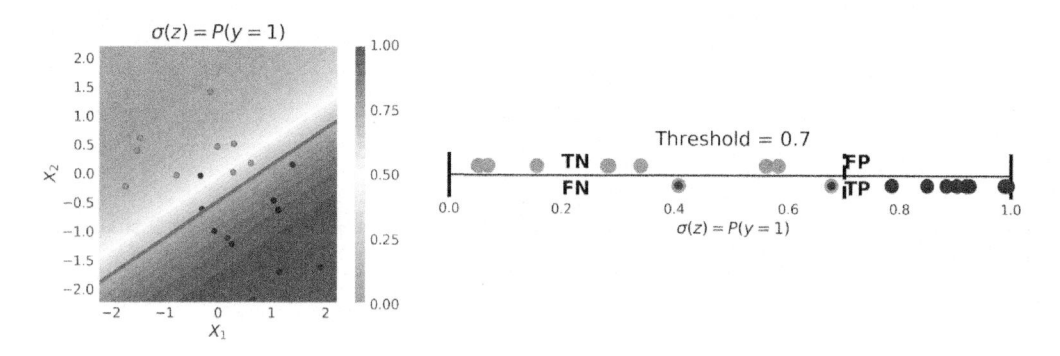

Figure 3.15 - Using a high threshold

You can see in the figure above that **raising the threshold** (moving it to the right on the probability line) **turned two false positives into true negatives** (red points close to 0.6), but it also **turned one true positive into a false negative** (blue point close to 0.6).

Let's double-check it with Scikit-Learn's confusion matrix:

```
confusion_matrix(y_val, (probabilities_val >= 0.7))
```

Output

```
array([[9, 0],
       [2, 9]])
```

OK, now let's plot the corresponding metrics again:

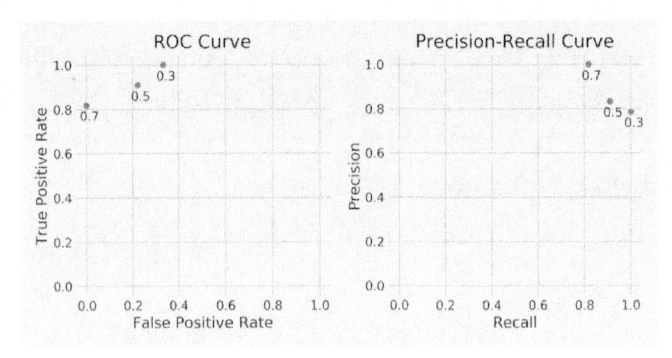

Figure 3.16 - Trade-offs for two different thresholds

I guess we earned the right to call it a curve now :-)

> **Raising the threshold moves you to the left along both curves.**

Can we just *connect the dots* and call it a curve for real? Actually, no, not yet.

ROC and PR Curves

We need to try out **more thresholds** to actually build a curve. Let's try multiples of 10%:

```
threshs = np.linspace(0,1,11)
```

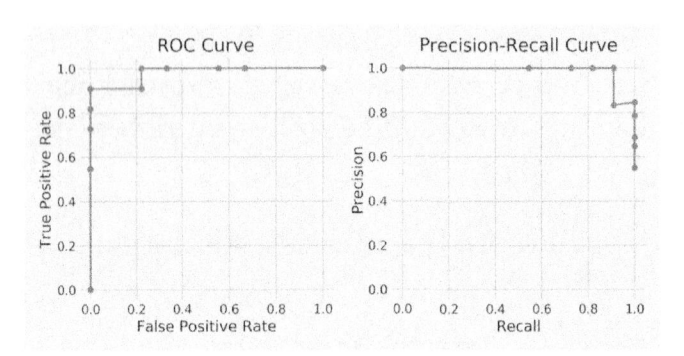

Figure 3.17 - Full curves

Cool! We finally have proper curves! I have some questions for you:

- In each plot, which point corresponds to a **threshold of zero (every prediction is positive)**?
- In each plot, which point corresponds to a **threshold of one (every prediction is negative)**?

- What does the **right-most point in the PR curve** represent?
- If I **raise the threshold**, how do I **move along the curve**?

You should be able to answer all of these questions by referring to the "Metrics" section. But, if you are eager to get the answers, here they are:

- The **threshold of zero** corresponds to the **right-most** point in both curves.
- The **threshold of one** corresponds to the **left-most** point in both curves.
- The **right-most point in the PR curve** represents the **proportion of positive examples in the dataset**.
- If I **raise the threshold**, I am **moving to the left** along both curves.

Now, let's double-check our curves with Scikit-Learn's roc_curve() and precision_recall_curve() methods:

```
fpr, tpr, thresholds1 = roc_curve(y_val, probabilities_val)
prec, rec, thresholds2 = \
    precision_recall_curve(y_val, probabilities_val)
```

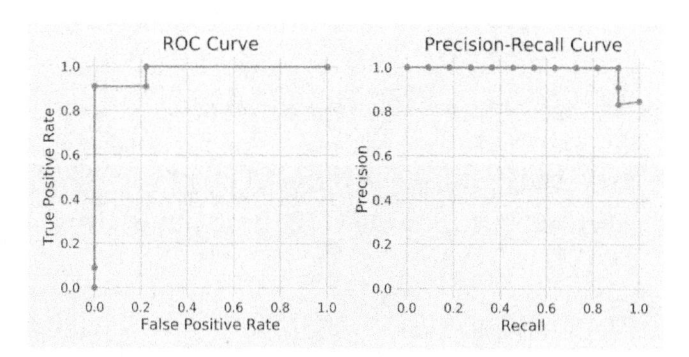

Figure 3.18 - Scikit-Learn's curves

Same shapes, different points.

*"Why do these curves have **different points** than ours?"*

Simply put, Scikit-Learn uses only **meaningful thresholds**; that is, those thresholds that **actually make a difference to the metrics**. If moving the threshold a bit does not modify the classification of any points, it doesn't matter for building a curve. Also, notice that the **two curves** have a **different number of points** because different metrics have different sets of meaningful thresholds. Moreover, these

thresholds do not necessarily include the extremes: zero and one. In Scikit-Learn's PR curve, the right-most point is clearly different than ours.

> *"How come the PR curve **dips to lower precision**? Shouldn't it always go up as we raise the threshold, moving to the left along the curve?"*

The Precision Quirk

Glad you asked! This is very annoying and somewhat counterintuitive, but it happens often, so let's take a closer look at it. To illustrate **why this happens**, I will plot the probability lines for three distinct thresholds: 0.4, 0.5, and 0.57.

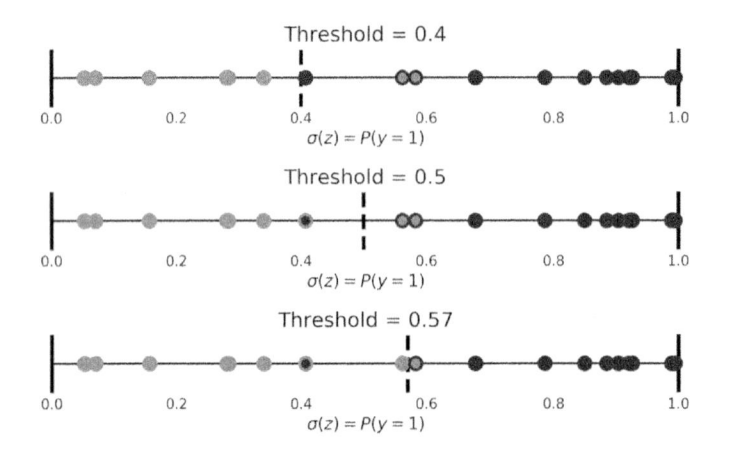

Figure 3.19 - The precision quirk

At the top, with a threshold of 0.4, we have **15 points** on the right (classified as **positive**), **two of which are false positives**. The **precision** is given by:

$$\text{Precision}(\text{thresh} = 0.40) = \frac{13}{13 + 2} = 0.8666$$

But if we move the threshold to the right, up to 0.5, we **lose one true positive**, effectively **reducing precision**:

$$\text{Precision}(\text{thresh} = 0.50) = \frac{(13 - 1)}{(13 - 1) + 2} = \frac{12}{12 + 2} = 0.8571$$

This is a **temporary side effect**, though. As we raise the threshold even further to 0.57, we get the benefit of **getting rid of a false positive**, thus **increasing precision**:

$$\text{Precision}(\text{thresh} = 0.57) = \frac{12}{12 + (2-1)} = \frac{12}{12+1} = 0.9230$$

In general, **raising the threshold** will **reduce the number of false positives** and **increase precision**.

But, along the way, we **may lose some of the true positives**, which will **temporarily reduce precision**. *Quirky*, right?

Best and Worst Curves

Let's ask ourselves: What would the **best possible** (and, of course, the **worst possible**) curve look like?

The **best** curve belongs to a model that predicts everything perfectly: It gives us a 100% probability to all actual positive data points and 0% probability to all actual negative data points. Of course, such a model *does not exist* in real life. But *cheating* does exist. So, let's cheat and use the **true labels** as the **probabilities**. These are the curves we get:

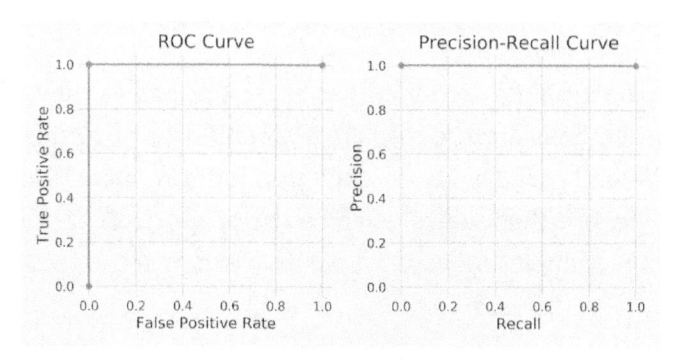

Figure 3.20 - Perfect curves

Nice! If a perfect model exists, its curves are actually **squares**! The **top-left corner** on the **ROC curve**, as well as the **top-right corner** on the **PR curve**, are the (unattainable) sweet spots. Our logistic regression was *not bad*, actually—but, of course, our validation set was ridiculously easy.

"And the Oscar for the **worst curve** goes to..."

"...the *random model*!"

If a model spits out **probabilities all over the place**, without any regard to the

Classification Threshold | 255

actual data, it is as bad as it can be. We can simply **generate uniformly distributed values between zero and one** as our **random probabilities**:

```
np.random.seed(39)
random_probs = np.random.uniform(size=y_val.shape)

fpr_random, tpr_random, thresholds1_random = \
    roc_curve(y_val, random_probs)
prec_random, rec_random, thresholds2_random = \
    precision_recall_curve(y_val, random_probs)
```

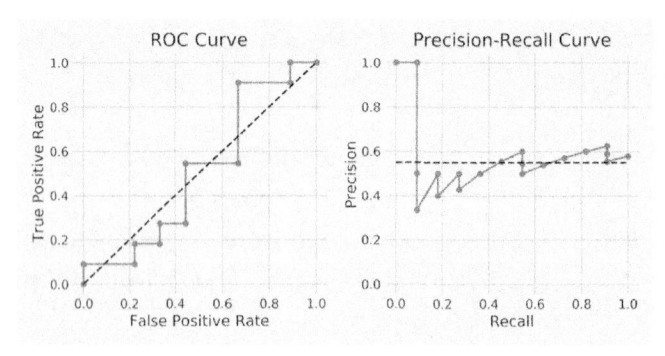

Figure 3.21 - Worst curves ever

We have only 20 data points, so our curves are not **as bad as they theoretically are** :-) The black dashed lines are the *theoretical worst* for both curves. On the left, the **diagonal line** is as bad as it can be. On the right, it is a *bit* more nuanced: The **worst is a horizontal line**, but the **level** is given by the **proportion of positive samples** in the dataset. In our example, we have 11 positive examples out of 20 data points, so the line sits at the level of 0.55.

Comparing Models

"*If I have two models, how do I choose the best one?*"

"*The best model is the one with the best curve.*"

Captain Obvious

Thank you, Captain. The real question here is: How do you compare curves? The **closer** they are to **squares**, the **better** they are, this much we already know. Besides, if **one curve has all its points above all the points of another curve**, the one above is clearly the best. The problem is, two different models may produce curves that **intersect each other** at some point. If that's the case, **there is no clear winner**.

One possible solution to this dilemma is to look at the **area under the curve**. The curve with **more area** under it **wins**! Luckily, Scikit-Learn has an auc() (area under the curve) method, which we can use to compute the area under the curves for our (good) model:

```
# Area under the curves of our model
auroc = auc(fpr, tpr)
aupr = auc(rec, prec)
print(auroc, aupr)
```

Output

```
0.9797979797979798 0.9854312354312356
```

Very close to the perfect value of one! But then again, this is a test example—you shouldn't expect figures so high in real-life problems. What about the random model? The theoretical minimum for the **area under the worst ROC curve is 0.5**, which is the area under the diagonal. The theoretical minimum for the **area under the worst PR curve is the proportion of positive samples in the dataset**, which is 0.55 in our case.

```
# Area under the curves of the random model
auroc_random = auc(fpr_random, tpr_random)
aupr_random = auc(rec_random, prec_random)
print(auroc_random, aupr_random)
```

Output

```
0.505050505050505 0.570559046216941
```

Close enough; after all, the curves produced by our random model were only roughly approximating the theoretical ones.

> If you want to learn more about both curves, you can check Scikit-Learn's documentation for "Receiver Operating Characteristic (ROC)"[70] and "Precision-Recall"[71]. Another good resource is Jason Brownlee's Machine Learning Mastery blog: "How to Use ROC Curves and Precision-Recall Curves for Classification in Python"[72] and "ROC Curves and Precision-Recall Curves for Imbalanced Classification."[73]

Putting It All Together

In this chapter, we haven't modified the training pipeline much. The data preparation part is roughly the same as in the previous chapter, except for the fact that we performed the split using Scikit-Learn this time. The model configuration part is largely the same as well, but we **changed the loss function**, so it is the appropriate one for a **classification** problem. The model training part is quite straightforward given the development of the `StepByStep` class in the last chapter.

But now, after training a model, we can use our class' `predict()` method to get predictions for our validation set and use Scikit-Learn's `metrics` module to compute a wide range of classification metrics, like the confusion matrix, for example.

Data Preparation

```
1  torch.manual_seed(13)
2
3  # Builds tensors from Numpy arrays
4  x_train_tensor = torch.as_tensor(X_train).float()
5  y_train_tensor = torch.as_tensor(y_train.reshape(-1, 1)).float()
6
7  x_val_tensor = torch.as_tensor(X_val).float()
8  y_val_tensor = torch.as_tensor(y_val.reshape(-1, 1)).float()
9
10 # Builds dataset containing ALL data points
11 train_dataset = TensorDataset(x_train_tensor, y_train_tensor)
12 val_dataset = TensorDataset(x_val_tensor, y_val_tensor)
13
14 # Builds a loader of each set
15 train_loader = DataLoader(
16     dataset=train_dataset,
17     batch_size=16,
18     shuffle=True
19 )
20 val_loader = DataLoader(dataset=val_dataset, batch_size=16)
```

Model Configuration

```
1  # Sets learning rate - this is "eta" ~ the "n"-like Greek letter
2  lr = 0.1
3
4  torch.manual_seed(42)
5  model = nn.Sequential()
6  model.add_module('linear', nn.Linear(2, 1))
7
8  # Defines an SGD optimizer to update the parameters
9  optimizer = optim.SGD(model.parameters(), lr=lr)
10
11 # Defines a BCE loss function
12 loss_fn = nn.BCEWithLogitsLoss()
```

Model Training

```
1 n_epochs = 100
2
3 sbs = StepByStep(model, loss_fn, optimizer)
4 sbs.set_loaders(train_loader, val_loader)
5 sbs.train(n_epochs)
```

```
print(model.state_dict())
```

Output

```
OrderedDict([('linear.weight', tensor([[ 1.1822, -1.8684]], device
='cuda:0')),
            ('linear.bias', tensor([-0.0587], device='cuda:0'))])
```

Evaluating

```
logits_val = sbs.predict(X_val)
probabilities_val = sigmoid(logits_val).squeeze()
cm_thresh50 = confusion_matrix(y_val, (probabilities_val >= 0.5))
cm_thresh50
```

Output

```
array([[ 7,  2],
       [ 1, 10]])
```

Recap

In this chapter, we've gone through many concepts related to classification problems. This is what we've covered:

- defining a **binary classification problem**
- generating and preparing a toy dataset using Scikit-Learn's `make_moons()` method
- defining **logits** as the result of a **linear combination of features**

260 | Chapter 3: A Simple Classification Problem

- understanding what **odds ratios** and **log odds ratios** are
- figuring out we can **interpret logits as log odds ratios**
- mapping **logits into probabilities** using a **sigmoid function**
- defining a **logistic regression** as a **simple neural network with a sigmoid function in the output**
- understanding the **binary cross-entropy loss** and its PyTorch implementation `nn.BCELoss()`
- understanding the difference between `nn.BCELoss()` and `nn.BCEWithLogitsLoss()`
- highlighting the **importance of choosing the correct combination of the last layer and loss function**
- using PyTorch's loss functions' arguments to handle **imbalanced datasets**
- **configuring** model, loss function, and optimizer for a classification problem
- **training** a model using the `StepByStep` class
- understanding that the validation loss **may be lower** than the training loss
- **making predictions** and mapping **predicted logits to probabilities**
- **using a classification threshold** to convert **probabilities into classes**
- understanding the definition of a **decision boundary**
- understanding the concept of **separability of classes** and how it's related to **dimensionality**
- exploring **different classification thresholds** and their effect on the **confusion matrix**
- reviewing typical **metrics** for evaluating classification algorithms, like true and false positive rates, precision, and recall
- building **ROC** and **precision-recall** curves out of **metrics computed for multiple thresholds**
- understanding the reason behind the **quirk of losing precision** while raising the classification threshold
- defining the **best** and **worst** possible ROC and PR curves
- using the **area under the curve** to **compare different models**

Wow! That's a *whole lot* of material! Congratulations on finishing yet another big step in your journey! What's next? In the second volume, *Computer Vision*, we'll **build upon this knowledge** to tackle **image classification problems** in general. We'll learn about activation functions, convolutions, optimizers, schedulers, vanishing and exploding gradients, transfer learning, and more!

See you there!

Thank You!

I really hope you enjoyed reading and learning about all these topics as much as I enjoyed writing (and learning, too!) about them.

If you have any suggestions, or if you find any errors, please don't hesitate to contact me through GitHub (dvgodoy), Twitter (@dvgodoy), or LinkedIn.

I'm looking forward to hearing back from you!

Daniel Voigt Godoy, December 5, 2021

[67] https://github.com/dvgodoy/PyTorchStepByStep/blob/master/Chapter03.ipynb
[68] https://colab.research.google.com/github/dvgodoy/PyTorchStepByStep/blob/master/Chapter03.ipynb
[69] https://bit.ly/2GlmLO0
[70] https://bit.ly/34IPAlx
[71] https://bit.ly/30xB9JZ
[72] https://bit.ly/30vF7TE
[73] https://bit.ly/2GCEL6A

Index

A

accuracy, 248-249
activation function, 240, 60
    ReLU, 218
    Sigmoid, 218
    Tanh, 218
AUC, 257
autograd, 84

B

backpropagation, 40
backward
    method, 84-85, 88
batch, 30
bias, 23
binary cross-entropy, 220-225

C

chain rule, 37, 40, 84
class
    negative, 206, 211, 220, 222, 234-235
    positive, 206, 211, 220, 222, 234-235
class method
    private, 183
    protected, 183
    public, 183
classification
    binary, 206, 220
    metrics, 240, 244
    threshold, 234-235, 240-243, 249-256
confusion matrix, 242-243
context manager
    no_grad, 149, 91
CUDA, 76

curve
    area under the, 257
    comparison, 256
    precision-recall (PR), 249-255, 258
    receiver operating characteristic (ROC), 249-253, 258

D

data
    dimensionality, 238-240
    generation, 193, 207, 24, 61
    leakage, 26
    loader, 135, 138-139, 142
        device, 140
        getitem, 140
        mini-batch size, 136
        sampler, 136
    preparation, 114-115, 138, 145, 169, 194, 202, 208-209, 259
    separability, 237-239
    synthetic, 207, 23-24, 61
dataset
    class, 133, 138
        custom, 134
        getitem, 133
        init, 133
        len, 134
        TensorDataset, 135
    imbalanced, 136, 223, 226-229, 248
decision boundary, 211, 235-237, 239, 241
derivative, 37
    partial, 36-37, 64, 84
device, 106, 140, 142, 176-177, 76, 78
    sending to, 78
dynamic computation graph, 74, 85, 90-91, 93-95

E

epoch, 53, 66
error, 29
    computing, 33
    mean squared, 30
    term, 210, 23
evaluation, 146

F

false positive rate (FPR), 244-245
feature
    scale, 47-49
    standardizing, 208, 50-53
forward pass, 106, 28, 63, 67

G

gradient, 36-41, 47, 50, 64, 67
    accumulation, 87
    descent, 22-23, 26-27, 35, 40, 62
        batch, 30, 53, 55-56, 63-64, 66-67
        mini-batch, 30, 53, 55-56, 64, 66
        path of, 55
        stochastic, 30, 53, 55-56, 64, 66
    vanishing, 52
    visualizing, 38
    zeroing, 87-88
gradient descent
    mini-batch, 139-140, 143

H

higher-order function, 125-129, 180-181, 223, 98
hook, 103

I

in-place, 82
initialization
    random, 27-28, 63, 67

    scheme, 27
intercept, 23

K

kernel
    polynomial, 239
    trick, 239

L

layer, 111-113
    types, 114
learning rate, 22, 40-44, 47, 50, 65, 96
    high, 44-45
    low, 43-44
    very high, 45-46
linear regression, 210, 23, 60, 66
log odds ratio, 213-215
logistic regression, 209-210, 217-218, 237
logit, 210-211, 213-214, 224, 226, 232-235
loss, 29, 37, 39, 84
    binary cross-entropy, 220-223, 225
    binary cross-entropy with logits, 224-225, 229-230
    cross-section, 35-36, 38, 49, 53
    function, 116-117, 220, 30, 40, 98-99
    increasing, 46
    mean squared error, 34, 63-64, 98-99
    minimizing, 29, 38, 40, 65
    minimum, 34
    surface, 31, 34-37, 49, 53, 55
    training, 232, 237
    validation, 146, 149, 232, 237
    visualizing, 150

M

magic commands, 116, 175
matrix, 70
mean squared error, 30, 34, 37
mini-batch, 137, 142, 30
    inner loop, 142
    size, 136, 96
model
    add_module, 113
    checkpoint, 163-165, 168, 198
    class, 102
        custom, 104
        device, 106
        forward, 103, 106, 110
        init, 103, 110
        nested, 108-110
        parameters, 104
        state_dict, 105, 110
    configuration, 114, 116-117, 131, 148, 159, 170, 195, 203, 230-231, 259
    deploying, 167-168
    evaluation, 260
    evaluation mode, 146, 168
    layer, 111-113
    loading, 164-165, 199
    parameters, 23, 63
    resuming training, 164-165
    saving, 163, 198
    sequential, 111-113, 219
    state_dict, 163
    training, 114, 117-118, 132, 139, 143, 149, 160, 171, 196, 200, 203, 231, 260
    training mode, 108, 165, 168

N

neural network, 218, 60-61
noise, 23
    Gaussian, 24, 61
nonlinearity, 218
no_grad, 91

O

object oriented programming, 102, 175
odds ratio, 211-212
    log, 213
optimizer, 116-117, 95-96
    Adam, 96
    SGD, 96
    state_dict, 105
    step, 96
    zero_grad, 96

P

parameter
    creating, 81-84
    hyper-, 22, 42, 67
    tensor, 80
    update, 40-41, 53, 56, 65-67, 88, 91
precision, 246-247
    -recall curve, 249
prediction
    making, 106, 28, 32, 63, 67
probability, 210-215, 220, 233-234, 236

R

random seed, 25, 67, 81, 84
recall, 246-247
regression
    linear, 210, 217, 23, 60, 66
    logistic, 209-210, 218, 237
reproducibility, 141, 188, 25, 67, 81
ROC curve, 249

S

scalar, 70
seed

random, 25, 67, 81, 84
sequential model, 111-113, 219
    add_module, 113
setattr, 183-186
shuffle, 136, 25-26, 61
sigmoid function, 215-218, 220, 233-234
slope, 23
standardizing, 50-53
state_dict, 105
StepByStep class
    arguments, 176
    constructor, 176-177
    data loaders, 178
    device, 177
    functions / methods, 179-180
    loading checkpoint, 190
    mini-batch, 186-187
    placeholders, 177-178
    predict, 191
    saving checkpoint, 190
    seed, 188
    TensorBoard, 178, 192
    training loop, 189
    training step, 181
    validation step, 181
    variables / attributes, 179
    visualizing losses, 191-192
support vector machine, 239

T

tensor, 70
    backward, 84-85, 88
    clone, 73-74
    CPU, 76, 78
    creating, 71
    dataset, 135
    detach, 101, 74
    device, 76, 78

from Numpy, 75, 79
GPU, 76, 78
grad, 86
gradient-requiring, 80-84, 93
item, 102
parameter, 80, 93
precision, 75
reshape, 73
shape, 72
size, 72
to Numpy, 101, 76, 80
tolist, 102
view, 73
zero_, 87-88
TensorBoard, 151-153
    losses, 161-162
    writing to, 154-158
time series, 26
trade-off
    precision vs recall, 248
    TPR vs FPR, 246
train, 108
train-validation-test split, 144, 207, 26, 61
training
    loop, 118, 123, 125, 129, 53
    step, 129-132, 139, 142
training loop, 66
true positive rate (TPR), 244-245

V

validation step, 147-148
vanishing gradient, 52
vector, 70

W

weight, 23, 40
    initialization, 27, 63, 67

Printed in Great Britain
by Amazon